P

Finding Recovery
A Daily Spiritual Path to Wholeness

"Lively, highly readable.... Challenges us to create lives of purpose, meaning, integrity and transparency.... A unique, valuable addition to the spiritual treatment of addictive disorders."

—**Dr. David Friedman**, addiction psychiatrist; assistant clinical professor, UCLA Geffen School of Medicine

"The strength of the commentary is in the straightforward messages [Rabbi Mark] teaches from Torah.... Certainly needed."

—**Arnold Eisen, PhD**, chancellor, The Jewish Theological Seminary

"Provides a simple yet profound spiritual practice to facilitate recovery.... I will keep this book on my breakfast table, for daily nourishment and inspiration!"

—**Rabbi Laura Owens**, Congregation B'nai Horin, Children of Freedom; chair of the board, Academy for Jewish Religion, California

"Weave[s] stories from the Torah with issues confronting us every day. Intriguing questions stimulate self-reflection, encouraging you to look inside in a non-threatening way. Read this book and it will surely enrich your soul. I know it did mine."

—**Dr. Susan Krevoy**, founding director, Susan B. Krevoy Eating Disorders Program

"An essential companion for anyone who wants to experience the life-changing gifts of daily practice that leads to holiness and wholeness.... There is no more sure-footed guide to the immersion of Torah and recovery in our lives."

—**Rabbi Jodie Siff**, Reconstructionist Synagogue of the North Shore

"Offers ... immediate access to the power of Torah to repair the world—the world of the individual and family seeking recovery.... Remarkable.... Anyone who seeks guidance will find it here in abundance."

—**Leonard Buschel**, certified substance abuse counselor; founder, Writers in Treatment; creator, Reel Recovery Film Festival

"This richly buoyant book propels us all forward to find luminous meaning in our lives. So at home in both the Torah and the 12 Steps, this book will help a wide audience live in the soul and discover joy and wholeness there."

—**Fr. Gregory Boyle, SJ**, founder/executive director, Homeboy Industries; author, *Tattoos on the Heart*

"A wellspring of inspiration and practical, spiritual guidance certain to support all who walk the path of recovery."

—**Rabbi Edwin S. Harris, PhD**, visiting assistant professor of pastoral counseling, Hebrew Union College–Jewish Institute of Religion, Los Angeles

"Rabbi Mark's … extraordinary teaching brings Torah to life. His book is a gift to all who search for a truth to live by."

—**Rabbi Edward Feinstein**, author, *Tough Questions Jews Ask: A Young Adult's Guide to Building a Jewish Life* and *The Chutzpah Imperative: Empowering Today's Jews for a Life That Matters*

"Give[s] you the right questions in order to enhance the way you live. I've worked with Rabbi Mark in various ways and he has helped me in ways I never thought possible."

—**Jimmy Iovine**, record and film producer; co-founder, Interscope Records; chairman, Interscope Geffen A&M.

"An invaluable resource for all of us who yearn to live with a sense of meaning.... [It]nvites us to grapple with questions that help us integrate the wisdom of Torah into the fabric of our lives."

—**Rabbi Mychal Springer**, chaplain; director, The Center for Pastoral Education at The Jewish Theological Seminary

Who Should Read This Book

You don't have to be an addict to find recovery in Torah. You don't have to be Jewish to learn from the wisdom of the Hebrew Bible. This book is meant for all seekers—anyone searching for a deeper connection with themselves, with their communities, and with a power greater than themselves, that is to say, God. This book offers a clear path to receiving the wisdom of the Jewish tradition to everyone willing to be honest with themselves, asking the questions laid out for each day and allowing for time to reflect and listen to the answers contained within their souls.

- People living in recovery from addiction.
- People searching for a Jewish path to recovery.
- People wanting to be immersed in the wisdom of the Torah.
- People who are seeking a path to connect with their soul.
- Families of people living in recovery or who are still in active addiction.
- Clergy who want to help their congregants find recovery, and the families of those who have struggled with addiction.
- Clergy of all denominations who want to begin or deepen their recovery through Hebrew Bible study.
- Rabbis and educators who want to teach a living and relevant Torah to their students.

- Psychiatrists, psychologists, therapists, and counselors who seek practical tools to introduce clients to a spiritual practice rooted in scripture.
- Jews and non-Jews alike who seek tools to help themselves live well.
- Anyone who has read any of the books in the Jewish Lights Publishing Recovery Series including:

Twelve Jewish Steps to Recovery: A Personal Guide for Turning from Alcoholism and Other Addictions

100 Blessings Every Day: Daily Twelve Step Recovery Affirmations, Exercises for Personal Growth and Renewal Reflecting Seasons of the Jewish Year

Renewed Each Day: Daily Twelve Step Recovery Meditations Based on the Bible

Recovery from Codependence: A Jewish Twelve Steps Guide to Healing Your Soul

Recovery—The Sacred Art: The Twelve Steps as Spiritual Practice

Recovery, the 12 Steps and Jewish Spirituality: Reclaiming Hope, Courage and Wholeness

A note on the cover art: Many recovery programs and treatment centers throughout the world use recovery medallions to mark sobriety anniversaries and to provide hope and encouragement to people struggling with addiction.

Finding Recovery *and* Yourself *in* Torah

A DAILY SPIRITUAL PATH TO WHOLENESS

RABBI MARK BOROVITZ

Foreword by Rabbi Kerry M. Olitzky

Afterword by Harriet Rossetto

For People of All Faiths, All Backgrounds

JEWISH LIGHTS Publishing

Woodstock, Vermont

Finding Recovery and Yourself in Torah:
A Daily Spiritual Path to Wholeness

2016 Quality Paperback Edition, First Printing

Library of Congress Cataloging-in-Publication Data
Names: Borovitz, Mark, 1951– author.
Title: Finding recovery and yourself in Torah : a daily spiritual path to wholeness / Rabbi Mark Borovitz ; foreword by Rabbi Kerry M. Olitzky ; afterword by Harriet Rossetto.
Description: Woodstock, VT : Jewish Lights Publishing, a division of LongHill Partners, Inc., [2016] | Includes bibliographical references.
Identifiers: LCCN 2015050737| ISBN 9781580238571 (pbk.) | ISBN 9781580238625 (ebook)
Subjects: LCSH: Bible. Pentateuch—Sermons. | Twelve-step programs—Religious aspects—Judaism. | Self-actualization (Psychology)—Religious aspects—Judaism. | Spiritual life—Judaism.
Classification: LCC BS1225.54 .B67 2016 | DDC 296.7/6—dc23 LC record available at http://lccn.loc.gov/2015050737

10 9 8 7 6 5 4 3 2 1

Manufactured in the United States of America
Cover Design: Tim Holtz
Interior Design: Tim Holtz

Published by Jewish Lights Publishing
A Division of LongHill Partners, Inc.
Sunset Farm Offices, Route 4, P.O. Box 237
Woodstock, VT 05091
Tel: (802) 457-4000 Fax: (802) 457-4004
www.jewishlights.com

This book is dedicated to all of my teachers of Torah:
Rabbi Neal Borovitz
Heather Garrett
Harriet Rossetto
Rabbi Mel Silverman, *z"l*
Rabbi Jonathan Omer-Man
Rabbi Edward Feinstein
Rabbi Harold Schulweis, *z"l*
Dr. Garrett O'Connor, *z"l*
Rabbi Abraham Joshua Heschel, *z"l*
Alumni and residents of Beit T'Shuvah
Board of Directors of Beit T'Shuvah
Community of Beit T'Shuvah

Contents

Foreword

If the Torah is the all-encompassing moral compass that it claims to be, and I believe it to be so, then we can find anything in it, including the support needed for recovery. Jewish resources, especially in sacred literature, are available for those in recovery from alcoholism and other addictions and compulsive behaviors. We just have to help people access those resources. That's why the Rabbis quipped, referring to Torah, "Turn it, turn it—for everything is in it" (*Pirkei Avot* 5:22). The great medieval Jewish philosopher and physician Moses Maimonides went so far as to say, "Torah is a healing balm." In it are the remedies for all spiritual maladies—we just have to probe the text, dig deeply in it, and drink of its life-giving waters. Some even suggest that the Torah is like a love letter. We handle it the way we would a missive from our lover. Every aspect of it offers meaning, particularly in its nuances and subtleties, all expressions of love.

The process of recovery shares a great deal in common with the practice of Torah study. This is clearly demonstrated in the pages ahead. Both the Twelve Steps of Alcoholics Anonymous and Torah study are lifelong endeavors that carry us forward, providing spiritual buoyancy for our lives—one hour, one day, one week at a time. We read these texts over and over, digesting each word, searching for meaning and insight, as if we have never reviewed them before. The Rabbis provide us with this guidance about the study of Torah, loosely translated from the Hebrew as "There is no before or after in the Torah." In other words, chronology doesn't get in the way of our understanding the lessons of the sacred text. We read the Torah as if its stories unfold in a linear sequence of events. Yet, we also read the Torah as if the stories happen somewhat simultaneously or even in a different temporal order. At the same time, we follow the entire Torah narrative and the journey of the Jewish people as if we don't know what will happen next while fully aware of all of the Torah's dramatic events.

The Torah and Twelve-Step spirituality are a perfect fit. They both provide us with a spiritual discipline that helps guide and anchor our lives. They both offer us community and fellowship. While those who study Torah—whether student or teacher—know that the study of Torah can aid recovery, only those in recovery know that the process of recovery can also enhance our study of Torah. And that is what is mystical and even magical about this book by my colleague Rabbi Mark Borovitz. He is immersed in both Torah and recovery; he has journeyed through both and continues to do so. Torah fuels his recovery, and recovery feeds his study of the Torah. Both nurture the individual who is in recovery, who is a student of Torah. Rabbi Borovitz—and the pages that he has penned for all of us—is a testament of both.

—Rabbi Kerry M. Olitzky

Acknowledgments

This book is a book of love and learning. I have to acknowledge so many people. First and foremost I want to acknowledge my grandfather, Abe Borovitz, *z"l*, for always wanting to learn and instilling that thirst and hunger for learning in my father, Jerry Borovitz, *z"l*. My dad taught me the joy of learning and how to immerse myself in whatever was/is in front of me. I forgot those lessons for a period of time, and this is my *t'shuvah* to both of these great men.

This book would not be possible without the sages of our tradition, from the Rabbis of old to the rabbis of today who continue to teach and inspire me. Rabbis Harold Schulweis, *z"l*, and Abraham Joshua Heschel, *z"l*, taught me how to immerse myself in text and to recover my authenticity through the Torah. I cannot thank them enough; they saved and grew my soul, my intellect, and my humanity. Rabbi Heschel continues to inspire, motivate, and disturb me.

I have been blessed with amazing teachers along this journey. My love of *Yiddishkeit* (Jewishness) was nurtured by Cantor Saul Meisels, *z"l*, at Temple on the Heights in Cleveland, Ohio, and by the "old men" of the minyan that I attended to say *Kaddish* after my father died. My teachers at rabbinical school were (and still are) fantastic and taught me so much. Rabbi Alan Shranz, *z"l*, taught me the beauty of Torah, and I hope that I have done him proud in my writing. I also need to thank Rabbi Daniel Gordis for taking a chance on an ex-con for the first full year of the Ziegler School of Rabbinic Studies and, of course, Ruth Ziegler for her gift of an opportunity for me to become a rabbi.

I am blessed to be a student and friend of Rabbi Edward Feinstein. Ed has taken me by the hand and guided me in what it means to be a rabbi, teacher, and friend. Thank you so much, my friend. My other rabbi, who is also my brother, Rabbi Neal Borovitz, has kept holding on to me my entire life. I am so grateful for our love and connection. I am honored that my friend and colleague Rabbi Kerry Olitzky has reviewed this work and contributed the foreword. Kerry has done outstanding work to help advance the integration of Torah study with Twelve Steps, helping many with whom I work to discover their own truth and path to wholeness.

Harriet Rossetto and Heather Garrett are my wife and daughter, respectively, and each continues to push me beyond what I believe I am capable of. You both are my rock and my go-to people. You have pushed me for years to finish this book, and I am so grateful to have you both in my corner.

Chloe Grey has done an amazing job putting everything together and editing my writing. Thanks so much, Chloe, for keeping me on task. The people at Jewish Lights Publishing—beginning with Stuart M. Matlins, publisher, and Emily Wichland, vice president of Editorial and Production—have been so amazing and patient with me. Your enthusiasm for this project has meant everything to me.

Jon Esformes and Matt Shapiro represent two groups of people who have taught me and learned with me over the years. Jon represents all of the alumni of Beit T'Shuvah, who have pushed me to "keep it real and useful" for the past fifteen years. Matt is the quintessential rabbinic intern, who has challenged all of my ideas and thoughts and actions to better understand how I live Torah and how our interns can spread the word of a Living Torah throughout the world.

I am humbled by this opportunity to share what I have learned with all of you.

Introduction

This book is the result of a spiritual awakening that I had in December of 1986, after my last arrest for fraud, forgery, and bad checks. An LAPD detective, Jim Bashira, who had arrested me in January of 1981, again arrested me. He saw me crossing a street and remembered a wanted poster that was sent from Santa Barbara County about a month before. Everything clicked for him in an instant, and I was arrested for the umpteenth time. While sitting in a holding cell and speaking to my first wife on the phone, I uttered these words: "Don't call anyone, the Man Upstairs is trying to tell me something, and I have to sit here until I figure it out." To this day, twenty-nine years later, I have no idea where those words came from, except from God/my Soul. This spiritual awakening would mean nothing if I did not stay committed to it. I knew right then that I had to change my life and my actions.

I spoke to my brother, Rabbi Neal Borovitz, and asked him to send me a *Chumash* and a prayer book. He did, and I began to study Torah again and pray again, each day that I was in the Santa Barbara County Jail and in state prison. I also began to read the writings of Rabbi Abraham Joshua Heschel, *z"l*, and learned about being immersed in Torah and that prayer had to move us forward in our living. Rabbi Harold Schulweis, *z"l*, taught me that study is a form of prayer also. This started me on a journey of recovering my soul, my search for truth, and finding myself in the text of the Torah as my story/our story. The Bible is a book of eternal wisdom and truth; many of us feel too inadequate to unlock this wisdom and truth, yet we all have the tools to do so. The Torah is not for the learned to study and take apart with biblical criticism; rather, it is a gift to immerse ourselves in. I found that being immersed means seeing the Torah as my guidebook for living. I have found that the more I am immersed in studying and seeing myself in the text, the more I am able to grow and have solutions to situations that used to baffle me.

This book takes all of us on a personal journey through the first five books of the Bible. In each of the fifty-two weeks of the year, we find the text speaking to both our inner and our outer worlds. From one of my teachers, Rabbi Jonathan Omer-Man, I learned that the text is the answer and we just have to find the right questions. This resonated deeply with me. I began to understand that I always had the "right" answers, I was simply asking the wrong questions. I set my mind, emotions, and spirit on the quest to find the right questions that each chapter/section of Torah was asking. This book is the result of my quest thus far. I still study and pray each day; I still seek new and deeper questions of and for myself and the world around me. I am still recovering my spirit and my questions in these five books of the Bible.

The format is to read a page each day and to either answer the questions that I have put forth or ask yourself the questions that come to you. I have given you my understanding of different parts of each section of Torah, based on my life and the work I do helping people recover their passion and discover their purpose, in my role as the senior rabbi and CEO of Beit T'Shuvah, a residential addiction treatment center in Los Angeles. I use these questions and understandings with people who have been residents and congregants, people who seek me out for spiritual and life coaching, the staff at Beit T'Shuvah, and the many rabbinic interns who have come to Beit T'Shuvah to learn and help grow their spirits and the souls of our residents.

I have been honored and humbled and joyous to be on this journey. Rabbi Mel Silverman, *z"l*, my first rabbi as an adult, was the Jewish chaplain at the California Institution for Men, and he encouraged me to look at the text in a personal way. We studied together for two and a half years, and each day I was amazed and awed to learn with and from him. Rabbi Jonathan Omer-Man was my first rabbi in Los Angeles. Not only did he teach me the importance of asking the right questions, but he also encouraged my insights and my work. Rabbi Edward Feinstein has been my rabbi and friend since 1993. Ed and I have learned together and argued together. Ed pushed me to go to rabbinical school and helped me in all of my darkest hours. Ed is, in my opinion, one of the greatest teachers in America, and I am blessed to have him and to have had Rabbi Mel and Rabbi Jonathan as my mentors and guides.

My hope is that this book shines some light on your greatness and gives fuel to the inner spark of holiness and divinity inside of you. I further hope it spurs you on to engage with a teacher, and others, in the magnificent exploration of how to live well, which can be found in the pages of our Bible. I am inviting you to find your own questions and recover the revelations that help guide you to find the purpose for which you were created.

You Matter,

Rabbi Mark Borovitz

Bereshit

Bereshit—day one

In the beginning ...

—Genesis 1:1

This week's parashah (Torah portion) is *Bereshit* (in the beginning), the first portion of the Torah. I am having a difficult time reining in my enthusiasm as we begin this year's cycle of reading, learning, and living Torah. Each year in reading this parashah, I find myself excited to learn more about the world and myself. I know that all of the challenges and joys I will experience are found in the Torah. I also know that the new questions about how to live well will be found here. Most of all, I know that I am able to make a new beginning each year.

What are you beginning anew this year?

How will you engage the Torah more to find new truths about yourself and living well?

What questions do you need to ask yourself this year that are different from those you asked last year?

Bereshit—day two

And the Spirit of God hovered
over the face of the waters.

—Genesis 1:2

The story of creation in the Torah is that in the beginning the universe consisted only of emptiness, chaos, and darkness, with the Spirit of God hovering above it all. I find this description to be true. Our inventions, our innovations are all created because of the emptiness and feeling of need that we experience. In the chaotic nature of life, we feel empty inside, that we are lacking something we truly need.

What are you lacking in your own life?

What is the emptiness you are currently experiencing?

How are you creating a healthy new
solution to this feeling of need?

Bereshit—day three

> And the earth was chaotic and void; and darkness was upon the face of the deep.
>
> —GENESIS 1:2

We learn that darkness gives form and order to the chaos and emptiness of creation. This is an interesting phenomenon. Most of us are afraid of darkness; we think that it is bad. I am reassured by Torah's teaching of how creation happens. Here we are being told that darkness is not only part of the creative process, it is actually necessary for creation to take place. So, when we are experiencing a dark mood or a dark place, we are really in the creative process, and something is going to happen. This darkness is not totally black; there is actually a pinpoint of light at its core. This pinpoint of light is God, the source of our own creative instincts. We reach down through the darkness and find this luminescence, and suddenly everything becomes brighter and the solution that we are creating comes to light.

What areas of darkness in your life are you running from rather than embracing?

How are you stopping the creative process by trying to run away from your own darkness?

At what times in your life are you aware of your need to stop and reach down and into your soul to find your own creative light?

Bereshit—day four

And God said …

—Genesis 1:3

The Torah teaches us about creation in a way that marries science and spirit. In the progression of the days of creation, we can see an evolutionary pattern leading from a black hole all the way to the magnificence of being human. In the teaching that there is a Creator of the universe, that we are here not as the result of a random event, we learn that we are both part of the pattern and also part of the Creator. The learning here, I believe, is that life is not about choosing sides, selecting between intellect or spirit; rather, life and living well are actually about the marriage of intellect and spirit.

Where do you belong in the divine pattern of life?

When do you find yourself living in an either/or experience of the world?

How can you become comfortable marrying both/and?

Bereshit—day five

And Adonai God … breathed into
his nostrils the breath of life.

—Genesis 2:7

In the first chapter of Genesis, we are called *tzelem Elohim* (image of God). In the second chapter of Genesis, we are created with *nishmat chayim* (the breath and spirit of life). *Tzelem Elohim* refers to our intellect, our problem-solving ability. *Nishmat chayim* is our spirit, our inner light. Therefore, to abdicate either would be to disown the basic foundation and principles upon which we are created. My intellect instructs me, offering creative solutions to my challenges. My spirit tells me things that my intellect can't yet know. Both intellect and spirit receive messages from God. My mind is bombarded with so many different messages from others, from my emotions, and from my surroundings. My spirit gets blocked because of the walls I build and the schmutz I collect, in order to avoid hearing my own conscience. Both my intellect and my soul need to be open, learning, and developing.

Do you recognize and relate to others as
divine images or as objects, and how?

What schmutz still blocks you from your soul
and the voice of your conscience or God?

How are you raising your soul, your intellect,
and your emotions to better serve God,
others, and your authentic self?

Bereshit—day six

> And they heard … and Adam and his wife hid themselves from the presence of God.
>
> —Genesis 3:8

Adam and Eve are disloyal to God when they hide from God, not because they did not obey God. Loyalty to God is not in obeying, as we will see with Abraham and the rest of our ancestors. They did not always obey; in fact, many times they argued with God. Adam and Eve were disloyal because they took an action and then were unwilling to stand up and acknowledge their action; they went against a principle and did not want to experience the consequences. Sound familiar? Loyalty to God and principles means that I must be responsible for *all* of my actions.

How are you hiding from God, from others, and from yourself?

Whom are you blaming for your life not going the way you wanted or believed it should?

How can you take responsibility for all of your actions, doing *t'shuvah* (repentance), whenever it is necessary?

Bereshit—day seven

And God called to Adam and said
to him, "Where are you?"

—Genesis 3:9

Searching for God is the ultimate principle to which we must remain loyal. We do this by searching for our true essence, searching to grow our intellect and our spirit, searching for our place, and searching for wholeness. We do this by allowing God to find us as well. In his 1972 interview with Carl Stern, Rabbi Abraham Joshua Heschel, *z"l*, said that "God is in search of man"—yet we keep hiding just like our ancestors Adam and Eve did. We seek God when we continue to refine and define our purpose in this world. We do this by acknowledging and living with passion. We do this through loving all people (even though not all people are likable at all times). We love all people by seeing their divine image even when they are trying to hide. We do this by erasing margins, experiencing our kinship with all of our brothers and sisters, while still maintaining healthy boundaries.

How are you seeking your authentic self and God?
How are you searching for and living your purpose?
How are you treating everyone as kinfolk?

Noach

Noach—day one

This is the line of Noah.

—Genesis 6:9

This week's parashah is *Noach* (comfort). It is interesting that the parashah that describes the Flood, the destruction of the world, is called "comfort." In thinking about this, I believe there are a couple of lessons that God and Torah are teaching us. The first lesson is that Noah is a simple and righteous man. Extrapolating a bit, this helps me understand and teach that comfort is simplicity, decency, and justice. God is comforted by the fact that there is at least one person who not only possesses these qualities—because we all do—but who also lives these qualities. This is the challenge to all of us. Torah is teaching us that for the world to truly survive, we all need to live comfort for ourselves, in our families, in our communities, and in the world. Without living these principles, the world falls apart.

How are you living decently?

How are you living loyally to your principles?

Even in times of hardship, how are you able to live as an example of decency in action?

Noach—day two

Noah was a righteous and simple man.

—Genesis 6:9

I speak often about living simply. I want to underscore that living a simple life is not the same as living a stupid life. It does not mean living as a simpleton. Living a simple life means making sure that I don't unnecessarily complicate things. Life is both complex and simple. Simple living means taking a breath. It means living for today and planning for tomorrow. Living a simple life involves doing what I can today to the best of my ability and knowing that I won't finish everything. Living a simple life entails doing what I am supposed to do, not everything that I want. Simple living is adhering to my authentic script, not some false script. Simple living is appreciating what I have. Simple living is accepting my place and purpose in the world.

How are you complicating life?

How are you living a simple life?

Are you able to go to sleep at night knowing you have done the very best you could each day; if not, what most frequently weighs upon your conscience?

Noach—day three

Noah walked with God.

—GENESIS 6:9

Rabbi Hillel the elder defines living a life of justice in the following way: "What is hateful to you, do not do to anyone else." Justice means caring about my actions. Living a life of justice means realizing my importance to God, my community, and the world. Also in his interview with Carl Stern, Rabbi Abraham Joshua Heschel, *z"l*, said that "we are each a divine need." Many of us have a hard time with this type of living because we do not accept that we are important. Too many people think that they are just "little fish." While this is true in one sense, in the bigger picture this feeling is a lie; given our essence, how can we be "little fish"? We are all created in the image of God, and we are all partners with God, as we were taught in last week's parashah. Living a life of justice means that I take my life and my actions seriously. Living a life of justice means that I have to discern what things are hateful. Living a life of justice entails not using the phrase "everyone else does it" as an excuse for my bad behavior. Living a life of justice involves me taking actions in the world, and it forces me to be an active participant rather than a passive victim. Living a life of justice requires commitment and action.

What hateful things that have been done to you are you in turn doing to others?

What hateful things are you committed to not doing to others?

How are you living as a divine need?

Noach—day four

The earth was also corrupt before God.

—GENESIS 6:11

Another lesson in this parashah is that when we are corrupt, we also corrupt the land in which we live. Think about this statement: when we corrupt, pollute, and destroy our souls, we also destroy the souls of others; we corrupt, pollute, and destroy the communities in which we live; and ultimately, we corrupt, pollute, and destroy the world in which we live. Think of how many examples of this you hear about on a daily basis. I believe that God did not just arbitrarily send the Flood; the Flood was the response to the corruption, pollution, and destruction that we humans had wrought on the land.

What are some of the ways in which you know you are corrupting your soul?

What causes you to stand idly by, watching others corrupt and destroy our world?

When has it taken a catastrophic event to get you to respond in a divine way?

Noach—day five

And God looked upon the earth ...
all flesh had corrupted its way.

—GENESIS 6:12

The generation in which Noah lived was, according to our tradition, the worst one ever. Some of the commentaries say that what made this generation so bad was their exploitation of the poor, the widow, the orphan, and the stranger. These people, the powerless, were used, abused, and killed by people who were stronger. It was truly survival of the fittest. God was incensed that his creations could treat other humans in this manner. In fact, the Torah says that the corruption of the people was so great that even the land was affected and infected. While this may seem over the top, I think that there is much truth in it; when something bad happens in a space, it seems as if the aura, the smell, the very air of the space itself becomes infected or at least a reminder of negativity. We have some rituals to cleanse the space, such as using a smudge stick, repainting, re-carpeting, changing the mezuzah, and remodeling the entire space. We do this as an acknowledgment of this lesson in the Torah, that our actions can and do influence the space in which we live.

Whom are you exploiting for your own personal gain?

What spaces do you need to clean up
because of past negative actions?

How are you influencing the spaces that you
occupy today, both positively and negatively?

Noach—day six

For the earth is filled with violence.

—GENESIS 6:13

Given the atmosphere of corruption and exploitation, Noah's ability to rise above this negativity is heroic. We all know the tremendous pull of negativity. We have all experienced the magnetic force that negativity has upon us. Yet, given all of this, Noah was a righteous man. Some people say that had he lived in a different generation he would not have been so righteous. I disagree; I think that it takes more commitment and more strength to be righteous in the presence of negativity than when surrounded by other positive people. Our prophets exemplify great courage by confronting the leaders of their time and rebuking them. All of the great social justice movements have come about because people were willing to challenge and stand up to leaders of the status quo.

What are the largest sources of corruption and exploitation in your life?

What are the kinds of negativity to which you are most susceptible?

How can you respond heroically, standing against these forces of negativity?

Noach—day seven

He drank of the wine and became drunk.... And Ham ... saw the nakedness of his father.

—Genesis 9:21–22

This parashah also teaches us that every storm ends and that our job is to renew creation by picking up the pieces after the storm has passed. Noah grows a vineyard and gets drunk. This is not the plan that God had in mind. God wanted Noah to plant the seeds of every tree, plant, fruit, and vegetable and to help them grow. Noah decided that what was needed first was a vineyard. Noah was so shaken by the Flood and the sight of destruction, he needed a drink! We all know what happened after that; his son, Ham, knew him. Ham made a mockery out of his father's drunkenness and took advantage of Noah. Ham did what he did because he could. Noah's part in this was getting drunk, dulling all of his senses.

How do you seek relief from the aftermath of disasters in your life?

What are some of the ways you rebuild the land and the lives of your fellows?

Instead of being like Noah or Ham, how can you act as a divine need?

Lech L'cha

Lech L'cha—day one

And Adonai said to Abram, "Go for yourself."

—Genesis 12:1

This week's Torah portion is *Lech L'cha* (go for yourself). This is the beginning of the story of Abraham. Abram is told to go to himself in order to find himself, by leaving his land and his father's home, and to live his own authentic life. This is a very important lesson for us; from childhood, where we live places certain demands on us. These demands are not necessarily bad, but as we all know, that which our social circle deems important may not really be in keeping with our ideals, morals, values, and purpose. So, in order to go to ourselves, we have to leave outside influences and find a space of our own in which we are able to hear the call of our soul. This is true for Abraham, Jacob, Joseph, Judah, Moses, Jesus, Muhammad, all the way to Bill Wilson, who was in a hospital bed, all alone, when he had his spiritual awakening. Too often we are so busy, hearing so much chatter, that we are unable to distinguish what is authentic from what is phony. The first move is to get away from the places that want to keep us pigeonholed so that we can find our true self.

How do you distinguish truth from chatter?

By whom and how do you feel you have been pigeonholed?

Where do you go to connect to God and your own soul?

Lech L'cha—day two

From your people …

—GENESIS 12:1

The second move that we have to make is to leave the people around us who have their own ideas of who we are or who we should be. We don't have to hate these people, as they usually have the best of intentions. Yet, even with the best of intentions, most people are still interested in their own needs, and their vision and ideas for others are tainted. Sometimes, these people want us to serve their needs and don't care about ours. Again, this may not be from a place of bad intention, just from a place of unconscious self-centeredness.

Whom do you have to leave in order to find yourself?

Upon whom are you trying to force your agenda?

How are you striking out on your own to find your true self, rather than just being like everyone else?

Lech L'cha—day three

From your father's house …

—Genesis 12:1

The third move is, in my opinion, the most important and the most difficult: Abram is told to leave his father's home. Honoring our parents is an extremely important value in our tradition. How can these two seemingly conflicting claims be reconciled? In Genesis 2:24 we are told that a human should leave his or her parents' home and cling or have union with a mate. Here again, we are being told to leave our father's house in order to find ourselves and be for ourselves. The reasons are similar; if we stay in our father's home, we are bound to live by our father's decrees. While these decrees may work for our fathers, they may not be what nourishes and grows our own soul. We can never be who we are truly meant to be when we live in the shadow of our parents. This is not an indictment of parents; it is simply the truth. Our parents want what is best for us, and while they may believe they know what that means, they cannot know our purpose. We have to find our own niche, our own path, and our own place in life—these cannot be given to us by someone else. We have to find it, claim it, and live it. We honor our parents by living our own authentic script. We honor them by becoming the person that they and God created. We honor them by listening to the call of our soul.

How are you certain you are living as your true self?

How do you reconcile conflicting claims in your life?

What are the ways you honor yourself, others, and God by living your unique script?

Lech L'cha—day four

So Abram departed as Adonai had spoken to him.

—Genesis 12:4

This parashah teaches us that even with our human foibles and frailties, we are able to be heroic. In the opening chapter of this parashah, God tells Abram and Sarai to leave their home in Haran, all of their neighbors and kinfolk, and even the home of their father and go on a journey without having any idea where they are going. They leave everything that they know. They leave the comfort and safety of their lives and they go on this journey without a definite destination. This is heroic to me: to leave everything that you are used to, to leave the comforts that you have obtained in order to go out for yourself and find yourself is a heroic journey. We learn that having everything without having ourselves is still empty living. Without having ourselves and without being grounded in our own souls, we can't have everything. Conversely, having a sense of self and being grounded in and living from our own souls truly means everything.

How do you acknowledge your own heroism by rising above your foibles to continue on your own life's journey?

What external trappings have distracted you from your inner life?

What are the practices you engage in to help build, nurture, and follow your inner voice or God's voice?

Lech L'cha—day five

Abram took Sarai his wife ... and the souls they made in Haran.

—GENESIS 12:5

We are also told in this parashah that Abram and Sarai, his wife, made souls in Haran. Since they were childless, there are many thoughts on what "making souls" means. I believe that it refers to their bringing people to believe in and follow the call of God, rather than the desire to worship idols. Making souls means helping others find their unique purpose and place in the world. I know that making souls has to include helping people trust their soul's knowledge over and above the voices of others and above their other inner voices. Making souls means being able to hear the call of the soul of another person and becoming concerned with his or her concerns, as Rabbi Abraham Joshua Heschel, *z"l*, teaches in his reflection on transitive concern in his book, *Man Is Not Alone*. Making souls must mean helping people realize the lies they tell themselves and how not to follow these lies.

How do you help others hear the call of God and their own soul?

What is your practice that helps you hear your soul's knowledge and trust this knowledge over and above the other voices in your life?

How often do you recognize the lies you tell yourself, and what are they?

Lech L'cha—day six

And the land was not able to bear them
... so they could not live together.
—GENESIS 13:6

Another lesson of this parashah comes when the herdsmen of Lot and Abram start quarreling. One of the ways to interpret this is that Lot needs to rebel against his uncle, Abram, in order to find his own place. He doesn't want to live in Abram's shadow. While this is natural and good, the way he goes about it is not. Too many people rebel instead of individuate. This is one of the great issues of our time and of all time. Lot's need to rebel, not to learn from his uncle, causes a split between the two relatives. Jealousy and envy cause strife, and we take actions that are not always in our own best interests and not in the best interests of God and others. Because of his rebellious attitude and actions, Lot chooses to dwell in greener pastures and goes into the bad neighborhood of Sodom. The Torah tells us that Sodom is a place of great negativity. Lot, in his rebellion and hubris, believes that he can live in the midst of negativity and not be affected. He does not proceed with care, nor does he plan for his future and the future of his family; he sees only what looks good in the moment.

How are you rebelling or individuating?

What are some of the possible consequences of the choices you are currently making?

When should you take charge, and when do you belong in a supporting role?

Lech L'cha—day seven

And when Abram heard … he
armed … and pursued them.

—Genesis 14:14

We also learn in this parashah about not putting someone out of our heart even when they have to leave our home. Abram hears that an enemy of Sodom has captured his nephew Lot, and even though Lot left Abram, Abram knows that he has to help his nephew and save him from captivity and worse. Abram goes with his community and rescues his nephew. For Abram there was no hesitation; his kinsman was in danger and he had to go and help. The fact that Lot rebelled against him did not matter. What mattered was the principle of being responsible for the concerns of others. Our tradition teaches that every Jew is responsible for every other Jew. Alcoholics Anonymous teaches that whenever anyone anywhere reaches out for help, those in recovery are responsible to help those still suffering from addiction. Abram embodies this teaching in this passage.

Whom are you ignoring because you were hurt?

Whom are you letting be captive to another person or to his or her own lies because you are hurt or angry?

How can you rise above your own feelings and be responsible for helping those you have been hurt by, to the best of your ability?

Va-yeira

Va-yeira—day one

And Adonai appeared to him.

—GENESIS 18:1

This week's Torah portion is *Va-yeira* (He appeared). The entire portion is about seeing and not seeing. The question that is continually being answered in this parashah is about differentiating between what we are seeing and what we are not seeing.

The theme of sight appears at the beginning of the portion. God sees and appears to Abraham. The Rabbis say that God came because Abraham was recuperating from his circumcision. This teaches us to see when people are ill, recuperating, or suffering, be it physically, emotionally, or spiritually. We not only have to see these facts, but we also have to respond by appearing and showing up for them to give them comfort.

In what ways are you showing up for those who need comfort?

How do you see the suffering of others?

What are some of the ways you are able to participate with others in their joy?

Va-yeira—day two

And he lifted up his eyes and saw …

—Genesis 18:2

While engaged with God through God appearing to him, Abraham lifts up his eyes and sees. What does he see? He sees three men who are walking on the path that leads by his tent. Abraham runs to meet them and asks them to accept his hospitality. There are at least three teachings from this story.

The first is that we have to lift up our eyes to see. I understand this interesting phrase to mean that we have to make a conscious effort in order to see. Merely looking does not do it. Too often we look and don't see. We lift up our eyes and see when we are engaged in pursuing truth. We lift up our eyes and see when we ask questions. We lift up our eyes and see when we are passionate about life. We lift up our eyes and see when we revel in the wonder of living. We lift up our eyes and see when we recognize and honor the sacredness of each event in our lives. We live in a world that is in dire need of sight. Our world has chosen to wear blinders and keep our narrow, egotistical, and selfish views.

How are you lifting up your eyes to see what is, the whole picture?

How and when do you blind yourself through selfishness and self-seeking?

How are you seeing the "sublime wonder of living," as Rabbi Abraham Joshua Heschel, *z"l*, teaches us in *God in Search of Man* (43)?

Va-yeira—day three

When he saw them, he ran to
meet them from the tent.
—Genesis 18:2

The second lesson is one of hospitality. Abraham does not wait for the three men to come by, half-heartedly asking if they need anything. He runs to meet them and asks them, even begs them, to let him be of service to them. He even offers to wash their feet. Abraham wants the men to know that he cares so much he even wants them to rest and refresh their feet so they can continue on their journey in strength. The men agree, and Abraham prepares a feast for them, watching over them to serve them anything that they need. He partakes of nothing himself so that the men know that their welfare is what is of paramount importance to him.

How do you feel burdened by helping others
when they ask or even beg you for help?

When and whom do you welcome
into your home and heart?

In which ways do you let people, all people, know
that they are important and have dignity?

Va-yeira—day four

If I have found favor in your eyes …

—GENESIS 18:3

The third lesson may be the most important of all. God appears to Abraham, and then Abraham lifts up his eyes and sees the three men. Think about this scenario for a moment. Here Abraham is hanging out with God and leaves God to serve three strangers. What chutzpah! Actually this teaches us that if we cannot serve God's creations, if we are indifferent to the needs of others even when we are meditating, praying, or studying, then we are not really connected to God. Too often people will say that they are too busy praying or meditating or studying to do a *mitzvah* (commandment). Too often people have to be forced to do the next right thing. Too often people act as if they themselves matter first, last, and always. Too often people say they know who is worthy of being served, and they serve only their own kind. These people are not people of God, they are people of the lie. The problem is that they sound convincing. They sound as if they are the guardians of faith and truth and God. They are liars. God, Torah, and our tradition teach us through Abraham's example that we can never be so busy, so engaged, so wrapped up that we fail to see the needs of others and be a person of faith and of God.

Whom have you run to help this week, this month, this year?

What opportunities to serve, help, and offer hospitality have you seized upon?

How do you see each person, yourself included, as a divine being?

Va-yeira—day five

Shall not the Judge of all the earth deal justly?
—Genesis 18:25

Later in this chapter is the famous bargaining scene between Abraham and God. Rabbi Harold Schulweis, *z"l*, taught me that these verses make it incumbent upon us to argue with God whenever we believe that God is not doing justly. Abraham's courage to stand up to God, while acknowledging his own place, continues to amaze me and disturb me. What disturbs me is that I have to question myself whether I am doing justly in all of my affairs. Second, I have to question myself about what injustices I ignore in my life and in the lives of others. Third, I am forced to accept responsibility for the injustices that are perpetrated in the name of freedom by the United States and Israel and other countries. As Rabbi Abraham Joshua Heschel, *z"l*, wrote in *Moral Grandeur and Spiritual Audacity*, "In a free society, some are guilty and all are responsible."

How are you treating seriously your responsibility to deal justly?

How are you arguing with God, others, and yourself to do the next right action?

How do you choose when to obey and when to disobey?

Va-yeira—day six

But God said to Abraham, "... Whatever
Sarah tells, do as she says."

—Genesis 21:12

In this parashah, after the argument with God, Abraham succumbs to his own fear and apathy. When Sarah decides to throw his son, Ishmael, out of the house and the community, Abraham is silent. While he does ask God what to do and God tells him to listen to Sarah, he does not argue this time. What happened to the person who could argue for nameless and faceless strangers? I am perplexed that Abraham, in this case, just accepts what God says. We know that he loves his son and Hagar from what happens later in the story, yet he does not argue in favor of their staying part of the family and community.

How are you caring for and about strangers
more than those closest to you?

What happens to your morality and sense of
justice when it comes to those closest to you?

How do you care for the widow, orphan,
stranger, and poor person in yourself and in
the inner lives of those closest to you?

Va-yeira—day seven

God opened her eyes and she saw a well of water.

—Genesis 21:19

Hagar falls into the same trap as Abraham. She forgets who she is and her experience with God. When the water that Abraham gave her for the trip runs out, she sits down and waits to die. Not only that, but she also moves away from her son because she doesn't want to watch him die of thirst. Hagar is oblivious to her surroundings and to the promise God gave her while she was pregnant. It is only when an angel comes to her, after her son has cried out, that she notices the well of water that was near her the entire time. She did not cry out for help; rather, she cried for herself. She was in such despair that she failed to see the solution that was in front of her eyes.

What are some of the ways in which your despair is blinding you to the solution that is so close at hand?

How are you giving in to your hopelessness and "why even bother" attitudes?

Which wells are you not seeing?

Chayei Sarah

Chayei Sarah—day one

Sarah's lifetime was one hundred years
and twenty years and seven years.

—Genesis 23:1

This week's parashah is *Chayei Sarah* (life of Sarah). The Torah portion starts out with Sarah's death. Yet, it is called "the life" or "the living of Sarah." This always puzzles me. This is a lovely *drash* (interpretation). I believe that the Torah is telling us about the Angel of Death.

Not the Angel of Death that comes at the end of our lives, but the Angel of Death that takes our living from us while we are still alive. The parashah is teaching us that we have to live until we die. Too many of us are just existing, not living. Sarah lived all of her years. She lived a difficult life. She was a partner with her husband in creating a people that worshipped Adonai, the one God. She helped Abraham steal people away from worshipping idols and, as the text says earlier, made souls who worshipped God.

How are you engaged in really living each day?

What are the ways you are staying open to new ideas and new experiences no matter how old you are?

Are you worshipping idols or God, and how?

Chayei Sarah—day two

These were the years of Sarah.

—GENESIS 23:1

Sarah had reasons to give up. She was barren for most of her life, and yet she kept believing and acting as a representative of God, as a divine need. Sarah never stopped living as a partner of God and a partner of her husband. Sarah never stopped caring for the other people in her household, with the exception of Hagar. Sarah, being human, had fears and worries. Instead of giving in to them, she continued to rise above her fears and disappointments to serve God.

What are you still in despair about?

How do you keep hope alive?

How are you rising above your fears in order to serve your higher purpose?

Chayei Sarah—day three

And Sarah died.

—Genesis 23:2

Not only does Sarah rise above her own fears and disappointments, but she also goes beyond her own self-interest to care for others, especially her husband. Twice she says that she is Abraham's sister so that the rulers of the countries they go to won't kill him. Twice she allows herself to be sold by her husband so that he can live. Each time she has faith and belief that God will protect her and Abraham. Each time her faith and belief are proved correct. She also goes beyond her own self-interest when she gives her maidservant, Hagar, to Abraham to have a child. Sarah knows how much Abraham wants a child, and in caring for her husband's interest, she goes beyond her own ego and interest to fill a need of Abraham's.

Whose interests do you serve?

Who is so dear to you that you will let go of your self-interest for their betterment?

How does your ego help you serve others, and how does it help you serve only you?

Chayei Sarah—day four

Abraham came to eulogize for Sarah.

—Genesis 23:2

Another lesson in this parashah is shown to us when Abraham comes to mourn for Sarah; in a *hesped* (eulogy) I believe we should extol the deceased person's virtues and then teach the lessons from their life. We are taught, by Abraham and Sarah, that life never truly ends. Sarah's life lessons are taught and used by others, including the other matriarchs. In this way, she is still alive and living, *chayah* (to live). We learn that after Abraham extols her and teaches the lessons of her life, he cries. Do we cry when we realize the void that is created when a loved one dies? Do we cry when we realize the void that we create whenever we stop living our authentic life script? Do we cry because we are aware of the lessons that the world has forgotten and the destruction that results from this forgetting?

What actions are you committed to doing each day, week, month, and year to honor and fill the void of a loved one who has died?

What are some of the lessons you have learned about yourself by trying to live someone else's life?

What lessons do you forget over and over, having to learn the hard way from the destruction that forgetting can cause?

Chayei Sarah—day five

To weep for her ...

—GENESIS 23:2

The Angel of Death continues to lie to us, and these lies are so believable. We have to use Sarah as an example and continue to uncover the lies and defeat this spiritual enemy. We have to examine ourselves each day, acknowledge the lies we tell ourselves, and examine them for the destruction that they cause ourselves and others.

Make a daily list of the lies that the Angel of Death tells you so that you can recognize the enemy.

Make a list of the ways you do not give in to the despairing attitude of "why bother?"

Each day write down the ways in which you have lived in joy and hope.

Chayei Sarah—day six

Abraham buried Sarah.

—Genesis 23:19

Sarah teaches us to really live until we die. She never gave in to the Angel of Death, who wanted her to give up on the joy of living, simply existing until she died physically. Sarah did not buy the lies of the Angel of Death that life was pure suffering and then you die. Sarah did not allow herself to become overwhelmed by despair and live a life ruled by an attitude of "why bother?" Sarah continues to teach us that it is not only possible but mandatory to make lemonade out of lemons.

How are you resisting the temptation of the Angel of Death to give up on living?

What actions are you taking so that you remember and celebrate the joy of living?

When despair starts to overtake you, what can remind you that you are a divine need?

Chayei Sarah—day seven

His sons Isaac and Ishmael buried him.

—Genesis 25:9

A third lesson happens at the end of this parashah; Isaac and Ishmael come together to bury their father Abraham. In our text, the first time that Isaac and Ishmael come together as adults is to bury their father. How incredibly sad this is.

When do you regularly join family for *simchas* (times of joy or celebrations) each year?

How are you making time to see people more often than just at funerals?

Whom do you consider family; with whom do you choose to share and celebrate life, recovery, and rituals?

Toledot

Toledot—day one

Isaac pleaded with God for his wife
because she was barren.

—Genesis 25:21

This week's parashah is *Toledot* (story); in it we begin the story of Jacob. At the start, we learn that Rebekah, like Sarah, has been barren for about twenty years. Isaac prays to God for Rebekah, and she becomes pregnant. There is an interesting difference, however, between Isaac and Abraham. Like Sarah, Rebekah is barren; she is unable to have children, and Isaac pleads to God on her behalf. This is completely different from what his father did. Abraham never asked God to help Sarah. He asked for heirs for himself, never for Sarah. We see here that Isaac learned about the importance of family from his father's errors. Isaac shows great love and compassion for his wife; he wants to relieve her suffering. Because of his prayers, we are told, Rebekah conceives.

Whom are you more like, Abraham or Isaac?

How do you show Isaac's type of love and compassion for the people you love?

Do you relieve their suffering, add to it, or stay indifferent?

Toledot—day two

She said, "If it is this, why is this happening to me?"
—Genesis 25:22

Once Rebekah becomes pregnant, she feels anguish because she is constantly experiencing a war inside. She has no idea what pregnancy is like and wants to know why she feels her twins battling inside of her. She cries out, "Why is this happening to me?" How many of us identify with this experience? We often ask the question why and try to figure out a reason. Rebekah teaches us a different path for finding the solution to the experiences that baffle us. Rebekah goes to ask God what is happening.

When do you experience a battle between two opposing thoughts or feelings?

How long do you stay in this war?

When do you seek the counsel of God and others?

Toledot—day three

And she went to inquire of Adonai.
—Genesis 25:22

Another lesson that Rebekah teaches us is shown in her waiting for an answer from God. God reveals to Rebekah what is happening and what will happen. Rebekah is in a state where she is capable, available, and worthy of God's revelations. Her state is one of vulnerability, sincerity, and teachability. Rebekah is present in the moment and wants to find a solution, rather than needing to have the answer. This is an important distinction, and she, like we, does not always stay in this state. In fact, as we see later in the parashah, Rebekah does not continue to ask God how to handle things but decides what the right decisions are, asking no one for guidance.

Are you open to solutions, or do you usually wallow in your problems?

How are you showing yourself to be capable, available, and worthy?

When do you wait for a response from God or your mentors, and when do you make decisions without consulting anyone else?

Toledot—day four

Esau said to Jacob, "Give me some of that red stuff to gulp down, for I am famished."

—Genesis 25:30

We learn that Esau is born to Rebekah first, followed by Jacob. Jacob's character is hinted at by the way the text describes his entry into the world. He is holding on to Esau's heel, as if he were fighting to come out first. *Yaakov*, "Jacob" in Hebrew, means "heel" or "supplanter." The narrative about Jacob in this parashah tells us how Jacob tries and succeeds in taking his brother's place in the family. Esau, we learn, is a really simple man of passion and impulse. He supplies the food for the family and is looked down upon by his brother, Jacob. Jacob knows that he can take advantage of Esau's impulsive nature. In a moment of Esau's vulnerability, Jacob is able to swap some lentil stew for Esau's birthright. While it seems as if Esau does not value this birthright, there is another way to view this story: Esau is so focused on his hunger, believing that he is going to die without food at that precise moment, he is willing to do anything to live.

How often do you use someone's vulnerability against them so that you can take advantage and control of a situation?

When do you allow your own vulnerabilities to hurt you?

Are you embracing your own life, really living it, or are you trying to live someone else's life? How?

Toledot—day five

Jacob said, "First sell me your birthright."
—GENESIS 25:31

One of the saddest lessons we learn is about disconnection—disconnection from God, our partner, our families, and ourselves. Jacob is a twin, and he disconnects from his own twin brother, Esau, in order to get what he wants. He does not care what effect this disconnection and trickery has on his brother or on himself. I can relate to this because, while my brother Neal is not my twin, in my indecent years of using and stealing I used any and all means of trickery to take advantage of Neal's vulnerabilities and get what I wanted when I wanted it. The real crime of Jacob's, of mine, and of anyone else who has engaged in this type of behavior is having stolen the dignity of another person. We have treated them as objects for our pleasure and not honored their divinity.

What are some times you have let the feeling of disconnection drive you toward destructive behavior?

How have you tried to steal the dignity of another?

How have you forgotten your own dignity?

Rebekah said to her son Jacob, "... in order
that he might bless you before he dies."

—Genesis 27:6–10

Rebekah disconnects from her husband, Isaac, by not telling him of God's revelation to her and by thwarting his efforts and taking advantage of his kindness and love. Isaac is an honest person who does not believe that his wife, his partner, would ever trick him. Rebekah tricks Isaac and lies to him by omitting God's prophecy. Any time we act like Rebekah or Jacob, we disconnect from God because we are not honoring either our own divinity or the divinity of others.

How have you used deceit to hurt or
disconnect from someone you love?

Of which of the subtle shades of deceit, the lies
you tell yourself and others, are you aware?

How do your lies of omission keep you
from being your best self?

Toledot—day seven

Your curse be upon me—do as I say
and go fetch them for me.

—Genesis 27:13

Rebekah creates a situation where relationships are broken and set afire. I call this "relationship arson." We create this when we set two people against each other and then stand back and watch them blow. It happens when we say to one person how much better they are than the other and how the other one is going to get something that the first will not. It happens when we condone bad behavior by one person because it is "for the best" or because "God wants it this way." God, as I understand God, never wants us to treat others as less than human. God wants us to live together in harmony, not in strife. Rebekah sets up the rivalry between Jacob and Esau, and both then play their roles. Isaac becomes a pawn in the drama that Rebekah set up. Everyone suffers. While it seems as if the commentators clean up Jacob's actions, the Torah never mentions Rebekah again, not even her death.

How do you set fire to relationships so that
you can then be seen as a hero?

What bad behavior are you condoning in others
because the "end justifies the means"?

Who becomes "collateral damage" in your
zeal to set fire to relationships?

Va-yetzei

Va-yetzei—day one

Jacob went out from Beer-Sheva and set out for Haran.

—GENESIS 28:10

This week's parashah is *Va-yetzei* (he went out). This is the continuation of the story of Jacob, as he is running away from his brother Esau's anger.

Jacob's dream has a ladder in it stretching from earth to heaven. On the ladder are angels going up and down. I have come to understand the entire dream sequence as God's answer to Jacob's unspoken fear of leaving home and the unknown journey ahead of him. I think that we can all identify with this fear. Remember the first time you went to school, the first time you slept over someplace other than your home, the first time away at camp? The fear of leaving everything we knew, even for a night, was, maybe still is, terribly strong for most of us. Couple that with feeling unknown and uprooted, having no idea when and if you will return home, and your entire life, which you thought you had planned out, feels overwhelmingly out of control. I think we can all understand Jacob's unspoken fear.

From what or whom are you running?

What are some of your unspoken fears of the unknown?

When you find yourself leaving the familiar, how can you respond with faith instead of responding out of fear?

Va-yetzei—day two

A ladder was set up on the ground and … angels of God were going up and coming down.

—Genesis 28:12

I believe what we are all seeking is a canopy of wholeness, a symbol of safety and security that makes us feel protected. The ladder may represent the protection that is all around us, which we sometimes fail to see. This protection is twofold: we are surrounded by the angels of God going up and down the ladder; these angels are among us, and we are also, ourselves, angels of God. These angels are friends, family, doctors, spiritual guides, and others who want to help us live well and care for us when we are sick. Most of us are more afraid to accept help, for fear of looking weak, than we are of the situation for which we need help. Being an angel of God means that we have to help lift others up. As my brother, Rabbi Neal Borovitz, said to me, "This is the model for a community." Those who are able have to help those who are down; otherwise we will all fall down into the abyss. Those who are down need to accept the help of others; otherwise they will sink lower. We have to forgo our pride and prejudice to be angels of God. All of us have been in the position both to give help and of needing help; our place on the ladder is fluid.

How do you recognize the angels all around you?

What are the ways you act as an angel for others?

Do you live in accordance with Ben Franklin's saying "We must, indeed, all hang together or, most assuredly, we shall all hang separately"?

Va-yetzei—day three

Adonai is in this place and I did not know it.

—Genesis 28:16

How destructive is false pride and prejudice? In the first chapter of this parashah, Jacob says, "God is in this place and I did not know it." The Hebrew word for "I" here is *anochi*. The use of *anochi* is usually reserved for God and our godlike image. Also, in Hebrew the word *anochi* is superfluous given the form of the verb "to know" here, which is why, in his book by the same name, Rabbi Lawrence Kushner translates this sentence as "God was in this place and I, I did not know." Given this grammatical anomaly, I read this sentence as a powerful lesson: when I do not know and recognize that I, *anochi*, was created *b'tzelem Elohim* [in the image of God], then my ego, my puffed-up vision of myself, my I takes over, and I am unaware of God and/or anyone else's existence except in the context of my own personal use. The text goes on to say that this place is the house of God. Since it is not a special place, Torah is telling us that every place is the house of God and that God is in every place.

When are you aware of being *anochi*?

In which areas of your life does false pride, feeling less than or more than another, rule you?

How can you live in God's world more often?

Va-yetzei—day four

You are truly my bone and flesh.

—Genesis 29:14

This portion teaches us a lot about deception and the harms that deception brings to others, yourself, and the world. The first hint at the deception that is to happen is when Laban, Jacob's uncle, meets Jacob and hears his story of how he came to be there in the first place. Upon hearing Jacob's story, Laban says, "You are truly my bone and flesh," meaning, you and I are brothers in deception. Jacob does not at that time understand the full meaning of this phrase and thinks that his uncle is going to help him.

Jacob actually takes Laban at his word, thinking that if he works seven years for Rachel, Laban will deliver on his end of the deal. Jacob, the deceiver and trickster, believes that no one is sharp enough to trick him. This is the great lie that many of us tell ourselves. Jacob, as we all know, gets tricked and marries the other sister, Leah. He cannot believe that this has happened to him, that he has been so foolish. Laban then makes a new deal with Jacob and winds up getting fourteen years of work from Jacob as the bride price for Rachel. Jacob, who believes that Rachel is his true love, never comments on the fact that Rachel took part in this deception.

When do you let the arrogance of "being the smartest person in the room" rule you?

How do you know if someone is trustworthy in the areas in which you are placing trust in them?

Whose deception have you overlooked because of being blinded by lust, love, or greed?

Va-yetzei—day five

Adonai has seen my affliction.

—GENESIS 29:32

Another lesson comes from Leah, the unloved wife. Leah thinks that if she has children, then Jacob will finally love her. After she has three sons, Reuben, Shimon, and Levi, she realizes the folly of her fantasy. The names of these three represent Leah's hope that God will open Jacob's heart toward her. They translate as "seeing," "hearing," and "joining." Leah names her first three sons in accordance with her hopes of Jacob seeing her, hearing her, and joining her in love and pain. None of this works; Leah is still unloved.

How is your need to be loved blinding you to the truth of your relationships?

When do you try to buy someone's love or friendship?

How do you deal with the pain of unrequited love?

Va-yetzei—day six

This time I will praise Adonai.

—Genesis 29:35

Leah finally gets it; with the birth of her fourth son, Judah, she realizes that children are a gift from God. "Judah" translates to "praise" or "gratitude." Leah finally has given up her fantasy about Jacob and realizes that God's love is enough for her. She comes to believe that God has given her the gift of children, and she has to be grateful for what she has, not resentful about what she does not. While many may call this settling, I believe that this is the nature of true acceptance.

How do you live in gratitude for what you have?

What does it take for you to have self-love and accept God's Love?

How do you experience the difference between acceptance and settling?

Va-yetzei—day seven

And in that dream … and I answered, "Here I am."

—Genesis 31:11

An important teaching from this parashah is about loyalty. Too often we are loyal to people instead of being loyal to principles. Jacob has been loyal to his mother and even to his uncle, both of whom are deceivers. Jacob has been loyal to Rachel, who also turns out to be a deceiver. Toward the end of this parashah, God calls out to Jacob, and he answers, "*Hineni*" (Here I am). Jacob then hears the call of return, return to his homeland, return to his father, return to his proper place. Jacob could have ignored this call. Instead, he changes his loyalty. He goes from being loyal to people to being loyal to God and God's principles—not completely, but he starts his change. When accused by Laban of stealing his idols, Jacob tells Laban to search his entire camp and if someone has stolen these idols or anything else from Laban, they will die. Jacob is no longer loyal to a person; Jacob becomes loyal to the principle of truth and honest dealings.

This is so important for all of us; when we are loyal to a person, we lose our integrity and sometimes our good name. Being loyal to principles allows us to practice the utmost loyalty. When we are able to be loyal to God, we are able to live as our authentic selves. Only then can we be loyal to the people we care about.

What principles do you hold most dear?

How do you practice loyalty to these principles?

Which old behaviors have you let go of by adopting God's will?

Va-yishlach

Va-yishlach—day one

Jacob sent messengers ahead to his brother Esau.

—Genesis 32:4

This week's parashah is *Va-yishlach* (he sent). This is the third Torah portion about Jacob. He has left Laban and is on his way back home. Jacob is returning after twenty years away, still afraid of Esau, his twin brother. Jacob sends messengers ahead of him to let Esau know that he is coming. Here is the first lesson of our portion: we should not just pop in on someone after a long absence; it is important to let the person know that we are coming. This gives them the choice and opportunity to greet us and prepare for our visit. This is especially true when it involves someone we have harmed. It is important to give the injured party notice of our arrival so that they have a choice about whether to see us and time to prepare for our meeting.

How are you allowing your guilt over past actions rule what you do today?

With whom do you need to make contact in order to do *t'shuvah* (repentance)?

What is stopping you from doing this?

Va-yishlach—day two

The messengers returned to Jacob, saying, "... Esau is coming to meet you with four hundred men."

—GENESIS 32:7

The word used here for "messengers" is not the one usually used in Hebrew. Usually messengers are called *sheluchim*; in this parashah, however, the word used is *malachim* (usually translated as "angels"). I think that the Torah is telling us that Jacob is protected and, once again, he is unaware of God's protection. When these messengers or angels return to tell him that Esau is coming to meet him with four hundred men, Jacob is scared. He does not notice that the people speaking to him are also angels. He forgets that God's angels protect him, and he does not think that Esau is coming to meet him in peace, bringing men to protect and honor Jacob. Why is Jacob so scared? Jacob is afraid because he knows that he is guilty for the ways in which he treated and mistreated his brother. Jacob has carried his guilt for twenty years. Interestingly, he is just as afraid today of his brother as he was when he hurriedly left his home twenty years before. He must also be projecting onto Esau his own belief that he, Jacob, would carry a grudge for all these years.

How do you experience the *malachim* (angels) that surround you and protect you?

What are the situations from your past that still cause you to feel extremely guilty?

In which situations in your life do you carry the same fears as Jacob, believing that *t'shuvah* and redemption are not possible?

Va-yishlach—day three

Jacob was greatly afraid; … he divided
the people … into two camps.

—GENESIS 32:8

Jacob, in his fear, separates his camp. This teaches us to take every precaution in order to protect ourselves and the lives of those around us. After dividing the camps, Jacob prays to God for God's help. Jacob's approach is interesting: he states that he knows that he is "made small from all of God's kindnesses and truth." This awareness is one that many of us could and probably should adopt. It is in direct opposition to what many people believe: that they, themselves, make good things happen and that God and others make bad things happen.

How are you actually becoming more safe by being open to a different experience with others?

How are you aware of the kindness and truth that God and others, acting as God's angels, offer you?

Are you still taking all of the credit for the positive aspects in your life and blaming God and others for the negative?

Va-yishlach—day four

I have been made small from all the kindnesses.

—Genesis 32:11

It is inconceivable to Jacob that Esau could be coming to meet him for any reason other than revenge. In fact, Jacob is so scared that he again prays to God. In this prayer, Jacob reminds God of God's promise and asks God to save him from his brother Esau, whom he assumes is coming to destroy him. While this prayer is mostly self-serving, Jacob gives us the formula for humility: he says, "I have been made small from all of [Your] kindnesses." This is not self-effacing; rather, it is the truth. Whenever someone else or God is kind to us, we are made small. Why? Because when we recognize truth and see that who we are, what we are, and our successes are the result of our hard work and the help of others, including God, we lose a lot of our egotism and narcissism. When we acknowledge this truth, we become more right-sized. Right-sized means owning our part in our success as well as the help we have received from teachers, helpers, parents, and the gifts that God has given us. So, Jacob again hits upon truth even when he tries to bribe God by making this return God's idea and plan.

To whom do you owe gratitude for
their kindnesses and help?

How are you acting grateful to God, who has given
you your abilities, gifts, and uniqueness?

How are you living in egotism, and
how are you living in humility?

Va-yishlach—day five

And a man wrestled with Jacob
until the break of dawn.

—Genesis 32:25

This is the encounter that many of us have when we are in distress over where our lives are at the moment and what our next move will be. This distress is not only about addiction or criminality; this distress is about the way we live in the world. All of us behave in ways that are not holy, ways that feed our most profane self; therefore, all of us need to have this wrestling match with our souls. All of us, at one time or another, have had a choice to treat someone as a divine image or to take advantage of them, treating them as an object. We do this when we don't think of how our actions and decisions will affect others. We do this when we ignore the cries and pleadings of others. We do this when we don't take our own inventories and when we refuse to make *t'shuvah*. Jacob teaches us that all of us, no matter how righteous we think we are, no matter how much we want to see ourselves as the good guys, need to wrestle with our souls. In *The Lonely Man of Faith*, Rabbi Joseph B. Soloveitchik, *z"l*, adds that we must also allow ourselves to "be confronted and defeated by a Higher and Truer Being."

When and how are you aware of your soul's calling to you?

How are you allowing your soul to wrestle
with your baser desires and actions?

Are you allowing God or your higher self
to defeat you? If not now, when?

Va-yishlach—day six

I will not let you go until you bless me.

—Genesis 32:27

The night before he meets Esau, Jacob spends alone. He has another dream where he is struggling with a man/angel. They wrestle all night, and at dawn the angel/man says he has to go. Jacob's hip gets wrenched, and Jacob still hangs on and wrestles this angel/man to a draw. Some commentators say that this is Esau's guardian angel, and others say that this angel/man is Jacob's negativity. Either way, at the end of the night, Jacob is given a new name as a blessing. This name is Israel, "one who struggles with God and others." Again, Jacob realizes that he has been in the presence of the Divine. This time, however, the real Jacob won—not the trickster, but the Jacob who wants to live well and honor the kindnesses and truth that God has bestowed upon him.

How are you wrestling with your negative nature and allowing your soul to win?

How do you realize when you are in the presence of the Divine?

Have you accepted the Hebrew name that you were given at birth, and how are you living the spirit of this name?

Va-yishlach—day seven

So Jacob named the place Peniel.

—Genesis 32:31

Jacob wins the match not because he is stronger; rather, it is because he finally decides to allow himself to be confronted and defeated by a higher and truer being, a higher truth. Jacob wins the match because even though he is injured, he holds on until the end of the contest. Jacob wins the match because this time when he is asked his name, he responds, "Jacob." Jacob wins the match because while he did hide from and lie to his father, now he is open and in truth with his own soul. This is why the place is called Peniel (seeing God face to face). When we confront and hold on to our own souls, we see God. When we face and hold on to another, we see God.

How are you allowing yourself to be confronted and defeated by a higher truth?

When are you open to hearing from and able to follow your soul's direction?

How are you recognizing and seeing God in nature and in other people?

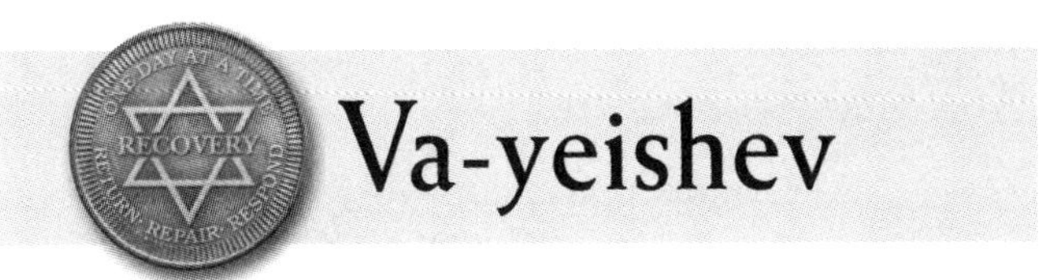

Va-yeishev

Va-yeishev—day one

Now Jacob was settled in the land.

—Genesis 37:1

This week's parashah is *Va-yeishev* (and he settled). After his return from Haran, this is how Jacob's time in the land of Canaan is described. It is interesting that the Torah chose this word, *va-yeishev*, because Jacob never really settles in the land.

What does it mean to settle in a place?

Have you found your place, and how have you really settled into it?

How could you feel more settled in your life?

Va-yeishev—day two

At seventeen years of age, Joseph …

—Genesis 37:2

The parashah begins by telling us about Jacob's lineage, and it starts and stops with Joseph. The Torah is making it seem as if Joseph is the only one of Jacob's children who matters to him, and in fact, the rest of the story seems to underscore this further. Jacob treats Joseph differently from the rest of his children, which is good and bad. It is good because, as parents, we have to treat each of our children as a unique individual. No two children are exactly the same, and we learn in Proverbs 22:6 to teach each child according to his or her own understanding. It is bad because Jacob concentrates on Joseph to the exclusion of the rest of his children. Joseph is not just the favorite—it seems as if he is the only one Jacob cares about, causing the normal sibling rivalry to escalate.

How do you try to be the main attraction in your family to the exclusion of everyone else?

Whom are you ignoring because you want to favor one child, parent, or friend?

What causes you to seek the love of those who are withholding their love?

Va-yeishev—day three

And Joseph brought bad reports.

—Genesis 37:2

Because of his status, Joseph thought that he had privilege rather than responsibility. He was a talebearer about his brothers and never thought he did anything wrong. This is such a prevalent theme in today's society as well. Many people look at their gifts, their status, and their wealth as privileges rather than responsibilities. When we have been blessed, we are obligated to care for others, not put them down. We are commanded to care for the widow, the orphan, the poor, and the stranger, not take advantage of them. Rather than be exclusive, the prophets tell us that we are to be "a light unto the nations" (Isaiah 49:6). In other words, we have to share our good fortune, our intellect, and our wisdom with others, not use it to lord over them.

Of whom are you taking advantage because you can?

What gifts are you using to have power over others instead of raising them up?

When do you use the vulnerabilities of others against them instead of helping strengthen them?

Va-yeishev—day four

Now Israel loved Joseph best of all his sons.

—GENESIS 37:3

This parashah is a continuation of the story of Jacob and begins the story of Joseph and Judah. The irony of this story is, of course, that Jacob was never really settled in the land of his father and grandfather. He made the same errors as his parents and caused great strife in his own life and for his own family.

What errors do you continue to make that are the same as those that your ancestors made?

How are these errors continuing to cause strife in your life and the lives of your family members?

Which of your ancestors' mistakes are you repairing, and how are these repairs bringing peace and harmony to those you interact with?

Va-yeishev—day five

Once Joseph had a dream.

—Genesis 37:5

Joseph is a dreamer. He is able to see a larger picture, which is a great gift. Unfortunately, in the beginning of this parashah, he is only able to see himself as the center of the universe. He thinks it is all about him. He has no consideration for others, not even his own father. We haven't progressed much further, have we? The Bernard Madoff scandal proves this so powerfully; Mr. Madoff used his skill to take advantage of others, not to help them. He used his gifts to reach people for his own gain. He used the vulnerability of people who wanted to be special and in an "exclusive" club to bilk them out of billions of dollars. To be fair, the people who were taken advantage of failed to see their own specialness. They felt that someone else had to recognize them in order for them to truly feel special and deserving. We are all special and deserving; we all matter. There is no club that can confirm this; if we need external validation in order to think that we matter, we probably wouldn't believe it anyway. Joseph kept trying to promote himself and instead wound up in prison.

What does it take for you to realize your uniqueness?

Why do you find it difficult to believe your inner voice about this?

What will it take for you to become part of the oneness of the world?

Va-yeishev—day six

All his sons and daughters sought to
comfort him, but he refused.

—Genesis 37:35

Joseph is sold by his brothers to the Midianites. He is sold into slavery by the ones who should have been protecting him. Their jealousy is so powerful that they commit a grave miscarriage of justice. The brothers want their father to notice them and he doesn't; he is too overcome with grief to care about them. Joseph wins even in death.

Whom are you enslaving instead of protecting?

Whom are you so jealous of that you breach the tenth commandment, coveting something of your neighbor's?

How has this covetousness harmed both yourself and the other person?

Va-yeishev—day seven

So Joseph's master had him put in jail.

—Genesis 39:20

Joseph had to learn the lesson of humility by going back into a pit. This pit was jail in Egypt. To his credit, he did learn this lesson. He found God in the darkest part of his life. This is also, unfortunately, a recurring theme in the world. Many of us have to go all the way down into a pit to find God and learn/relearn how to use our gifts to help others, rather than lord over them.

What has been your deepest bottom?

How can you stop digging, and are you ready to accept your proper place in the world?

How will you live your gratitude for being alive?

Miketz

Miketz—day one

Yet the chief cupbearer did not think of Joseph; he forgot him.

—Genesis 40:23

This week's Torah portion, *Miketz* (at the end), is about the story of Joseph and his journey from the pit. We can easily see this in terms of our own lives both as addicts and simply as people. Many people see themselves as black sheep. Joseph feels persecuted and unloved by his brothers and his father. He feels forgotten, *einenu* (nonexistent). While we were delving deeper into our addictions and self-loathing, we became *einenu*. We destroyed our relationships with our families, and we punished them for their wrongdoings, or what we perceived as wrongdoings, to us.

When do you feel forgotten or nonexistent?

What resentments are you still holding on to?

How are you making yourself a victim, and how does being a victim serve you?

Miketz—day two

T'shuvah … averts the severity of the decree.

—High Holy Day *machzor*

I have lived a couple of lifetimes: one as a thief, alcoholic, con man, convict; one as a man struggling to be human and holy, a rabbi, leader of a community, CEO, father, husband, brother, and son. While I use my past to enhance my present and future, I find that I don't see myself as that person anymore, even while knowing that is a part of me. If I continue to live from and in the past, I become stuck there. I have to live in today, to be present in my life and not carry the baggage of my past with me. I have done *t'shuvah* for my errors and seen the parts of my past that I can use for good. I can no longer define myself by my past nor hold resentments and blame toward the people who I feel are responsible for my woes.

How are you still living in the past?

How heavy is the baggage of the past weighing you down?

How can you use your past to enhance your present?

Miketz—day three

A Hebrew youth … interpreted them
for us … and so it came to pass.
—Genesis 41:12–13

Joseph is brought out of prison because the pharaoh had a dream that no one could interpret. The chief cupbearer finally makes good on his commitment to remember Joseph, telling the pharaoh about how Joseph told him and the chief baker what their dreams meant and how each of those dreams came true. When he interpreted the dreams for the two men, Joseph said, "Surely God can interpret; tell me your dreams" (Genesis 40:8). This can be understood in a few ways: one is that Joseph had started to truly understand humility, and another is that Joseph still thought too highly of himself. When he comes to Pharaoh, however, the change in Joseph is immediately seen. Joseph responds to Pharaoh's statement about his being an interpreter of dreams by saying, "Not I! God will see to Pharaoh's welfare" (Genesis 41:16). Joseph has true humility in this moment. He has realized that trying to be too puffed up, too full of himself, has worked against him. He has finally come to believe that God is God and all things emanate from God, even Joseph's own wisdom. This is, I believe, Joseph's spiritual awakening.

What and when was your spiritual awakening?

How have you followed through on the enlightenment that you received at the time of your spiritual awakening?

How have you changed because of your experience with the Divine?

Miketz—day four

Joseph named his son ... "God has made me forget completely the suffering of my father's house."

—GENESIS 41:51

In this week's parashah, Joseph names his first son Manasseh, meaning "God has made me forget completely the suffering of my father's house." Joseph has never left the past nor done his own *t'shuvah* and *cheshbon hanefesh* (accounting of the soul). He keeps blaming others for everything that has happened to him. He does not, evidently, believe in his father's love and devotion. Perhaps being the favorite was too much and too burdensome for him. When Joseph has the opportunity to contact his father, he does not. When his brothers come to get food from him and he recognizes them, he gets even instead of hearing and seeing how they have changed. Joseph does not put an end to his own earlier misery; he wants to inflict harm on others because of his own pain.

How are you not hearing the *t'shuvah* of others?

How are you refusing to let go of the past and indulging in your feelings of being oppressed and abused?

How does not putting an end to something painful help you do the same kinds of things that were so harmful to you?

Miketz—day five

When Joseph saw his brothers he
recognized them ... and acted harshly.

—Genesis 42:7

Like Joseph, we cannot begin to heal until we face our demons (many in the form of long-held resentments). Like Joseph, when we begin to face the truth of our circumstances, we can truly emerge from the pit. We can begin to be not only externally successful, but also internally serene.

It is not Joseph who is entirely to blame, however, for the rift between him and his family. Joseph's older brothers and his father are not able to see their way past Joseph's youthful, arrogant delivery when, as a child, he told them his dreams. They cannot accept the light of the insights that God gave him. They miss out, and they push him away.

How do you respond when others shine?
What is the truth of your circumstances?
What pit are you still trapped in?

Miketz—day six

And Joseph remembered the dreams which he dreamed of them, and said to them, "You are spies; to see the nakedness of the land you have come."

—Genesis 42:9

Joseph's siblings react out of jealousy when they decide to throw him away. Hopefully, this is not our reaction when it is another's time to shine. On the Hanukkah menorah, when the shammes (literally, "servant"; the ninth candle) lights the flame of each of the other candles, its own fire remains undiminished. This shows us that there is enough light in the world for us all. As Peter Yarrow wrote in the song *Light One Candle*, "Don't let the light go out! It's lasted for so many years! Don't let the light go out! Let it shine through our love and our tears."

What is your reward for comparing and competing?

In which ways are you still being greedy?

When and how are you sharing and shining your light?

Miketz—day seven

Alas we are being punished on account of our brother.

—Genesis 42:21

Perhaps it would have been helpful to Joseph to do a personal inventory. When his brothers come to Egypt to get food, Joseph recognizes them, but he is now unrecognizable to them. For many of us who have lived in active addiction, this is a familiar story; we, too, became unrecognizable to our families and friends. In not recognizing Joseph, his family begins to speak to him about himself. Joseph accuses them of being spies. He demands that they bring Benjamin, his full brother, to Egypt. They understand this as a punishment for their treatment of Joseph. When Joseph becomes aware that his family still thinks of him, he begins to cry; he can no longer hold on to the idea that he has been forgotten.

What does it take to remember that you are missed?

How do you know that you are loved?

How do you acknowledge your part in all of your interactions?

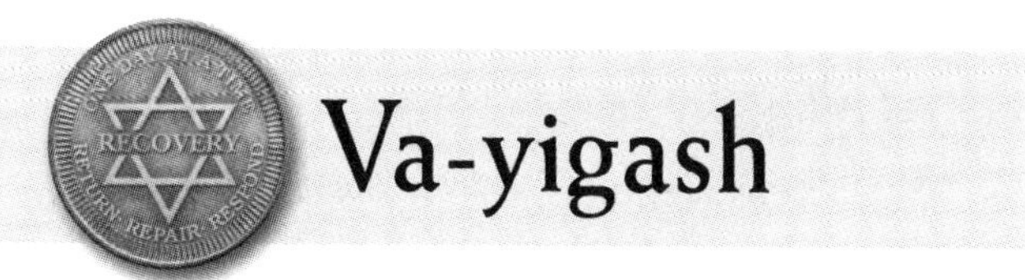

Va-yigash

Va-yigash—day one

Then Judah approached.

—Genesis 44:18

This week's parashah is *Va-yigash* (and he drew near). The first words of the parashah, "he approached," are interesting to me; I have often observed myself and others talk at each other instead of to each other. This seems to happen when we decide to cling to a position or response to an issue and we want to let others know how smart we are. It happens when we let our resentments and fears get in the way of communicating our true desires and passions. Judah knows that he has to come close enough to Joseph so that Joseph can't just disregard him. Judah keeps his focus on convincing Joseph not to put Benjamin in jail and to let him go back to his father.

How can you remember to talk to others rather than at them?

Are you passionate enough about your life to approach others to help them also live well?

Whom do you need to approach so that you can help save a life?

Va-yigash—day two

Please let me speak into your ears.

—Genesis 44:18

In this parashah Joseph's brothers and his father, Jacob, find out that Joseph is still alive and is second in command to Pharaoh in Egypt. In our tradition, and for all people, study is incredibly important. To paraphrase from Rabbi Abraham Joshua Heschel, *z"l*, in his interview with Carl Stern, a life without learning is not worth living. I know that once we stop learning, we stop growing, and once we stop growing, we become dead both intellectually and spiritually. We learn many things in this parashah and in the whole of Torah.

In this story of Judah, Joseph, and reconciliation of the family, Judah approaches Joseph, still not knowing who he is. Judah "speaks into his ears" so that Joseph hears the words through his soul, not his brain. This is an interesting phrase to consider.

What is your practice of study that helps keep you learning and growing?

What reconciliations do you still need to make in your family, in your community, and in the world?

How often do you hear people with your brain rather than with your soul?

Va-yigash—day three

Don't let your anger flare up against your servant.

—Genesis 44:18

Really hearing what someone else is actually saying is a great challenge for most of us. We usually start to think of a response as soon as someone starts speaking to us. In doing this, we miss a lot of what the other person is trying to convey. I have noticed that many successful people, true leaders, fully hear the other person out, sometimes taking notes to remember specific points, and then take a breath before responding. Judah spoke into Joseph's ears so that he would hear everything being conveyed. By doing this, Judah allowed Joseph to respond rather than react.

Do you hear others out or start answering them in your mind before they are done talking?

Are you more interested in needing to be right than understanding the whole picture?

What stops you from taking a breath and responding rather than reacting to what others say?

Va-yigash—day four

So Israel set out ... where he offered offerings to God.
—GENESIS 46:1

One of the lessons of this parashah is that when we hear news that is good we should make an offering to God. This offering should not be considered quid pro quo; rather, it is an acknowledgment that we did not make good happen on our own. With our offering we are proclaiming our enduring need to keep approaching God for strength, courage, and wisdom. It is also our way of thanking God for the grace that God has given us. We learn this because Jacob, when he starts his journey to Egypt for his reunion with Joseph, stops and makes an offering to God for his good fortune. We do this today when we do the *mitzvah* (commandment) of *tzedakah* (the righteous duty to give charitably) upon experiencing good fortune. We do this when we send tributes to people who have shown us some particular kindness. When we recognize people who have helped us and been kind to us, we are saluting and acknowledging their divine image. We are stating that these people have revealed their *tzelem Elohim* (divine image) and seen our divine image, responding to the needs of our soul. This is a basic concept and action in our tradition. Without these acknowledgments, it is easy to slide into entitlement and apathy.

Whom do you need to acknowledge through offering *tzedakah* for the kindnesses they have shown you?

How are you living through your divine image to see the needs of the souls of others?

What are your offerings for the courage and wisdom God has given you?

Va-yigash—day five

God called to Israel.

—Genesis 46:2

Another lesson is shown to us by what happens when Jacob shares his offering. God appears to Jacob, calling to him. The text says, "God called to Israel, calling, 'Jacob, Jacob!'" (Genesis 46:2). How interesting that God calls to "Israel" and calls him by the name "Jacob." What is the importance of this? God tells Jacob that God is going down to Egypt with him, God will bring him up from Egypt, and Joseph will bury him.

This is an important teaching for everyone: God is always with us. God is with us in slavery, and God is with us in freedom. God is never far away from us. As Menachem Mendel of Kotzk, known as the Kotzker Rebbe, said, "Where do we find God? Wherever and whenever we invite God in." I have to invite God into my life, and as soon as I do, God is there. Many of us think that darkness and slavery mean that God is not around. The psalmist says, "Adonai is near unto all, unto all who call upon God in truth" (Psalm 145:18). In the story of Hanukkah, Mattathias calls for people to join him and his sons by saying, "All who are for God follow me!" (1 Maccabees 2:17). In this, the darkest time of the year, calling on God and inviting other people to call out for and invite God in allow us to be victorious.

When does darkness overwhelm you?

What are the names to which you answer?

When and where do you consciously invite God into your life?

Va-yigash—day six

I myself will go down with you to Egypt.
—GENESIS 46:4

Another teaching shown here comes when God tells Jacob, viewed now as the negative aspect of Israel, that Israel's decency and light have God's help in fighting off the lies that the Jacob voice spews. We have all experienced the loudness of negative self-talk. God is telling the negative voice of Israel and teaching us that the voice that calls, usually softly, to do the next right thing, to be decent, is going to be aided by the strength and energy that is God. This is especially important because Egypt is a place that feeds the negative voice. God is telling Israel/Jacob that the negativity will not win the war; it may win a few battles, but it will not, however, prevail. God is going down to the narrow place called Egypt and will assist Israel in prevailing there.

Where are the places that negativity gets fed in your life?

Are you calling on the strength, energy, wisdom, and truth that are God to help your soul prevail over your own negativity?

How can you do this more often?

Va-yigash—day seven

He wept on his neck a lot.

—Genesis 46:29

From this parashah we know that Jacob/Israel calls on and uses God's help. We know this because when he sees Joseph, Jacob does not ask why Joseph hasn't called or written in all this time. Jacob weeps and says that upon seeing Joseph, he can now die in peace. I interpret this to mean that Jacob does not dwell on the past; he is truly grateful for this moment. He does not need to recriminate Joseph for not letting him know sooner that Joseph was alive. Jacob is present in this moment and does not need to hold on to any resentment. He is teaching us that we have a choice: we can stay stuck in the past, which may be the most pervasive slavery in which we find ourselves, or we can be present to enjoy and experience this exact moment. Again, to quote Rabbi Heschel, *z"l*, from *Moral Grandeur and Spiritual Audacity*, "No two moments are alike."

What are some of the old resentments that keep you stuck in the past?

What are you doing to live in today, rather than in the past or future?

Is there anyone with whom you would like to reconnect but your resentments against them have prevented you from doing so?

Va-yechi

Va-yechi—day one

And Jacob lived ...

—GENESIS 47:28

This week's parashah is *Va-yechi* (and he lived). Again, as in *Chayei Sarah*, the Torah teaches us that when someone is about to die, we talk about that person's life and living, not his or her death. The lesson here is that we have to live all of our life; we are obligated to stay present and keep growing until we die. Too many of us stop living long before we die physically. We stop living by not continuing to grow and learn. We stop living by staying stuck in the past. We stop living by being consumed by resentment and entitlement.

Usually during the week of this parashah, I recite the name of my father, Jerry Borovitz, *z"l*; his name is a blessing. My father lived until he died. Although he died at a young age, he really lived those years. My father knew that his time was limited after his first heart attack. Rather than taking the easy way out, sitting at home and collecting disability benefits, he kept working. He never complained that life was unfair. He loved, lived, and celebrated life with the same gusto throughout all forty-two of his years.

How are you living your entire life?

How are you living in complaint and fear or resentment?

How are you able to live in gratitude each day?

Va-yechi—day two

The whole life of Jacob …

—GENESIS 47:28

This parashah addresses a problem that is prevalent in our society: the why bother, whatever, poor me syndrome. I know many people in all walks of life, in all socioeconomic groups, who live in this mentality; I call them the walking dead. You know some of these people. You can see it in their eyes—they are flat. You can hear it in their voices—their tone is listless. You experience it in their actions, which are taken half-heartedly. This kind of apathy is the great lie of our time.

How are you lying to yourself and others?

In what situations does your early trauma still rule your behavior and thinking?

Are you willing to leave these experiences in the past and live facing forward?

Va-yechi—day three

When I lie down with my fathers ... bury
me in their burial place ... swear to me.

—GENESIS 47:30–31

Jacob calls for Joseph to request that Joseph not bury him in Egypt. He asks his son, his favorite son, to bury him in the land of his fathers. He is so worried about his burial that he makes Joseph swear to do it this way. He is asked to swear not once, but twice; I keep asking myself, what is the reason?

One reason is that Joseph has not demonstrated his forgiveness of his father. My wife, Harriet Rossetto, says that forgiving those whom we have harmed is the greatest spiritual challenge. Joseph seems to be demonstrating this fact; he harmed his father by not getting in touch with him for the nine years that Joseph was in charge of Egypt. Jacob must be questioning his own relationship with Joseph, even after the seventeen years that they have lived together in Egypt. Jacob does not feel certain of his son's devotion and love.

Joseph, like many of us, did not want to let his father off the hook. Jacob was so overcome with joy and awe that his son was alive, and still he is unsure that his son loves him enough to be able to simply accept Joseph's statement. Rather, he demands that Joseph swear to follow his request.

Whom do you keep on the hook or off-balance,
for a harm that you actually did to them?

Whom do you love with reservation?

When will you forgive him or her and deeply reconnect?

Va-yechi—day four

Israel said …, "I never expected to see you again. And here God has let me see your children as well."

—Genesis 48:11

Both my father and my brother, Stuart, taught me that life is not always easy but it is always joyful. My brother suffered from multiple sclerosis, and he decided one day, because of my father's gift of wisdom to us, to no longer suffer. He kept a smile on his face; he said hello to everyone he passed and those who passed him. He brought joy to the caregivers at the Montefiore Home, where he spent the last ten years of his life. He would talk about the challenges, victories, and defeats that he experienced without whining or complaining about them. We all need to wake up and see the beauty of life. Far too many people become indifferent to the sublime wonder of living, which, in *God in Search of Man,* Rabbi Abraham Joshua Heschel, *z"l*, says, "is the root of sin." The sin, in this context, is sleeping through your life.

Do you say hello and thank you with a smile to the people who serve you in stores or restaurants? To coworkers you pass in the hallway? To whom could you be more consistently friendly?

How do you appreciate your gifts and use them wisely?

Are you truly seeing the people in your life, or are you taking them for granted, and how?

Va-yechi—day five

God make you like Ephraim and Manasseh.

—Genesis 48:20

In this parashah Jacob blesses the sons of Joseph and takes them as his own. Our tradition teaches us to bless our male children, saying, "May you be like Ephraim and Manasseh." The sages teach us that this is said because these two stayed true to the tenets of Judaism even though they were raised in Egypt. They welcomed the stranger, they saw each person as a holy soul, and they lived with compassion and justice. Each of us needs to remember to bless those around us each week, each day, each moment.

What are some of the ways you ignore the strangers with whom you come in contact?

How do you acknowledge everyone as a holy soul, as infinitely worthy?

How can you treat everyone you encounter with more compassion and justice?

Va-yechi—day six

Assemble and listen, sons of Jacob.

—GENESIS 49:2

Jacob is concerned that his children keep their faith. There is a midrash (ancient commentary on Hebrew scriptures) that says: Jacob asked his children, "Who is your God?" They responded, "Hear, Israel, Adonai is our God, and Adonai is One." This is an explanation of why the *Shema* (literally, "to hear"; it is both a daily morning and an evening prayer) is so central to our tradition. Jacob's fear in this midrash says a lot about how he sees himself as a parent. He asks himself questions about his parenting skills, and we must do the same, asking ourselves these questions.

How have you imparted good and
decent values to your children?

In which ways do you live these values so that your
children know how to act and be decent?

How do you treat others as divine images
and allow them to see the real you?

Va-yechi—day seven

So they sent this message to Joseph,
"... Forgive I urge you."
—GENESIS 50:16–17

Joseph's behavior carries over to his brothers. After their father dies, the brothers go to Joseph and tell him that their father wanted Joseph to pardon their offense, and they again ask for his forgiveness. Joseph had said that he forgave them and would care for them, and he treated them kindly, according to the Torah. My question is, why would the brothers still feel this need to go to Joseph? Although he did what was right, helping and caring for the family, Joseph still did not convey that he truly forgave his brothers and wanted a full and true reconciliation. Joseph did not demonstrate his reconnection to either his father or his brothers.

Whom do you need to assure of your forgiveness?

From whom do you need assurance about their forgiveness?

How do your actions of forgiveness and reconnection match your words?

Shemot

Shemot—day one

These are the names of the sons of
Israel who came to Egypt.

—Exodus 1:1

This week's parashah is *Shemot* (names), which begins with retelling the names of the sons of Jacob who came to Egypt when Joseph summoned them all to live with him. It lists the entire lineage, corresponding to their mothers. This is an interesting beginning; we are again hearing the names of Jacob, his sons, and his grandchildren. I believe this is meant to remind us of where we came from. Lineage is important to and for us. Remembering our lineage and the lineages of others allows us to see our similarities and repair any old wounds from past generations that still impact us today.

Where did your family come from, and what are some of the lessons, morals, and ethics your ancestors held dear?

What are the lessons you need to learn from them?

Whom and what are you ignoring because acknowledgment would force you to change your actions?

Shemot—day two

Reuben, Simeon, Levi, and Judah; Issachar, Zebulun …

—Exodus 1:2–3

Shemot translates to "names" and is also the name of the second book of the Torah. In English, the name of this second book is Exodus. The English name tells us what happens in the story. This can be likened to the material world. In the history of the Jewish people, this book describes both the descent into slavery and the ascent to freedom. The Hebrew name of the book, which means "names," tells us what happens inside the people Israel and each individual Israelite. The inner life of each of us happens in stages, and each of these stages has a name. More importantly, the inner name we choose to call ourselves is significant. Our tradition teaches that there are three crowns—the crown of royalty, the crown of wealth, and the crown of priesthood—but the crown of a good name exceeds them all.

What are the names you are known by?

What are the names you call yourself?

What does it mean for you to wear
the crown of a good name?

Shemot—day three

A new king arose over Egypt who
did not know Joseph.

—EXODUS 1:8

This parashah tells us that the new pharaoh did not know Joseph, which is impossible. Yet, it also teaches us what happens when we don't remember to whom we should be grateful. When we allow ourselves to think too highly of ourselves, we forget all the people who have helped us on our journeys. The new pharaoh thought that he could harm Joseph's people by forgetting Joseph's accomplishments. If Pharaoh had remembered what Joseph had done for Egypt, he would have no choice but to be grateful for and treat Joseph's descendants with respect and care. Instead, by not knowing Joseph, the new pharaoh was able to make the Israelites into the cause of all problems in Egypt. This in turn allowed him to convince the Egyptian people that all of the Israelites were responsible for the problems of Egypt and together the pharaoh and the people could enslave Joseph's descendants, saying this was for the good of all Egypt. While we know this story is a ruse, how many of us use the same sorts of ploys to justify our own lack of gratitude?

To whom have you forgotten to be grateful
for where you are in your life?

How do you show your gratitude to the
descendants of those who have helped you?

What are the ways in which you get others
to deny the help you and they receive so
that you don't have to pay it forward?

Shemot—day four

The midwives, fearing God, did not do
as the king of Egypt told them.

—EXODUS 1:17

Another lesson is also found in this first chapter of *Shemot*: it is always possible to say no to tyranny. Here, there are two midwives, Shifrah and Puah, who are instructed by Pharaoh to kill all male babies at birth; they don't do this though—they defy Pharaoh. And, the babies live. When the pharaoh asks the midwives why they are not killing the male children, they respond with some simple excuse. Pharaoh believes them or at least does not harm them for not having followed his direction. I think many of us are afraid to say yes to freedom. Saying yes to freedom obligates us to follow a path toward truth and wholeness. The bricks that make up this path are the 613 commandments given to us by God. These commandments help us find our authentic selves. We can say no to slavery only when we choose to say yes to freedom.

How many times have you been afraid of authority and followed directions that you knew were wrong?

How often are you afraid to say no to slavery? Why?

What will it take for you to say yes to freedom?

Shemot—day five

And God said to Moses, *"Ehyeh Asher Ehyeh."*

—Exodus 3:14

God tells us God's name in this parashah: *Ehyeh Asher Ehyeh* (Exodus 3:14), often translated as "I will be what I will be," from which we get the Hebrew *Yud Hey Vav Hey*. I believe this is what Rabbi Heschel, *z"l*, meant when he told Carl Stern that God is "waiting … [for] a righteous generation." This name of God screams at me that unless you and I participate in redeeming the world, one person at a time, God remains mere potentiality. We have the power and obligation to call ourselves God's representatives and to do our part for redemption. Redemption requires that we repair our inner lives, returning to our true selves and responding to life in a manner proper and befitting of the person we wish to become.

How are you participating in your own redemption?

How are you helping others to redeem themselves?

How are you helping to move the world closer to wholeness?

Shemot—day six

But Moses said to Adonai, "… I am slow of speech."
—EXODUS 4:10

Moses is called by God to lead the Israelites out of Egypt, and he keeps saying no. Each year I wonder, how could Moses not feel honored to be chosen for this mission, and rush to do God's bidding? I finally have an answer to my own question: Moses calls himself by names that are not truthful for his soul. He fled Egypt because he stood up for a Hebrew who was being beaten. He redeemed that soul and became frightened. Then he began to call himself names other than redeemer, names other than one who was redeemed. In other words, Moses forgot his history, his purpose, and his debt for having been redeemed.

What calls has God made to you that you have ignored?

Which opportunities to redeem yourself
and others have you missed?

Which opportunities have you taken?

Shemot—day seven

I have strengthened his heart.

—Exodus 4:21

There is a direct correlation between Moses's defiance and God saying that God will strengthen Pharaoh's heart. Both Moses and Pharaoh want to continue to argue against God. Neither wants to accept the yoke of obligation that comes with heeding the call of God. Moses finally is strong enough to realize that God wants him to accept the call from a place of inner strength. Pharaoh never accepts that his strength comes from God, not from himself. Pharaoh is invested in his outer strength, but Moses learns that without inner strength, there is no truly lasting outer strength.

Whom are you acting most like in this story this year?

How are you like Pharaoh, who is interested in outer strength and its trappings?

How are you like Moses, who realizes that without inner strength, the outer strength and trappings are ethereal?

Va-eira

Va-eira—day one

I appeared as El Shaddai.

—Exodus 6:3

This week's parashah is *Va-eira* (and God appeared). Rabbi Heschel, *z"l*, explains in *Moral Grandeur and Spiritual Audacity* that we are all created in the divine image and therefore are all reminders of God. It is hard to adopt this idea as a way of living. If we want to choose freedom rather than slavery, we have to continually strive to improve by one grain of sand each day. We must learn not to take anyone or anything in our lives for granted, or else we risk slipping into the slavery of inertia and apathy. As Rabbi Heschel, *z"l*, says in *God in Search of Man*, "Indifference to the sublime wonder of living is the root of sin." Every time we fail to see the beauty and divinity in living, we are one step closer to existing in slavery. Each time that we forget to care for God's creatures and creations, including ourselves, we are one step closer to becoming an enslaver.

Whom and what do you take for granted?

How do you help cultivate the unique divine image found in your children, spouse, and/or partners?

How can you be reminded to see the divine image in the people you know best, those with whom you spend most of your time?

Va-eira—day two

But I did not make Myself known to
them by My name *YHVH*.

—Exodus 6:3

I am thinking about the entire verse: "I appeared to Abraham, Isaac, and Jacob as El Shaddai [God Almighty], but I did not make Myself known to them by My name *YHVH* [four-letter unutterable name of God, commonly substituted by using *Adonai*, 'my Lord']." God makes God known to each of us in different ways, as each name of God represents a different attribute. I see how I know only certain parts of the people in my life, and this saddens me. Sadness is a difficult emotion for me to experience; typically I move quickly to feeling angry when I realize that people are hiding from me. It also makes me wonder if and how I am hiding myself from other people. We all are ashamed of parts of ourselves, afraid what people will think, and conditioned to politely put on "company manners" for the world to see. Considering my own history, I find that this kind of hiding is what led me to addictive behaviors, and even in my active addiction I was still hiding parts of myself. I now know that God is calling to us to come closer, to become partners. Shabbat is considered the day of union with a second soul from God. Our prayers and psalms call out from our deepest places to God, the One and only One, who can hear our cries.

How do you relate to God, and in what ways do you honor this relationship?

How do you appear to different people?

What is the reason you do not make yourself known to everyone, completely?

Va-eira—day three

Say, therefore, to the Israelites: I am Adonai.

—Exodus 6:6

Another idea about the name *YHVH* is, as I learned from my colleague, friend, and esteemed teacher Rabbi Harold Schulweis, *z"l*, this name of God is in the form of a verb. I learned that God is action. *YHVH* is the third-person singular future tense meaning "God will be." In Hebrew, the future tense is used to denote an action not yet complete. Nachmanides calls *YHVH* the name by which all that exists has its being. So, *YHVH* is the root, the basic fundamental energy that causes the life force to exist and flourish. When we call God by the name *YHVH*, we are connecting to the basic energy in the world and, since *YHVH* breathes into us this life force, we are also calling on God to help us, not do everything for us. We are acknowledging that we are a part of the basic energy in the world. In this parashah, therefore, because God is telling us that *YHVH* is the name for the Israelites to use, God is telling us that once we get out of slavery we have to be part of the solution. Once we have been brought out of the narrow places that trap us, we can no longer sit around waiting for someone else to take care of us; entitlement is not the proper way of being in the world. Rather, *YHVH* teaches us that we, the redeemed, have to add our part to the world, taking actions in partnership with God's will.

In what ways are you God's partner?

How are you flourishing in your living?

What are the ways you enhance your life force and the life force of others?

Va-eira—day four

I, Adonai, will take you from under
the hardships of Egypt.

—Exodus 6:6

In this parashah we find the covenant or promises from God. The difference between a covenant and a contract is that a covenant involves God, and God does not break God's covenant. In each covenant is a promise of hope and purpose. The first promise is that God will bring us out from under the burdens of the Egyptians. This promises that physical bondage will end. There is no place in God's world for one person to own another and give that person undue and unwarranted burdens. People are not animals or chattel. This promise is realized every day when we acknowledge and act upon our ability to live our own lives not under the rule of tyranny.

To what are you a slave?

How do you treat others as human beings or
as chattel, here to serve your own needs?

What are the ways you are reaching out to others to
redeem them from the physical bonds of another?

Va-eira—day five

I will save you from your slavery.

—Exodus 6:6

The second covenant is that God will rescue us from the labors. This promise refers to the difficulty of leaving the psychological scars of slavery behind. Many of us believe that we have either come out of slavery or have never been enslaved and are therefore immune to the scars of slavery. The truth is that it is much easier to be released from physical bondage than it is to leave slavery's internal scars in the past. We see this throughout the rest of the Torah. As we've learned from epigenetic studies, the slave mentality is passed down at a cellular level. Many people feel trapped by their circumstances, another form of inner slavery. Becoming stuck in a rut or routine that causes us to become numb and indifferent to our own lives is a form of psychological slavery. All of these are slaveries that we witness and unwittingly participate in every day. With this covenant God is promising that we can and will be rescued from this psychological hell.

How are you still enslaved by old ideas and messages?

How are you a slave to the good old days?

Are you asking to be rescued? If so, are you actively working with, not against, your rescuers?

Va-eira—day six

I will redeem you with an outstretched arm.

—Exodus 6:6

The third covenant is that God will redeem us with an outstretched arm. Redemption in this sense means that we will see ourselves as free people. Redemption does not happen without God or other people. We are able to make choices based on our own free will, not because we are driven by feeling less than or more than. We will have the inner strength not to become stuck in the routines of slavery. We will raise our souls to mature adulthood rather than staying stuck in adolescence. We will not need to rebel against ourselves and God because we have actively chosen to live as partners, friends, and lovers with God, ourselves, and others. We will be rich because we are happy with our lives and because we want everything we have.

How do you allow yourself to hold on to the outstretched arms of those who are trying to help?

What are some ways you are helping others to be redeemed?

How do you show your gratitude for what you have and for your life?

Va-eira—day seven

Yet Pharaoh's heart strengthened.

—Exodus 7:13

The Torah says that Pharaoh's heart stiffened; the exact translation is "got stronger." Many people question whether this is a setup. Does God set Pharaoh up to fail? This line of reasoning leads many people to say that their failures are divinely ordained and therefore not their fault. I would like to offer a different perspective: perhaps God does not want us to draw near simply because we are desperate and beaten down. When we reach up only in times of trouble, as soon as we are strong again, we will rebel against the authority that we, erroneously, believe has enslaved us. Imagine, our thinking can get so topsy-turvy that we believe that God is enslaving us.

How much like Pharaoh are you, believing that a strong heart means that you don't have to hear and follow God's call?

Do you believe that following God's call will enslave you? If so, why?

What continues to keep you in rejection of this call that will enhance your life and the lives of others?

Bo

Bo—day one

Then Adonai said to Moses, "Come to Pharaoh."

—Exodus 10:1

This week's parashah is *Bo* (come). This is an interesting choice of words for the Torah: "Then God said to Moses, 'Come to Pharaoh'" (Exodus 10:1). God is telling Moses to come to Pharaoh, but where is God? God must be with Pharaoh. This teaches us no matter what we think of someone, that person is still created in the image of God. Knowing this enables us never to give up trying to reach someone, to connect with this *tzelem Elohim* (divine image or image of God). As Rabbi Adin Steinsaltz teaches in *The Thirteen Petalled Rose*, "Everything that is not in the right measure, that relates out of proportion to a situation, tends to be bad." Love can turn to evil when it is out of proper measure, as with Pharaoh. Coming to wrestle with light that is out of proper measure forces me to find God in evil and gives me more strength to combat evil and wrestle light back into balance. It also obligates me not to run away from evil.

How do you remember that others are *b'tzelem Elohim* and treat them as such?

What areas of your life are out of proper measure?

What tools and/or whose help do you need to get those areas into proper measure?

Bo—day two

I have made his heart heavy with honor.

—Exodus 10:1

The Torah and commentators also tell us that Pharaoh had gone too far in his stubbornness and evildoing. Many in our tradition believe that after the first five plagues, Pharaoh was too stubborn and too proud to change. He had caused himself to be incapable of doing *t'shuvah*. Unfortunately, there are people like this living among us. There are people who are so committed to doing evil, to enslaving others, they can no longer see the wrongdoings they are committing. Some of us have become oblivious to the harm that we cause and even deceive ourselves into believing that we are doing the right thing when we are in fact causing chaos and pain. This is the kind of evil that many people practice each and every day; it is the evil that is our way of continuing to be like Pharaoh. Remember, there is a pharaoh inside us all. We, too, are able to enslave others in order to make ourselves feel better. I ask myself, and am asking that we all investigate how we are doing this in our own lives, how are we using others to their detriment? We must break the denial and self-deception in which we live. We can do this by having a spiritual guide and spiritually inclined friends who tell us the truth. When we hear their truth, we can then search inside to see how we need to change.

Who is your spiritual guide?

Who are your spiritual friends?

What truths are you still blocking out?

What I have done in Egypt . . .

—Exodus 10:2

God must be telling us that God is also in Pharaoh. This means that even evil has the potentiality of having God inside. Evil cannot simply be all bad; there is a possibility of finding evil and transforming it. This is our challenge from God; this challenge has to be met by us. As John F. Kennedy stated in his 1961 address to the Canadian Parliament, "As the great parliamentarian Edmund Burke said, 'The only thing necessary for the triumph of evil is for good men to do nothing.'" Too many of us run away from the evil that is both inside and outside of all. We are too afraid to confront it because evil seems so strong and overpowering. This week's parashah is telling us that God is within evil to help us confront and defeat it. We have to use our skills, our wits, and our souls to defeat evil. This is a radical concept, yet I ask you to consider its possibility.

How can you connect to the godlike image inside of evil?

How are you able to speak to the holiness and light that is within evil?

How are you allowing God and others to confront and defeat the evil inside of you?

Bo—day four

My signs that I have done among them …

—Exodus 10:2

This brings us to the question, if Pharaoh still has the divine image inside, then what stops him from hearing God, through Moses, and changing himself? This verse defines one of the greatest challenges of being human. Every human being is created in the image of God. Being human requires that we grow and live from this image rather than the false image we want to create or portray. To hear the call of God, we must listen from and with our soul. When we keep denying and destroying the pathways to our soul, our ability to hear God and others diminishes; this is Pharaoh's problem. He believed his own press and spin doctors. Pharaoh got so enamored by himself, his power, and his ego that he forgot that there was a power greater than him to which he was accountable. Each of us has a *yetzer hara* (evil inclination) that, left unchecked, will convince us that we are the be-all and end-all. "Come to Pharaoh" means we have to continue to see the divine image in everyone, including ourselves, and help to grow and respect this image.

How are you too full of yourself to hear the call of God?

How have you destroyed the passageways to your soul to such an extent that you don't even know how to hear its call?

How have you become the same type of person that you dislike being around?

Bo—day five

How long will you refuse to humble yourself …?

—Exodus 10:3

One question that people always ask is, does God set Pharaoh up? The reason I believe that God does not set Pharaoh up is because Pharaoh's advisors tell him the truth about the situation, and still he refuses to listen and follow their advice. They tell Pharaoh that he is trapped by his ego by telling him that Moses is a snare. The setup here is that Pharaoh gets caught in a war of wills between himself and Moses. Most wars happen because of a similar war of wills. Is this God's way of setting us up? Is God hardening our hearts? Actually, I believe many of us have underdeveloped souls. When our egos become larger than our spirits, we find ourselves fighting a battle of wills, rather than fighting for the will of God. When parents fight for what is supposedly best for their child, it is usually their will and ego telling them what is best, not necessarily their souls speaking. When employees see themselves working for the man, rather than seeing the privilege of being able to add to the world, it is their inflated ego speaking. When we see the world as adversarial, it is our egos that are hardening our hearts and minds.

When do you most often find yourself in a battle of wills?

How is your need to be right hurting your soul and the souls of others?

When and how are you aware that your heart or mind has become hardened?

Bo—day six

How long shall this one be a snare to us?

—Exodus 10:7

Also, in this parashah is one of my favorite questions: *Od matai?*—"Until when?" or "How long?" This phrase is used by Moses after seven of the plagues have been brought to Egypt. Moses asks Pharaoh, *Od matai*, "How long will you not humble yourself before God?" I understand this question so well; it took me more than twenty years to surrender. We have to give up our false egos, our false selves, in order to live with God; otherwise, we will live a barren and lonely existence with no real connection to ourselves, God, or others. Pharaoh represents the archetype of the false self and inauthentic living. Moses is speaking to the godlike image in Pharaoh, the little spark of light that is in all of us. Moses is begging Pharaoh to let this spark rule instead of his false pride and the desire to win.

When is your Pharaoh running your life? *Od matai*—until when will you refuse yourself an authentic, holy life?

Whose voice can you hear when you are coming from your false sense of self?

For whom are you acting like Moses? When is your real self allowed to direct your life?

Bo—day seven

This month shall mark for you the
beginning of the months.

—Exodus 12:2

Also in this chapter is found the commandment by God to change the numbering of months in the year. The first month was Tishrei, the month of Rosh Hashanah (literally, "head of the year"), the beginning of the world. Now, since the Exodus from Egypt, the first month of the calendar has become Nisan, the month in which the Israelites left Egypt. God is telling us that whenever we get out of slavery is our time of new beginning. While time does not stop nor does the sequence of years change, we recognize our new beginnings by counting the days, months, and years of our life from our release from bondage. Just as in Alcoholics Anonymous, we are given the power and responsibility to number the months and the time so that we can differentiate between our time spent in slavery and our time in freedom.

How do you mark your new beginnings?

How have you acknowledged whether or not you are currently living in slavery?

What does freedom from bondage mean for you?

Beshalach

Beshalach—day one

And when Pharaoh sent the people away …

—Exodus 13:17

This week's parashah is *Beshalach* (and he sent). The Torah is saying that Pharaoh sent the Israelites out of Egypt. This is puzzling. Had not God brought the Israelites out of Egypt? There is an important lesson here: we still need our enslaver to send us away. We cannot truly get out of slavery until slavery is no longer comfortable. Even though the text says Pharaoh sent us out, and it is true, it is also true that we cannot get out of slavery until we have help. That help is God. Here again, we see the both/and of living. We need to be aware that slavery is no longer working for us, and that only with God's help through God's messengers and miracles can we truly get out of our own narrow places, our Egypt. We all believe, to a greater or lesser degree, that we are unable to leave our slaveries or do not even recognize that we are enslaved.

How are you still living in slavery and to what or whom?

What help do you need from God or others to be lifted up and sent out by your Pharaoh?

In what ways can your community help you, and how can you help those in your community?

Beshalach—day two

And one-fifth of the Israelites went up from Egypt.
—EXODUS 13:18

This week we learn a lot about people who have been enslaved. According to many commentators, Torah says that only 20 percent of the Israelites actually left Egypt. Can you believe this? The gates are opened, you have the opportunity to leave your own particular Egypt, and yet most of us stay. This seems ridiculous. Yet, if we look at history, we clearly see that this happens over and over again. Statistically, we have seen that fewer than 20 percent of the people who go to their first AA meeting stay sober for 365 continuous days. While this figure is staggering, I would ask you to look at yourself and determine if you have left the different enslavements in your own life.

What, if any, relationships are you engaged in that are convenient but enslaving?

Are you working in a job that is enslaving you? How does it enslave you?

How are you afraid to live your true purpose and passion?

Beshalach—day three

Then Adonai said to Moses, "Why do you cry out to Me? Tell the Israelites to go forward."

—Exodus 14:15

There is an instance that I believe is of extreme importance to and for us all in this parashah. At the Red Sea, with the Egyptians chasing them and the sea in front of them, the Israelites complain to Moses. Moses then looks up toward God in a pleading motion. God says, "Why do you cry out to Me? Tell the Israelites to go forward!" From this moment we learn an important principle of Jewish spirituality about our relationship with God. We do not and cannot depend on God to do for us what we can do for ourselves. God acts as our partner, giving us the respect of believing that we can and will do our part. The Israelites were taught an important lesson: you have to do things for yourself. What we are able to do, we must do; when we need help, we must ask for it. Too many of us still want someone else to do our work for us. God believes in us and has faith that we can and will honor our part of the covenant, owning our lives and asking for help when we need it, and God will do the same.

How are you doing your part in taking all of the necessary actions to live well?

In which areas of your life do you know you need to ask for help? From whom and when will you be willing to ask for what you need?

Where are you still trying to play God either in your life or in the lives of others?

Beshalach—day four

And the waters returned and covered
the chariots and horsemen.

—EXODUS 14:28

Pharaoh and the Egyptians drown in the Red Sea—not because God wants them to, but because they are unable to accept reality and truth. They drown in the Red Sea because they think they know the right way even though it is different from God's way, the way of truth and reality. Rather than redeem themselves, they care more about being right and appearing strong. Because of their addiction to being right, the Egyptians die and God cries.

How are you unable to accept truth and reality
because of your own need to be right?

How are you still trying to save face by trying
to destroy or twist truth and reality?

How can you participate in your own redemption?

Beshalach—day five

Pharaoh's entire army … not one of them remained.

—Exodus 14:28

The story goes on to describe what happens when we surrender because of being beaten down rather than because we realize that we want to allow ourselves to be confronted and defeated by a higher truth. I believe that God wants us to surrender with a strong heart, with the resolve and purpose of living well. Pharaoh, who let the Israelites go, comes to his senses and decides that he should pursue the Israelites and either kill them or bring them back to slavery. Pharaoh is incapable of seeing truth. He refuses to surrender to reality; he wants to keep his fantasy of being right, of power and prestige.

How often do you surrender to a higher truth and the realities of your life?

How often do you find yourself trying to warp reality to serve your ego?

What character traits keep you blind to the higher truths and reality of your life?

Beshalach—day six

They had faith in Adonai.

—Exodus 14:31

Many people think that if you kill the enslaver, you will be set free. The truth is that the pharaoh never dies because there is always a new one to take his place. We have to learn how to live freely in order to truly be free of Pharaoh. Our tradition teaches us that through spirituality, sometimes our own unique practice of spirituality, we can and will find freedom. Only through connection to our higher selves will we be able to see the miracles and beauty in life.

Who are you: the one who wants to kill Pharaoh or the one who lives with and through God's principles?

How are you living: free or in the hell of your own or someone else's making?

What helps you to be connected to your higher self and the higher selves of others?

Beshalach—day seven

Amalek came and fought with Israel at Rephidim.

—Exodus 17:8

Also in this parashah, we have the attack of Amalek. Amalek has been associated with evil in our tradition because he attacked the weakest part of the Israelite people, the ones at the back of the group, the stragglers, the children, the infirm. This is the nature of evil—it attacks at our weakest points. Evil takes our most vulnerable parts and exploits them. In our morning prayers, we ask that God keep us away from evil and show us how to subdue our own evil inclination in order to better serve God. Amalek represents both the people in our lives and the force within us that causes us to believe the lies we hear. We must be aware of the lies of others and the lies we tell ourselves.

How are you being like Amalek to others and to yourself?

Who is playing the role of Amalek in your life?

What evil lies are you most susceptible to believing?

Yitro

Yitro—day one

God spoke all these words …

—Exodus 20:1

This week's Torah portion is *Yitro* (Jethro). In this portion, we receive the ten sayings also known as the Ten Commandments. Also, these ten sayings make up the *b'rit* (covenant) between God and the Israelite people. These agreements apply for everyone, providing a guide for living well and recovering our holy souls.

I understand this parashah to show us the specific moment of surrender by the Israelite people. Paraphrasing from a teaching of Rabbi Joseph B. Soloveitchik, *z"l*, surrender occurs when humans allow themselves to be confronted and defeated by a higher and truer being and/or a higher truth. All of the Ten Commandments are higher truths, and we have to allow ourselves to be defeated by them rather than continue to find the loopholes for us to fight against God and these higher truths.

When do you allow yourself to be defeated by a higher truth?

When and in which situations are you fighting against this higher truth?

How are you living in a covenantal relationship with God and others?

Yitro—day two

Remember the Sabbath day and keep it holy.

—EXODUS 20:8

The fourth commandment: "Remember the Sabbath day and keep it holy. Six days shall you do labor and work, but the seventh day is a day of rest, unto Adonai, your God. You shall not do any *m'lachah* [work]; not you, your son, your daughter, your male or female slave, your cattle, or the stranger who is within your settlement" (Exodus 10:8–10).

Covenant: I will take an hour each day for myself.

Following the wisdom of Rabbi Moshe Leib of Sassov, who said, "A person who does not take at least one hour every day for himself, for his own soul, and make a reckoning of his world is not considered a person," I am reminded of just how important doing this is for everyone.

What will you do with this time for yourself each day?

How will you use this time to learn more about yourself?

How will you remind or facilitate others to take this time for themselves each day?

Yitro—day three

You shall not murder.

—Exodus 20:13

The sixth commandment: "You shall not murder" (Exodus 20:13).

Covenant: I will engage in soul-affirming actions throughout my day.

What soul-affirming actions did you take today?

What soul-destroying activities did you engage in today?

How did you affirm or destroy the soul of another person today?

Yitro—day four

You shall not commit adultery.

—Exodus 20:13

The seventh commandment: "You shall not commit adultery" (Exodus 20:13).

Covenant: I will not sell my soul, my portion, my blessing, or my integrity.

What are some of the ways you have stayed true to yourself today?

How have you lived in and with integrity today?

Where and when have you prostituted yourself, exchanging your values for some perceived reward?

Yitro—day five

You shall not steal.

—Exodus 20:13

The eighth commandment: "You shall not steal" (Exodus 20:13).

Covenant: I will rejoice in my uniqueness and be happy and use my gifts to the fullest that I can in the moment.

List the qualities you possess that you value most.

How do you appreciate these things about yourself each and every day?

How did you use your unique gifts today?

Yitro—day six

You shall not bear false witness.

—Exodus 20:13

The ninth commandment: "You shall not bear false witness" (Exodus 20:13).

Covenant: I will acknowledge daily who I am and where I am.

How have you lived as your divine image today?

What are some of the divine needs you fulfilled today, acting as God's partner on earth?

What are the lies you most frequently tell yourself?

Yitro—day seven

> You shall not covet your neighbor's house.
>
> —Exodus 20:14

The tenth commandment: "You shall not covet" (Exodus 20:14).

Covenant: I will live my own soul's script, my purpose, and add to my corner of the world.

How did you live your own life today?

How did you succumb to other people's pressure to live the life they wanted today?

How do you rejoice in who you are and what you have each and every day?

Mishpatim

Mishpatim—day one

These are the social ordinances.

—Exodus 21:1

This week's parashah is *Mishpatim*. This translates to "laws," "justice," and "social ordinances." These are the first words of Torah that we read after we receive the Ten Commandments. There is an incredibly strong message here about the importance of treating each other well in order to fulfill the spirit and the letter of God's will. This parashah reminds me of the words of Rabbi Abraham Joshua Heschel, *z"l*, who wrote in *Moral Grandeur and Spiritual Audacity*, "In a free society, some are guilty, but all are responsible."

In this parashah we learn to treat people decently. We are told that if we knock out the tooth of our slave, the slave must go free. Even though we have paid for our slaves, we are still not allowed to hurt them. It is also important that we treat people who are sick as people who are sick, and not expect them to be well. It is an obligation to see people for who they are and not who we want them to be.

Where do you still find it difficult to treat people decently, particularly those whom you oversee?

How can you have more compassion for people who are sick, accepting them exactly as they are?

How can you have more patience about your own illnesses?

Eye for eye, tooth for tooth ...

—Exodus 21:24

Another lesson in this parashah is about exchange, eye for eye, tooth for tooth, hand for hand, wound for wound. Many people have wrongly said that this means "tit for tat"—whatever you do to me, I can do back to you. How ridiculous! This is a way that fundamentalists try to justify their own desire for bloodletting. It is also a way for others to state that Torah and the Christian Bible have no place in our world. Both of these viewpoints are wrong and based on a faulty premise. Eye for eye, according to the Talmud, is about money. It is the basis for the system of paying damages in our tradition. We are told that when we harm another, we have to pay for five aspects of the injury: for actual damage, for pain, for healing, for loss of employment, and for humiliation. This teaches us that there is more damage than meets the eye when we harm another. We also need to understand that there is more damage than meets the eye when we harm another spiritually. When we forget to honor the dignity of others, we are harming them and God. When we hurt others physically, we are also hurting them spiritually.

Are you able to see the larger picture of harm that you cause when you treat people as objects? Name some instances in which you have created this harm.

How have you seen spiritual harm manifest in your life?

How are you contributing to making a community, and how are you contributing to destroying a community?

Mishpatim—day three

When a man opens a pit and does not cover it …

—EXODUS 21:33

We must think on this because Torah forces us to care for our friends, neighbors, and even our enemies. We are responsible for the damage caused when we dig a pit, leave it unmarked, and a neighbor falls into it. Our own blind spots can harm others who enter them. Later in this parashah, we learn that you can't take a lien on someone's last possession. If someone owes you and gives you the shirt that he sleeps in as a pledge, you have to return it before nightfall. Some markers can never be called. Even harder still, we have to return lost items to our enemies and even help them if they have a problem. Imagine seeing your worst enemy's car broken down on the highway—you have to stop and help him or her fix the vehicle or wait for a tow. Even your worst enemy, Torah says.

When and where are you a bad influence on others?

How does thinking about what you are owed cause you to ignore your own responsibilities?

How can you prepare yourself to forgive and to help even your worst enemy?

Mishpatim—day four

If it is known that the ox was in habit of goring …

—Exodus 21:36

Managing our affairs and the way we interact in community is a primary focus of this parashah. For example, Torah makes us responsible for damages caused by brushfires we start that burn out of control. Also, we're told that if we own an ox and it has a tendency to attack people and later kills a person, both the ox and its owner get put to death. The Talmud goes on to say that the only safe ox is one that is made into steak. Our actions, our inactions, and our tendencies all have consequences. Some, like fire, need to be managed and controlled. Others, like that ox, need to be put down.

What potentially damaging tendencies do you have that you are learning to manage?

When do your emotions burn out of control like brushfire and hurt others?

What are some of your most dangerous attributes and related actions?

Mishpatim—day five

If the thief is seized while tunneling …

—Exodus 22:1

Next, we learn from the verses that speak about the thief who is found in the dark. Since we don't know whether the thief is coming for us or not, we must take care of ourselves and seek safety. Here we also learn on a personal level to beware of people who look good but don't live good. If we suspect that others are hiding from us—and we all know whether they are real or not—then we are to treat them as a thief and take care not to let them steal our souls, our dignity, and our value. It is these types of people that Torah is most troubled by; our tradition is most distressed by the person who looks good and does bad. This is the epitome, according to the sages, of the *yetzer hara* (the evil inclination). We think that we know a person, and then his or her evil twin shows up. This evil twin will convince us that what we are seeing is really good and spiritual. This, the Rabbis say, is how the evil inclination works. The *yetzer hara* is so clever that it convinces us that we are the ones who are wrong. This is how we fall into the web of both an evil person and our own evil inclination.

When have you convinced yourself that something is okay when deep down you have doubt?

When have you been blindsided by a guru, letting one of these thieves steal your dignity, your money, or even your soul?

How have you let your own evil inclination trick you into believing you are being kind and spiritually minded when in fact you are hurting yourself or others?

Mishpatim—day six

You must not carry false rumors.

—Exodus 23:1

In chapter 23 of Exodus we are taught many lessons. The chapter begins with the commandment not to carry false rumors, not to join hands with the guilty as a false witness, and not to side with the rich out of deference nor with the poor out of pity. As I read this again this year, I am struck by how we transgress these commandments so often. We are not all liars; however, most of us do engage in *lashon hara* (evil speech). We carry rumors and seek out rumors in our daily lives, such as through our fascination with the dirt and negative reports about celebrities. We also carry false rumors about ourselves whenever we engage in negative self-talk.

How often do you lie to and about yourself?

What is your reward for doing this?

In what ways do you try to make yourself look good by putting others down?

Mishpatim—day seven

You shall not join hands with the guilty.

—Exodus 23:1

We join hands with the guilty when we go along with others out of loyalty to our friends even when we know that they are wrong. We say we want to support our friends. Yet, is it support when we go along with others knowing that they are not correct in their thinking or their actions? We join hands with the guilty when we say nothing in the face of evil. When we stand idly by and allow someone to use the vulnerabilities of another against him or her, we are joining hands with the guilty. When we don't say or do what is right out of fear that someone will get mad at us, we are transgressing this commandment. When we allow injustice to happen and to continue because of our fear of the rich and powerful or our pity for the poor, we are creating an unjust society.

When have you not only stood idly by, but encouraged or "cosigned" a friend's reasoning to harm another?

What helps you have the courage to stand up for what is right in the face of evil, power, and fear?

How have you succumbed to the lies of a society that says the one with the gold rules?

Terumah

Terumah—day one

Take for Me a gift or offering from
all whose heart moves them.

—EXODUS 25:2

This week's Torah portion is *Terumah* (a freewill offering). This portion examines what it takes for us to build a place where we can dwell with God. The parashah starts out with God telling Moses to "speak to the Israelite people and take for Me a gift or offering from all whose heart moves them." This is the great challenge for us and for God—we have to be willing and moved to give a gift to God. God is open and welcoming of all of our gifts. The next verses come to tell us what God wants as gifts, and the list, while specific, is also general in its nature. The gifts have to be the best that we have. They have to come from each individual and only from those who want to give.

When are you moved to give *terumah*, a freewill offering?

When do you give and feel like it is a bother or required, instead of coming from a true desire to make an offering, big or small?

How do you show up, giving what is needed and the absolute best you are able to share?

Terumah—day two

And these are the gifts that you shall accept …

—Exodus 25:3

This parashah continues from last week about what it is like to live in a community and what is needed from and for each person. This parashah focuses on the building of the Tabernacle. The Tabernacle was the meeting place for the community, and for the community with God. This is what synagogues are still supposed to be today—not just a place to worship, but a place to come together, meet each other, and meet God.

How could you better use your particular synagogue as a meeting place?

How often do you go to your synagogue? Why?

Where and when do you meet with your community and engage in dialogue about how to better yourself and your community as a whole?

Terumah—day three

Make for Me a holy/elevated space.

—Exodus 25:8

If we look closer, we see what the Israelites are building; they are building a place for God to dwell among them. The Children of Israel are instructed to create a vessel for them to take their experience of Sinai and try to keep it with them as best they can. The people of Israel cannot stay at Sinai forever; they need to move on, continuing on their journey to the Promised Land. So, they build the *Mishkan* (dwelling place; the Tabernacle), something that will allow them to take God with them on their journey. They figure out a way to keep God with them during the battles they fight both within themselves and against external enemies.

The Rabbis say that all of the Jewish souls were present at the giving of the Torah. We have all had moments of spiritual uplift; we have all experienced our own personal Sinai moments. At the time, these experiences can be intense and life-changing, and when they are over, we are left only with the memory of the experience. The further we get from our personal Sinai moments, the more we allow fear and doubt to creep in. If we allow them to, doubt and fear can make us rethink what, exactly, we experienced and make us play down the importance of these events.

How are you keeping the memories of your Sinai moments and the spiritual awakenings of your ancestors with you?

What is your way of downplaying or losing them?

Why do you think you might go into voluntary denial of these moments?

Terumah—day four

And … that I may dwell in them.

—Exodus 25:8

Many people find this parashah a little boring because of the in-depth details about how to build the Tabernacle. Since we don't have a Temple now and the building of the third Temple is not imminent, why bother with all of these details? I have thought about this often when reading this parashah, and each year I realize that we are reading this parashah for a reason. After we receive the Ten Commandments and the social ordinances, we have to take some action. It is not enough just to study the laws; we have to apply them to our lives. In fact, as Torah says at the end of last week's parashah, *na'aseh v'nishma*, "we will do and then we will understand" (Exodus 24:7). It is only in the doing that we truly learn and understand how to use the laws and teachings that Torah and God give us that fly in the face of modernity, saying, "I think, therefore I am." Judaism, as I understand it, says, "I am, I do, therefore I know how to think."

How often do you find yourself thinking about things rather than doing them?

Which laws do you live by in practice, not theory?

How are you still trying to think your way into right action rather than following the example of our tradition and acting your way into right thinking?

Terumah—day five

Exactly as I show you … so shall you make it.

—Exodus 25:9

In this vein, to act without knowing how to take the necessary action is unskillful. This week, Torah is giving us the teaching that when we don't know how to do something, it becomes necessary to learn the blueprint of how to take the required action from others. This parashah is also teaching us to take direction from others; we don't need to reinvent the wheel. Our hubris is thinking we have to do it all ourselves. Our portion this week is saying that it is good and right to learn the craft before we do what we want to. We send ourselves and our children to school, college, and graduate school to learn the tools necessary to be able to earn a good living. Why wouldn't we recognize that we need education in various other areas of life?

How are you teaching your children and yourself to live a life of joy, meaning, and purpose by using the blueprint given to us in Torah?

In which situations do you find yourself saying that you can do it all yourself, even when you know better?

How and with whom are you allowing yourself both to mentor and to be mentored?

Terumah—day six

The pattern of the Tabernacle ...

—Exodus 25:9

This parashah is also about following a plan. Torah gives us a detailed plan with measurements and weights for building the Tabernacle and its pieces. Many have wondered why the Torah would waste so much space with these details. While there will be areas in the building that allow us to express our individual creative spark, we still have to follow the plan. This is the hardest part for most of us to understand—God has a plan for us and for the world. This plan is for us to live well and make our corner of the world a little bit better. The plan is to add our unique gift to the world and live our authentic script. The plan is to live in cooperation, not competition. The plan is to live in harmony, not comparison. Another valuable lesson can be learned as the text teaches us not to be in such a hurry, simply assuming that people understand everything they need to complete what appear to be simple tasks. God is infinite, according to our tradition, and humans are finite. To assume that a finite mind is going to simply understand the words and thoughts of infinity is ridiculous. So, God is making sure that we are all on the same page.

How often do you speak in a cryptic manner, thinking that everyone else should be able to understand?

In which situations are you able to speak in a clear, detailed manner so that your words and your requests are understood?

When and about what are you truly satisfied when you are comparing yourself to others?

Terumah—day seven

They shall make an ark of …

—Exodus 25:10

There is also the inner gift that God is requesting. What is the inner gift God needs from us? God needs us to make a space in our lives and in our beings for God to dwell within. How do we do this? We do this by bringing the best that we have to God and to others. We have to be and bring the best that we have to ourselves, as well. We can no longer settle for the easier, softer way. The path of least resistance is no longer an option. We are able to do this. We can give to God, and others, a part of us that allows us to let God in; in that way, we, God, and others can truly dwell together. We will not always have the finest of the finest to offer, but we always have access to the best that we can give in any moment. This is truly all that God wants from us, the best we have to offer. We have to accept the best that we have in the moment. We have to accept the best that someone else can do and be in the moment. In this way, no one will have unrealistic expectations, and we can find ways to live and build better communities and a better world.

How are you doing the best in this moment and not comparing your best to anyone else's?

How are you learning right now to improve one grain of sand more each day?

How are you accepting the best from others without being competitive and comparative with them?

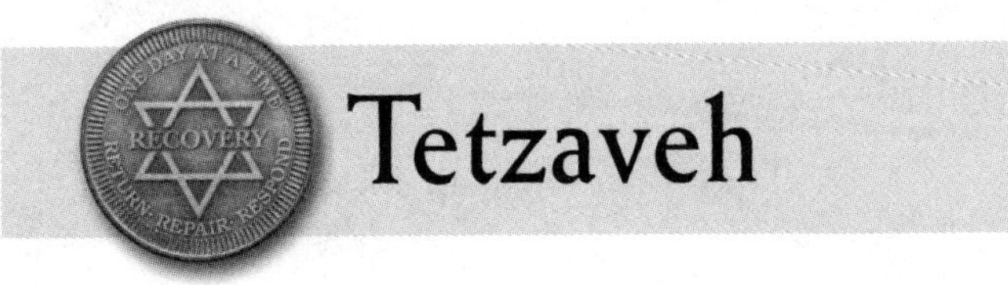

Tetzaveh

Tetzaveh—day one

For lighting always.

—Exodus 27:20

This week's parashah is *Tetzaveh* (you command). This parashah continues on from last week, telling us how to use the menorah (seven-branched candelabra) and how to make clothes for the priests. It also tells us that Aaron will be the High Priest and the priesthood will be inherited through his line.

In lighting the menorah, we are told that it is to be a *ner tamid* (an eternal light). We remember this and fulfill this *mitzvah* by having this light in front of the Ark in the synagogue. This light is to remind us that the covenant between us and God is forever, it is an active part of our daily lives, and the way to bring our living in line with our covenant—that is, to live a life of integrity—is to study and be with Torah. The *ner tamid* illuminates the teachings and the road map to living with God in God's world.

What is your most precious covenant with God?

What illuminates your path, keeping you in integrity and living well?

What is your practice of study and action that continually adds fuel to your *ner tamid*?

Tetzaveh—day two

Bring you clear oil of gently beaten olives …
—Exodus 27:20

To light the menorah, we have to use clear olive oil, according to the text. We are further commanded to gently beat the olives so that no pulp or schmutz gets into the oil, clogging the individual lights. The light of the menorah has to burn clear in order to give off enough brightness to illuminate the Covenant that is in the Ark. This is also true for us in our daily living; we have to use the fuel that is in our bodies, all of our energies, to live a life of integrity. We cannot just disown parts of ourselves. We have to be able to acknowledge all of our parts and to find ways to use all of ourselves to serve God.

What schmutz do you know you have
clogging up your spiritual arteries?

How do you cleanse the gunk that gets built up within you?

How are you using all of yourself to serve
God, others, and your higher self?

Tetzaveh—day three

Bring you clear oil …

—Exodus 27:20

This portion about the menorah and the oil is to be taken both literally and figuratively. Whenever I am fueling something, such as putting gas in the tank of my car or oil in its engine, I must use clean materials. If I put in the wrong kind of gas or dirty oil, there is a good chance that I will harm my car. This harm might not happen immediately, but it will most definitely take a toll over time. The same is true for us. Our physical, moral, and spiritual selves need to be nourished and filled with clean and clear fuel. We have access to healthy food and the knowledge about how to eat well, and still we often do not. We have the lessons from Torah, teaching us morality and how to live well, and we often do not heed them. We have our souls, our connection to God, and spiritual guides and friends to help us live spiritually fit, and we do not always use them. I am asking you to renew your commitment to living with cleaner and clearer fuel. I am asking you to renew your commitment to using your impulses in proper measure, and I am asking you to renew your commitment to living a life of integrity. We will not be perfect, but by renewing these commitments, we will become one grain of sand better each day.

What fuel are you putting into your body?

How do you fuel your discontent and angst?

How do you fuel your emotional, intellectual, and spiritual life?

Tetzaveh—day four

For the lamp to burn ...

—Exodus 27:20

The kind of fuel we use and what we choose to fuel can be one of the great challenges of being human. We can meet this challenge if we remember who and what we are. We are partners with God in making our corner of the world a little bit better, and we are divine images, reminders of God for each other. Each of us has a *yetzer hatov* (a good inclination) and a *yetzer hara* (an evil inclination). As Rabbi Harold Kushner told me over breakfast one morning, the *yetzer hatov* is our altruistic drive, our godly drive, and the *yetzer hara* is our egocentric drive. Both of these drives are needed, according to our holy tradition.

We need to use both aspects of ourselves wisely and in proper measure. If we used only our *yetzer hatov*, then we would not have the motivation to do things as human beings. If we used only our *yetzer hara*, then we would not have the motivation to do things godly; we would stop being human and would be superfluous to the world. We are created to take care of the world and care for each other. We have to do both in order to be fully human.

How do you determine proper measure
in each situation of daily living?

Knowing that both inclinations come from God, how can
you use them wisely rather than have them use you?

In which current situations in your life can you begin to think
of how to use both of these inclinations harmoniously?

Tetzaveh—day five

To burn from evening to morning before Adonai.

—Exodus 27:21

The *ner tamid* originally was meant to burn from evening to morning. At the darkest time of the day, this light, placed in front of the Ark of the Covenant, reminds us that God never leaves us. We do not have to fear disconnection from God when it is dark; rather, we can take comfort that God is always near. God never forsakes us. Now, I know that many of us feel lonely and lost when darkness in the form of illness or death comes upon us. This light does not guarantee that sickness will leave or that death will not arrive. It is a reminder to us and for us that the path to dealing with anything and everything that comes our way is through God and, by extension, our community. God being with us gives us the strength and courage to face all of life, the good and bad, with hope, determination, and certainty. The certainty is that with the help of God, family, and community we will be able to retain our dignity through all of life's situations. Healing in our tradition means being able to respond to any and all situations appropriately. When someone is ill, healing is being able to show up and give comfort to those who are sick and to their families.

How do you find yourself showing up for others currently?

How are you keeping your connection to God, others, and yourself when you are engulfed by darkness?

What are the spiritual exercises you engage in to strengthen yourself and face all of life with courage and integrity?

Tetzaveh—day six

Shall put their hands upon the head of the bull.

—Exodus 29:10

This beginning reminds me of my own imperfections. Studying, mastering a subject, earning a degree—none of these things necessarily confers expertise or perfection. We all get things right some of the time, and we all miss the mark sometimes. We have become a society obsessed with getting it right, hitting the bull's-eye all the time, and Torah is teaching us that this is impossible. We forget this fact and don't want to deal with our errors and the errors of others with truth, justice, compassion, kindness, and love. To deal with our errors in these gentle ways makes us more responsible to living a life being human, but we all want to be God. Getting it right requires a lot of trial and error. We want to hold others and ourselves to some ridiculous standard of perfection because we are afraid to face our authentic broken selves. This description of the beginning of the investiture of the High Priest teaches us that authenticity, truth, justice, love, kindness, and compassion are the most important ingredients for living well.

How can you practice being human more this week?

How are you being kind and loving when you or someone else misses the mark?

What are the actions you take to ensure you are living in truth, justice, and compassion more each and every day?

Tetzaveh—day seven

It is a sin offering.

—Exodus 29:14

Here God is instructing us about the investiture of Aaron and his sons. We are told that Aaron and his sons must bring a bull and a ram to the investiture. In reading this parashah, we are told the bull is a *chatat* (sin, or having missed the mark) offering. Aaron and his sons have to acknowledge that they have made mistakes before being invested into the priesthood. We know that they have erred and will err again. This understanding is so contrary to how we see our spiritual leaders today, or at least how we want to. No one is perfect, according to our holy tradition. The first act, actually the act prior to being invested into the priesthood, is to acknowledge humanness and human fallibility.

From which of your spiritual leaders
are you expecting perfection?

How are you still expecting or demanding
perfection from yourself?

How do you expect or demand perfection from family,
friends, mentors, coworkers, employees, or employers?

Ki Tisa

Ki Tisa—day one

When you take a census ...

—Exodus 30:12

This week's parashah is *Ki Tisa* (when you take). This portion has many seemingly different threads, but I believe that they are all intertwined. First, we learn that it is important to be engaged in some community. We have to decide on the community in which we want to become enrolled. God tells Moses to take a census by collecting a half-shekel from each male over the age of twenty. This was meant to ransom their souls and to pay for the upkeep of the Temple. No one may give more, and no one may give less. A half-shekel is equivalent to approximately five U.S. dollars; everyone could afford it. This is about more than giving; it is about being part of. It is about recognizing that we are all united in serving God and not being the one and only, having everyone serve us. This is the meaning of belonging; I serve you, me, us, and God.

What are you contributing to your community?

When and where do you see yourself as equal in worth and dignity to everyone else?

How are you demonstrating that you belong in all areas of your life?

Ki Tisa—day two

Each pay a ransom for himself … that no plague may come upon them.

—EXODUS 30:12

I am struck with the idea of the first few verses: each Israelite, over the age of twenty, must be enrolled or counted so that they do not suffer from the plagues. In other words, only when we enroll in the community of God can we be whole souls. Otherwise, we will be subject to plagues. Today, these are plagues of disunity, mistrust, competition, comparison, wrongful accusation. When we choose to enroll in a spiritual community that serves God, we are able to live as whole and complete human beings. When we do not enroll in a community, we are in a state of confusion, discontent, one-upping each other, relationship problems. These states of being lead us and our communities to be at war with each other and with everyone else.

How are your actions congruent with the community in which you are enrolled?

When and how do you find yourself living in opposition to others?

Which spiritual practices do you engage in that help you connect with yourself and others?

Ki Tisa—day three

> This is what everyone ... shall pay: a half-shekel.
> —Exodus 30:13

Another teaching in the opening of this parashah comes from each person being required to give a half-shekel in order to be enrolled in community. This was the smallest amount of money in that society. The Torah tells us that the poor shall give no less and the rich shall not give more. From this, we learn that each soul has the same worth. We cannot equate self-worth, or soul worth, with net worth. All of us are obligated, if we choose to enroll in the community of God, to see the worth of each and every individual. The half-shekel was to be used to support the Sanctuary. By contributing in this way, the Israelites would know that the Sanctuary was created with their participation. They had a part in its building and maintenance.

Giving a half-shekel also became the way of knowing how many adult males there were in the community. We used the half-shekel so that we did not have to count heads, teaching us that we can never put a number on a person or his or her worth. No one is ever always first or last. Using the half-shekel meant that no one had to push, lie, cheat, or steal in order to be first. Using it also meant that no one was ever left out or unimportant.

How are you putting a number or numerical value on yourself or others?

How are you lying about others so that you can feel better about yourself or get ahead?

What will it take for you to accept the infinitely equal value of every soul?

Ki Tisa—day four

It must not be rubbed on any person's body.

—Exodus 30:32

Another lesson this parashah teaches is to separate what we do that is sacred from that which is mundane. We are not to use the incense or the oil we use in the Sanctuary in our everyday activities. This is true in all areas of our lives. We have to separate the Sabbath from the other six days of work. We have to use each gift and tool that we possess in its proper way and in proper measure. We have to differentiate our many relationships, not confusing intimate with casual, personal with professional. When we are able to make these distinctions, we can experience the wisdom and skills we have been endowed with by God. We can also know how and when to use each of our gifts to the maximum benefit of God and our communities. When we confuse things, when we do not take a day of rest, when we use our gifts in ways other than how they were intended, we mix up the holy with the profane. This lesson is so important because without proper use and proper measure, we can easily bastardize our skills, muddle God's desires, and spiritually defile the souls of our communities.

What are some of the ways in which you are able to distinguish what is the next right action in any given moment?

How are you separating areas of your life to honor and recognize the sacred?

What is the greatest wisdom you are able to remember daily?

Ki Tisa—day five

See, I have singled out by name Bezalel.

—Exodus 31:2

The second chapter of this parashah tells us who will be in charge of the building of the Sanctuary. Bezalel is so named because he is filled with the Spirit of God and has wisdom, understanding, and knowledge. This description instructs us not to be enamored with wisdom alone. According to Kabbalah, wisdom without understanding is both dangerous and not valuable. Only when we understand how to use our wisdom do we gain and act in knowledge. Knowledge is the place where we are most godlike. In modernity, we worship information and forget how to use wisdom in many cases. We use information as clubs to beat and separate ourselves from those we deem less smart. This mentality is in direct opposition to that of being part of a community, acknowledging the truth that every soul has infinite worth and value.

How do you use information as a club and a means to separate yourself from others?

When do you act without understanding the nuances of a situation?

When do you find yourself believing or acting as if you are either more or less valuable or dignified than another person?

Ki Tisa—day six

Moreover, I have assigned to him Oholiab.

—EXODUS 31:6

We are told of others who will help Bezalel. All of the people who are willing to use their wisdom, understanding, and knowledge for the sake of heaven are to help with the construction and assembly of the *Mishkan*. These people are the ones who are willing to follow God's commands about what will be made and how it should be made. People who have knowledge don't need to rebel just because they want to do their own thing. People with knowledge can follow directions and still put their own unique stamp on everything they make.

Whom do you consider a person of wisdom, understanding, and knowledge?

When do you share your knowledge and the things you create with others?

Where are you able to follow directions while still being able to put your unique stamp on the things you create?

Ki Tisa—day seven

When the people saw that Moses was
so long in coming down …

—Exodus 32:1

This parashah also contains the story of the Golden Calf, one of the most disturbing incidents in our history. The people were impatient and counted incorrectly. Moses was not clear about when the forty days began. The people saw him go up in a cloud of smoke and fire; they got scared and held on for thirty-nine days and could not hang on for one day more. Aaron could not stand up to the people, and they knew that they could bully him. All of these factors led to the situation with the Golden Calf.

The Golden Calf represents our need to have something physically tangible to remind us of God. It represents our desire to worship idols. It teaches us that we can and will err, and we can be forgiven. God does not want to destroy us; rather, God wants Moses to really take ownership of his role as leader of the people. God knows what it is like to lose a lover to idolatry and wants Moses and the people to experience the feeling of love being taken away on a whim or because of an error. Moses will not let this happen. Moses's greatness is that he takes the responsibility of leadership seriously and wholeheartedly.

How are you standing up for our
community as Moses does?

What Golden Calves do you worship?

When do you still act like a fickle lover with
God, your partners, and your community?

Va-yakhel

Va-yakhel—day one

Moses then convoked the whole Israelite community.

—Exodus 35:1

The name of this week's Torah portion, *Va-yakhel*, can be translated to "and he convoked." Another way to translate this is "he (Moses) made a community." To make a community we have to make a statement as to who we are. In our Torah portion, we are called Children of Israel. When we congregate to make a community, each of us has to bring all of our parts, and all parts of the community have to come as well. We learn this from the first verse: "Moses then convoked the whole Israelite community." The Hebrew uses three different words to express this idea. The first word is *kol*, which means "all." The second word is *adat*, which means "entire community." The third word is "*B'nei Yisrael*," which means "Children of Israel." The text uses all three to emphasize the importance of bringing all of ourselves and not leaving any of our community behind.

How are you trying to bring all of your parts together and not hiding?

How are you assembling as an active and committed group member?

In what ways are you truly active in and committed to your own work life and company?

Va-yakhel—day two

These are the things Adonai has commanded.

—EXODUS 35:1

At first glance it seems like this parashah is redundant, since we learned about the *Mishkan*, its furnishings, and the priestly garments in earlier *parashiyot*. Why do we hear and read about it again? One reason is that the earlier *parashiyot* only gave the instructions for how to build it; they did not tell the story of the people actually building it. In this parashah, we learn that the people gave, from their own free will and because their heart moved them, the materials needed to build the *Mishkan* and did the work according to the plan.

How often do you talk about doing something
and then do not follow through?

What is the work you are capable of doing today?

How can you be satisfied with doing your part
and not feel the need to do everything?

Va-yakhel—day three

This is what Adonai has commanded.

—Exodus 35:4

To make community we have to be witnesses. This means we have to testify to the truth of what is going on. We cannot make a community by lying to and about ourselves. We have to be witnesses to truth rather than what we want to be true. We have to be witnesses to truth rather than wanting to be right. We have to be witnesses to God and for God, not false idols and ideas. We have to be witnesses for helping to improve our community and ourselves. We have to testify to the words of God, not our own words. We have to be like the prophets and testify to ways to help the widow, the poor, the orphan, and the needy.

What do your actions and words testify to?

Are you testifying to build a community or to tear down a community so that you can rule?

How do you answer these questions in all of your affairs—business, charitable work, social action, family, and social encounters?

Va-yakhel—day four

And let all among you who are skilled …

—Exodus 35:10

After the Golden Calf, God telling us to build the Tabernacle is God's way of telling us that we have been forgiven for our sin, I believe. This brings up an interesting concept. Do we accept the forgiveness of another? My contention is that without being forgiven and accepting the forgiveness of the other, we can never rebuild and/or repair the cracks that we have created in the structure of the relationship. God is teaching us that forgiveness is real. God is teaching us that forgiveness is necessary. God is teaching us that repairing relationships is an integral part of a communal structure. God is teaching us that just as we need God, so too does God need us. We can therefore deduce that since God needs us, we need each other. Since we need each other and we are not perfect, we have to do *t'shuvah* for our errors and accept the *t'shuvah* of others for their errors. Finally, we are obligated to forgive others and accept the forgiveness of others. Only through this spiritual action can we build the material structure of community, the Tabernacle, a meeting place for the community and God.

How are you doing *t'shuvah* with those you have harmed?

How are you forgiving those who have harmed you, once they have sought to make reparations?

In which areas of your life have you accepted other people's forgiveness?

Va-yakhel—day five

See, Adonai has singled out Bezalel.

—EXODUS 35:30

This verse reminds me that each of us has a unique task to complete during our lifetime. Here, Moses is telling us that God has singled out Bezalel to lead the task of building the Tabernacle. Rabbi Adin Steinsaltz, in his book *The Thirteen Petalled Rose*, says, "For each and every human has a specific task to perform in the world, a task that no one else can accomplish, though there may well be better and more gifted people around to do it. Only he can do it in a certain way...." Adonai singling out Bezalel tells us that only Bezalel possessed the spiritual and physical attributes to build the *Mishkan* in the way in which it had been designed by God. This is not to say that Bezalel was a puppet of God's, rather, this teaches us that Bezalel intuitively knew God's design and how to carry it to fruition.

How are you discerning what your unique gift or task is?

When do you let self-doubt stand in the way of living out your unique task?

How do you use your gift to better discern God's will and how to carry it out?

Va-yakhel—day six

He has filled him with the Spirit of God, with wisdom, understanding, and knowledge.

—Exodus 35:31

This is the parashah after the Golden Calf. This parashah also relates the building of the Sanctuary. We are not told about the plans of the building; rather, we are told how it was built. God tells Moses that Bezalel and Oholiab are to be the supervisors because they have been imbued with the Spirit of God, with wisdom, understanding, and knowledge. They are to have with them craftsmen who have been imbued with and utilize these same characteristics. What a beautiful choice of words. The people who are going to craft and build the structure that houses the Ten Commandments, the meeting place for both spiritual and communal affairs, are ones who have both the technical skills and the spiritual wisdom to do the job. The actions in this parashah are actions of completion.

What are you currently working on completing?

Which of your actions are still staying in the realm of planning?

How often do you have good ideas and not such good follow-through?

Va-yakhel—day seven

But when these continued to bring freewill offerings …

—Exodus 36:3

Another reason for the repetition of information in this parashah, I believe, is to show us that after the Golden Calf and our asking for forgiveness, God forgave us. If God had not forgiven the people Israel, then God would not have told Moses to go ahead and build the *Mishkan*. This is critical for us to understand. God accepts our *t'shuvah* when we make it. We have to accept God's forgiveness. This is the greater problem for most people. We think that whatever we have done is so terrible that no one, especially God, can forgive us. This is wrong. The greatest communal and individual sin is idolatry. The Golden Calf is the symbol of idolatry. God forgave us and told us to build a place where God dwells among us. This is the primary definition of love, in my opinion. Love is not some warm feeling; love is the action of accepting others for who and what they are. It is the action of knowing that all of us will err and being open for and to *t'shuvah*, the return of the other person. We are always able to do *t'shuvah*, and we are forgivable.

Where are you holding on to shame because you think that you cannot be forgiven and/or think you are supposed to be perfect?

How do you continue to deny your own foibles and blame others?

How are you able to love all of yourself and all others, as God does?

Pekudei

Pekudei—day one

Chazak, chazak, v'nitchazek.

—SAID AT THE END OF EACH OF THE FIVE BOOKS OF THE TORAH

This week's parashah, *Pekudei*, translates to "accounting." This is the last parashah of the book of Exodus. We will say, *Chazak, chazak, v'nitchazek*, "Be strong, be strong, we will be strengthened." This phrase comes at the end of each book of the Torah. We are being taught an important lesson: having finished a book of Torah, we have to be reminded that we have been made stronger because of our reading, comprehending, and using the lessons contained in that particular book. Also, we will be able to face more of life with strength and wisdom. A third teaching from this phrase is that in using the lessons of this book as well as previous books of the Torah, we will continue to strengthen ourselves.

What lessons are making you stronger today?

How are you using your past learning to live a stronger, more productive, and joyous life?

How are you helping others to be stronger by sharing your guidance and love?

Pekudei—day two

As it was counted …

—Exodus 38:21

Most of us have a record of our spending, even a record of our charity. Yet, how many of us keep a record of how we live? Our tradition tells us to do *t'shuvah* every day; this is one way of keeping a record of how we live. We are told to pray at least seven times a day—three services, after each meal, and before we go to sleep. Prayer, in Judaism, is about looking inside ourselves, another way of keeping a record. In the Twelve-Step movement, the tenth step is to continue to take personal inventory.

What makes this so interesting is that all of us take other people's inventory. We all have some judgment of the actions of others. We all remember the last person to slight us or denigrate us. We all engage in gossip of some kind. Our elected officials take the inventory of the opposing party. They also find all the errors of the poor, the afflicted, the disenchanted. This country is riveted every time a celebrity or politician explodes or implodes. Yet, do we take inventory of our daily living?

How often do you engage in a fearless and thorough moral inventory: each day, each week, each year?

How often do you hold yourself accountable as opposed to holding others accountable?

What prevents you from using prayer as your spiritual and emotional compass each day?

Pekudei—day three

These are the accountings ...

—Exodus 38:21

This parashah, *Pekudei*, starts out with an accounting of all the materials used in the making of the *Mishkan*. It seems rather boring and dull. What could this possibly teach us? Our sages of old say that with it we are taught to always make an accounting of what we have used, even in the service of God. Even a leader such as Moses, who seems beyond reproach, must account for all of the materials that have been placed in his keeping. Even though the people gave from their own free will, there still must be an accounting.

How do you account for all of the gifts that have been given to you?

How are you using the talents, gifts, and passion that God has given you to fulfill your unique mission?

How are you being accountable to others and to God?

Pekudei—day four

As Adonai had commanded …

—Exodus 39:1

The parashah goes on to tell us that each part was made "just as Adonai commanded Moses." This phrase appears seven times in this parashah. This seems a little redundant; if everything was not made according to God's command, we would not have had the plans to do it. What is the purpose of repeating this phrase so many times? It comes to teach us that some things have to be constructed exactly according to plan. Many times we can and must do things "outside of the box." And, there are times when we have to do things exactly as we have been instructed.

How can you tell when you have to do something exactly according to the plan?

When you need to be reminded of the precise instructions for carrying out an important task, are you willing to ask for them again?

How does following directions help you live better?

Pekudei—day five

As Adonai had commanded Moses.

—Exodus 39:5

Another reason for this repetition, I think, is so that no one would question the work of the people. They constructed all of the parts for the *Mishkan*. The repetition teaches us that we are able to follow directions as a group. Even the people who had special wisdom and skill did not have the need to do their own thing. They did not feel less than by following God's commands and direction.

When do you feel somewhat subordinated by following directions from your boss or Boss?

What do you believe stifles you when taking direction and conforming to precise ways of doing something?

How can you shift into being happy with a job well done, rather than feeling like you have to reinvent the wheel?

Pekudei—day six

When Moses saw that they had
performed all the work …

—Exodus 39:43

The parashah goes on to tell us that the *Mishkan* was truly constructed by all of the people. Everyone had a hand in building and/or contributing to the building of the *Mishkan*. No one was left out. Everyone had a part to play, and each person's presence mattered. Together they built a place where they could come together and dwell with God.

Are you leaving out someone important from helping to build your life today? If so, who?

Why are you leaving him or her out of this building process?

How are you contributing to building a space for people to come together and worship God?

Pekudei—day seven

Moses blessed them.

—Exodus 39:43

Moses blesses the Children of Israel after they bring all of the parts of the *Mishkan* to him. In *Moral Grandeur and Spiritual Audacity*, Rabbi Abraham Joshua Heschel, *z"l*, explains that prayer and blessings can come in the form of a chant, a song, a word of praise. Moses sings his praise to the people because they did what was asked of them. He praises them with a chant for being grateful to God for redeeming them from slavery by erecting the *Mishkan*.

What are some of the ways in which you praise yourself for doing the next right thing?

How are you singing other people's praises for doing what you ask of them?

With whom could you be more consistently generous in sharing your appreciation?

Va-yikra

Va-yikra—day one

Adonai called to Moses.

—LEVITICUS 1:1

This week's parashah is *Va-yikra* (and God called) and is the start of the book of Leviticus, the third book of the Torah. We believe that God called not just to Moses alone. We believe that God is calling to us all the time. One reason God calls out is that God is lonely when we are gone from God's presence. God wants us, as Rabbi Abraham Joshua Heschel, *z"l*, teaches in *God in Search of Man*; God is searching for us, and God needs us. What happened at Mount Sinai is still happening; what happened in the wilderness is still happening. God is still calling to us.

How and when do you realize that God is calling?

How do you distinguish between the voices in your head and God's call?

How do you respond to God's call?

Va-yikra—day two

Spoke to him …

—LEVITICUS 1:1

In the Hebrew, the last letter of the word *va-yikra*, the *aleph*, is smaller than the other letters in Torah. There are many commentaries on this fact, and I would like to relay the following teachings. The *aleph* is a silent consonant in Hebrew. It is also the first letter of the first-person pronoun for God, *Anochi*, and for humans, *ani*. In order for God to call to us, God has to contract Godself. God's voice shatters mountains and the cedars of Lebanon. As I understand from the story about Elijah the Prophet, we learn that God is the still small voice within (1 Kings 19:12). If God were to call out to us in full voice, we would be shattered and crumble to pieces. Therefore, God has to call to us in a small voice, hence the small *aleph*.

How often do you believe the loudest voice in the room, rather than what you know in your soul, to be true?

What are your practices to help strengthen the still small voice within?

How can you learn or enhance your ability to speak in a voice that others are able to hear?

Va-yikra—day three

Speak to the people of Israel.

—Leviticus 1:2

The human ego sometimes gets out of proper measure. When this happens, we are unable to hear the still small voice of God. We need to contract our egos in order to hear the call of God. We do not need to crush the ego—it is a gift from God; rather, we have to make sure our egos are right-sized, hence the small *aleph*.

What does your version of right-sized look like?

When do you contract yourself so that others have the opportunity to speak?

How are you using your ego as a gift rather than a weapon?

Va-yikra—day four

When any of you draw near ...

—LEVITICUS 1:2

How many of us have our egos functioning in proper measure? How many of us have too much plaque and fat in our spiritual arteries, in our minds and with our emotions, to hear the call of God? Are we too arrogant to hear God? Arrogance comes in different forms. The common feeling of not being good enough is actually borne of arrogance, I believe. When I say I am not good enough, I am denying God's truth that we are all holy souls, partners of and with God, and created in the image of the Divine with a divine purpose and message. Since this is true, how can any of us not be good enough? When we deny truth, we are being arrogant, thinking we know better.

What are some of the lies you tell yourself that keep you from hearing God's truth?

How do you manifest arrogance in your life?

How are you living your essence and authentic nature as a partner with the Divine?

Va-yikra—day five

Bring an offering …

—Leviticus 1:2

I believe the number one cause of strife, war, and misery is that we humans have not made ourselves small enough to hear the call of God. We are too full of ourselves. We are too self-absorbed. This is true of the person who has too big an ego and the person who has too small an ego; both of these types consider themselves to be the center of the universe. Those who have low or no self-esteem think only about how unworthy they are, how put upon they are, and how much of a victim they are. While this may seem like they have no ego, in truth their ego is so large that all they can think of is themselves. Those who believe themselves to be the center of the universe think that the world revolves around them. People in power, people who are filled with their own prestige, and those who think that because they have the gold, they can rule, all have egos so large that there is no room for God. There are some who have learned how to make themselves just the right size to be truly rich. Being rich, according to Ben Zoma in *Pirkei Avot* (literally, "Chapters of the Fathers," a compilation of the ethical teachings and maxims of the Rabbis of the Mishnaic period), is being happy with one's portion.

How are you self-absorbed with unworthiness, misery, and victimhood?

How are you self-absorbed with your power, prestige, and money?

How are you demonstrating that you are truly rich and happy with your portion and place in the world?

Va-yikra—day six

And Aaron's sons, the priests ...

—LEVITICUS 1:5

This, the third book, *Va-yikra*, is also called the Torah of the Priests, because it is filled with the priests' rituals. The ways in which the priests are to perform their duties are relayed in detail. Since there are no more priests, why spend so much time learning these rituals? The reason is twofold: the first is that we are called by God to be a "kingdom of priests and a holy nation" (Exodus 19:6), and therefore we are all enjoined to do these *mitzvot*; the second reason, in my opinion, is that we all err and need to know the way to return. The principles in this book are essential to fulfilling our goal of finding and living our authentic life scripts.

Which of your recent errors have you been able to acknowledge?

How do you act as a priest and minister to your soul and the souls of others?

How can you find your way back when you err? What is a good place to begin?

Va-yikra—day seven

When a person misses the mark …

—Leviticus 4:2

We are all moving closer to our authentic selves. Sometimes this movement comes by doing the next right thing, and sometimes it is through doing the next wrong thing. No, I have not completely lost my mind. When we do the next wrong thing, we are able to learn what path not to travel down. We can fail forward. There is a story of a man who was lost in the forest. He fell into despair, thinking he was lost forever. Suddenly, one day, he saw another person and became elated. He rushed over to the other person and said how happy he was that someone could lead him out of the forest. The other person smiled and said, "I am lost, also." The man crumbled into uncontrollable and inconsolable crying. The second person said to the man, "Stop crying. Don't you see, you know some of the ways not to go, and I know other paths not to travel down. By eliminating these wrong paths, we will be able to help each other find our way out of this dark forest and into the light of home." And they did. The same is true for all of us who feel lost, less than, not good enough, better than, and the like. Together, by right-sizing our egos and hearing the call of God, we will find the light of our places in the world.

What lesson did you learn the last time
you did the wrong thing?

How can you use this lesson to fail forward?

How can you better share your successes and
failures with others so together everyone can
find the right path for the moment?

Tzav

Tzav—day one

Command Aaron and his sons …

—Leviticus 6:2

This week's parashah is *Tzav* (command). God tells Moses to command Aaron and the priests to do certain things; these are most definitely not suggestions, they are commands. Many of us have problems with this word. We all want to be free to do as we please. "Command" connotes force, having to do something to which we are opposed. Here is a paradox for us: we are created with free will, we can make choices; but if we are commanded, then our free will is taken away. Yet, when we are controlled or commanded by our emotions or our thoughts, is this really free will? We are all compelled to do things by others, by our own needs, and by our desires.

How do you define free will?

What primarily governs your choices now—alignment with your will or God's will?

Which commands do you follow, and from whom do these commands originate?

Tzav—day two

This is the teaching/law of the …

—Leviticus 6:2

What do we do with this paradox about will? I believe the solution is found in our tradition. We are *chayav* (obligated). Obligation is what the force of command means for us. To reconcile our conception of free will with that of being commanded, we must be able to decide to fulfill the obligations that we have chosen. Many of us have problems with the ideas of command and obligation. This is because of mistaken identity, I believe. We mistake our identities for something separate from the world, separate from God, separate from our community or family. While we each have unique identities, they have to come together in order to serve the whole.

What obligations have you assumed?

How are these obligations helping you live well?

By fulfilling your obligations, to whom are you being responsible?

Tzav—day three

And the priest shall …

—LEVITICUS 6:3

The force of commandments allows us to know that life is a gift. To use the gift of life wisely, we must obligate ourselves to choose what is the next right thing to do in any given moment. Choosing a life following the commandments is living an obligated life. Living a life of obligation is living life on purpose. Living a life on purpose is living a life in and of God's will. Living a life based on God's will is living a life of gratitude.

How are you using your life as a gift?

How are you living on and with purpose?

How do you actively show your gratitude for everything you have?

Tzav—day four

Ritual of well-being ... if he offers it ...

—Leviticus 7:11–12

I have come to my understanding of free will from the teachings of Torah, Talmud, our sages, and my teachers, especially Rabbis Mel Silverman, *z"l*, Abraham Twerski, Abraham Joshua Heschel, *z"l*, Jonathan Omer-Man, and Edward Feinstein. According to these sources, free will is the ability to make moral choices and to ensure that the choices I make are moral. In order to do this, I must make a choice about what morality means. Our free will is a gift from God, a gift from our Creator. As we all know, most gifts come with instructions. Without life's instruction manual, Torah, we could easily make a mess of how to use the gift of free will. If we accept one of Rabbi Twerski's teachings from *The Spiritual Self*, that the ability for "an individual to make a free moral choice, something that is uniquely human and beyond the capabilities of even the most intelligent animal," then it is imperative to have a manual to teach us how to make these choices. This manual is the Torah.

What is your manual for moral living?

How are you acting as the sole interpreter of morality versus consulting with others?

How are you living: according to societal norms or according to God's commands?

Tzav—day five

This is the law of missing the mark; it is most holy.

—LEVITICUS 7:1

The Torah is, according to our prayers, a gift of love from God. We find this truth in the morning prayer *Ahavah Rabbah* and in the evening prayer *Ahavat Olam*. These two prayers express the belief that God shows love to humans by giving us Torah. Torah is described as the text that teaches us about commandments. Being commanded, according to our tradition, is the ultimate expression of love. Too often, especially in today's world, parents, teachers, and even employers are afraid to make commands and demands because someone will get upset and scream that it is a violation of personal civil rights. Historically, we all know many people's civil rights have been and continue to be violated; being commanded to be moral and being held responsible for this commandment does not constitute a civil rights violation, however. Holding to a standard that is determined by a higher authority, a Higher Power, God, seems to be the ultimate civil rights enhancement and the best way to enforce every person's rights. Judaism is concerned with obligations more than with rights. The obligations all lead to the same place, ensuring the rights of life, decency, compassion, justice, and love to and for all people.

How do you hold yourself and others responsible to ensure the civil rights of others?

How are you standing idly by the blood of your brothers and sisters?

How are you living a loving life through upholding obligations to your fellow humans?

Tzav—day six

The missing the mark offering is
a purification offering.

—LEVITICUS 7:7

God's unconditional love and continuous relationship with us is rooted in the idea of command. God commands us to be decent, respecting, and loving everyone, including and especially the voiceless and powerless in our society. This relationship is based on following the commandments of God so that we have an eternal, fixed code of ethics and morality. Without this code, we are able to live a life of situational ethics and morality where we alone decide what is ethical or moral in any given moment. We have seen the effects of this kind of morality in our world and the destruction that has been, continues to, and will be caused by humans being the arbiters of morality.

What would it look like for you to love yourself enough to follow God's commandments?

How are you loving others enough to hold them to this eternal moral code?

In which ways are you living a life of decency, simplicity, and love?

Tzav—day seven

He poured some of the anointing oil on
Aaron's head … to consecrate him.

—Leviticus 8:12

In this parashah, we are being taught that we can always be elevated, we can always rise above our previous errors. Aaron is elevated to a place of honor and reverence after his great mistake. When studying this parashah with my teacher Rabbi Edward Feinstein, he explains that it is, in fact, because of Aaron's experience of error that he is uniquely qualified for the job as High Priest. Too often, we shun the people who have erred; we get angry at the people we have counted on when they have not come through in the way we wanted and/or we did not get the results we wanted. God does not do this with Aaron, and God does not do this with any of us. God does not expect us to be perfect and does not have delusions that things will always work out the way God wants or in the way we want. Rather, God rewards us for our *t'shuvah*, for learning from our mistakes about how to live better.

How can you really accept the imperfections of others rather than getting angry when things do not work out the way you want?

Which experiences can you learn from instead of shunning those by whom you feel disappointed?

Which leaders can you allow to be imperfect, appreciating their foibles and seeing how they have learned from mistakes?

Shemini

Shemini—day one

On the eighth day …

—Leviticus 9:1

This week's parashah is *Shemini* (eight). The portion starts out by telling us that on the eighth day, the Sanctuary was completely dedicated, and Aaron and his sons were invested in the priesthood. In this we learn that the day after the completion of something is a significant day. In this case, the day after a week of celebration is important because it is a statement of what we are going to do with what we have gained. What we do the day after an event says a lot about how we want to be in the world. Are we changed on the day after Shabbat? Do we realize and take note of any new commitments? Are we even aware of the events that take place in our lives, or are we oblivious? This week's parashah teaches us not only to be moved by a great event, but also to be moved by the small happenings every day. Most of us get stuck thinking, "Same stuff, different day." This parashah is teaching us that this is not true. We have to be moved to do something different in order to honor all of life's moments.

How do you honor the special events in
your life after the day has passed?
How do you allow yourself to be changed by life's events?
How do these changes help you live well?

Shemini—day two

And speak to the Israelites … Take
a he-goat for purification.

—LEVITICUS 9:3

The text then tells us that the elders of Israel were instructed to bring a goat for their purification offering. Here we are taught that when a leader is installed, not only does the leader have to acknowledge his or her errors, but the people must also acknowledge theirs. Torah is teaching us to remember that both the new leader and the people have to clear themselves of their previous errors so that they can start anew. In this way, the leader is not subject to the prior negativity of either his or her predecessor or the population. We are being taught to see ourselves, each other, and our new leader with a new pair of eyes.

When do you clear yourself of your past mistakes?

How can you see your leaders, your peers,
and yourself with new eyes?

What do you gain by heaping old negativity onto new
situations, leaders, people, and even yourself?

Shemini—day three

Nadav and Avihu, the sons of Aaron …

—LEVITICUS 10:1

This is also the story of Nadav and Avihu, the eldest of Aaron's sons. We are told that Nadav and Avihu offered strange fire. We are not told what it was that made the fire strange. The Hebrew word used here for "strange," *zarah*, can be translated as "scatter" or "fan." Many commentators have said that these men were trying to do their own thing, and the fire got out of hand. Others say that they were disrespectful toward Aaron and Moses. Still others say that they were drunk. All of these interpretations are possible. In past years, I have understood that Nadav and Avihu were trying to get too close to God, and when they achieved this, they were burned. This, of course, is a familiar theme in addiction, getting too close, trying to achieve the ultimate high, and then overdosing and, sometimes, dying.

In which areas of your life are you trying
to take too much and overdosing?

What dangerous flames are you fanning in
your life out of habit or boredom?

How do you decide what to contain and what to scatter?

Shemini—day four

They offered alien fire before Adonai.

—LEVITICUS 10:1

In looking up the different meanings of the Hebrew for the word "strange," I found that it also means "scattered." This has helped me to understand the cause of Nadav and Avihu's deaths in a different way. They were scattered when they went to make their offering. They were not focused on the task at hand, and they were not focused on whom they were serving.

How often do you go through life in a scattered manner?

What is the result of your efforts when you approach things this way?

What are the consequences of losing your focus on what is truly important to you?

Shemini—day five

Put fire and incense on it …

—LEVITICUS 10:1

Another way of understanding "scattered" in this context is that the fire they brought was spread all over. They brought fire, and instead of keeping the fire contained and only for one purpose, Nadav and Avihu scattered the fire all over trying to fulfill different agendas, God's agenda and their own.

How are you bringing scattered fire to your life, trying to do too many things?

When you try to fulfill too many different agendas at the same time with the same fire, do you find yourself out of balance?

When does being scattered, trying to do too many things at once, ever really work for you?

Shemini—day six

These are the creatures you may eat
from among all the animals.

—Leviticus 11:2

We also learn about kosher food in this portion. What does this have to do with celebrating and consecrating life? Absolutely everything. In Hebrew, *kosher* means "fitting" and "proper." When we eat kosher, we are celebrating our commitment to follow God's words. We are celebrating our ability and desire to draw closer to God through *mitzvot*. We are consecrating ourselves by selecting what we eat carefully. We are consecrating ourselves by surrendering to eat what is considered fitting and proper in our tradition, not just eating anything and everything that is available. We are consecrating and celebrating being alive when we make conscious choices in all areas of our lives, including about how and what we eat.

How do you define what is kosher in your life?

How do you decide what is fitting and proper? What sources do you consult to make these determinations?

How are you living a kosher life, one that is fitting and proper for you and your community?

Shemini—day seven

Whatever parts the hoof, and is cloven footed, and chews the cud, among the beasts, that shall you eat.

—LEVITICUS 11:3

The Torah gives us some laws and explains the reasons for following them. Other guidelines are given to us without explaining why the boundaries are important to follow. Keeping kosher, *kashrut* (Jewish dietary laws), falls into this latter category. We are told that certain foods are kosher and others are not but not why these determinations have been made. It may not even be important to know the reasons behind these laws. What I believe is important is making distinctions about what is fitting and proper to eat, to wear, and to do in all facets of living. Too many people are living without limits. Too many people are still living according to what they can do, not what they should do. *Kashrut* reminds us and teaches us that just because we can does not mean that we should. In a lunch and learn held at Valley Beth Shalom, Encino, California, Dr. Meir Tamari, the author of the book *Al Chet: Sins in the Marketplace*, taught that there are twenty-eight laws concerning kosher food and over one hundred laws regarding kosher money.

How are the distinctions you make leading you to live in a fitting and proper way?

How can you learn to be as concerned and discerning about how you make and spend your money as you are about your food choices?

How are you making your soul kosher and helping others keep their souls kosher?

Tazria

Tazria—day one

When a woman at childbirth …

—Leviticus 12:2

This week's parashah is *Tazria* (she conceives). It deals with what to do when someone is ritually impure. We start out learning that no matter what we do, even something holy, there is going to be *tumah* (ritual impurity). I believe that the word "impure" connotes a state of being that is not grounded in this world; all instances of impurity I can think of have this same thing in common. The experience of childbirth gives a woman such a high that she becomes uprooted from this world. This is not a bad state per se, but it is a state in which she could easily err in performing her ritual duties, because of this high and because of the attention to her newborn.

Here again, we learn that Torah and God are concerned not only with what we think of as spiritual, but with elevating every aspect of life within the individual as well as the community. We have to understand that ritual duties are not the be-all end-all; they are a necessary part of living, and we all have them.

What are the "ritual duties" you perform each day, week, month?

How do they make the rest of your life work?

How do your rituals ground you in your daily living?

Tazria—day two

On the eighth day … circumcised.

—Leviticus 12:3

This parashah has gotten me to think about bringing children into the world. So many of us have no idea what to do to raise our children. We do the best we can, but I believe that we need a new way of responding to pregnancy and childbirth. I have developed a series of questions for prospective parents and for couples who already have children.

What is the *b'rit* (covenant) that you, the couple, are making with your child?

Which obligations to your child and your spouse exist now that there is another life you must nurture?

What is your plan for fulfilling each of these obligations?

Tazria—day three

She shall remain in a state … for sixty-six days.
—Leviticus 12:5

The focus in the first part of this chapter is on birth and how to bond with our children. It also teaches men that when our wives give birth, we have to think about them and the newborn rather than our own physical urges. Also, we are being taught to appreciate that childbirth creates a new reality for both mother and father. The father, especially, has to remember to stay out of the high chair. As many of us know, a newborn changes the entire dynamic of a family. There is another life to care about, nurture, and raise.

How are you committed to acting as an adult and raising, nurturing, and caring about your own children, the children you know, and the children of the world?

How do you, as an adult, get out of the high chair and become responsible for your actions, caring for the lives and welfare of others?

What are some of the ways you connect with your child?

Tazria—day four

> When a person has on the skin of his body a swelling or a discoloration ...
>
> —Leviticus 13:2

Torah describes different types of people who become impure. One type of person who becomes impure is one who has an outbreak called leprosy. This is not the same as the physical disease of leprosy; rather, it is a physical manifestation of a spiritual malady. God does not send us illnesses to punish us. We do, however, get outbreaks of physical symptoms because of both our internal maladies and our external actions. The person who manifests the first kind of leprosy, according to our holy tradition, causes this outbreak by speaking with *lashon hara* (evil tongue). The consequence for this behavior is to be put outside the camp, a form of quarantine. The reason behind this repercussion is that evil speech, *lashon hara*, is contagious and infectious.

How have you been infected with *lashon hara*?

How have you infected others with *lashon hara*?

Do you experience a physical reminder of the effects of engaging in *lashon hara*? If so, describe these sensations.

Tazria—day five

On the seventh day the priest shall examine him.

—Leviticus 13:5

We also learn about the obligations of the community when someone is suffering from a spiritual malady. Unlike in today's society, where keeping secrets is so treasured and seemingly honorable, Torah tells us that we have to know that people are ill in order to help them. In fact, we must let the priest, rabbi, or leader know about those who are suffering in order to help them. Likewise, we must identify addiction in ourselves and in our communities in order to be able to help those afflicted recover.

Which of your spiritual maladies are you keeping secret?

How are you complicit in hiding other people's illnesses from those who could provide help?

What is stopping you from asking for the help you need to get well?

Tazria—day six

Sages considered leprosy to be a punishment
for slander and malicious gossip.

—Leviticus Rabbah 16:1

This is one of the hardest commandments to follow: do not talk badly about another just because you can, whether or not the information is accurate. What makes this kind of speech so enticing? We have to look to our history to find both an answer and a solution. In Genesis 4:6–7, God says to Cain, "Why has your face fallen?… Negativity couches at your door; it desires you much." From this we learn that the negativity caused by *lashon hara* desires our company. Cain kills his brother Abel. Our sages teach that *lashon hara* is tantamount to murder because with it we destroy a person's name. This desire to destroy another seems almost natural to many of us, manifesting from the same source that God warned Cain about. This negativity desires us, waiting at the door of our mind and emotions. It allows us to feel better about ourselves by putting someone else down. We talk about killing the competition and doing whatever it takes to win—with sayings like these as our mantras, we don't even see that what we are doing is wrong.

When are you most susceptible to the
negativity that couches at your door?

How has the desire of this negativity
become your desire as well?

What is the specific cost to your soul of winning at all costs,
putting someone else down so that you can step up?

Tazria—day seven

Sages considered leprosy to be a punishment
for slander and malicious gossip.

—Leviticus Rabbah 16:1

Our tradition teaches us that the spreader of negativity must be quarantined, otherwise he or she will become a killer of many, using gossip and slander, pulling others down into negativity. Our tradition says three people are hurt by *lashon hara*: the speaker, the one being spoken about, and the listener. To avoid infecting a community, we have to separate the sick from the rest, ministering to them for healing. Putting someone outside of the camp is not punitive; rather, it is an act of *chesed* (kindness) to create separation for someone in order to help him or her heal. As all of us know, when we eat healthily, we have to separate ourselves from unhealthy foods, because if they are around, we will eat them. For those who want to speak healthily, they must be separated from the people to whom they talk unhealthily with and about; otherwise, they will continue to be tempted to go back to the old ways.

How do you make the determination to separate
from someone who is unhealthy for you?

When are you kind enough to tell someone
that what he or she is doing is a manifestation
of inner conflict and negativity?

What do you do to minster to those sick
with the dis-ease of *lashon hara*?

Metzora

Metzora—day one

This shall be the ritual for a leper at
the time he is to be purified.

—Leviticus 14:2

This week's parashah is *Metzora* (a diseased person). The portion talks about healing a person who has scales on his or her skin. The healing process is monitored by a priest, who, having determined that the gossiper has done the first part of *t'shuvah*, confession, allows this repentant to return to the camp. The priest still stays outside, observing the diseased person's house for a week. This is a way to ensure that a different action is being taken, that he or she is not engaging in *lashon hara*. In the next stage of healing, the priest makes offerings to allow others to again draw near the repentant person.

When do you see yourself as one who is with *tzaraat* (disease)?

When was the last time you felt remorse for gossiping?

What do you do to make reparations and again be able to draw near those in your community?

Metzora—day two

And the priest shall put it on the …

—LEVITICUS 14:14

There is an action that is different in the offering made to heal this kind of leprosy. The priest puts blood and oil on the right earlobe, right finger, and right big toe of the repentant. Interestingly, this is the same action that is done to anoint the priest into the priesthood. One reason for this is given in the commentary of the *Etz Hayim Chumash* (p. 662, verse 17), which says that this shows that healing spiritual maladies requires the combination of right action, right attitude, and divine grace. As most recovering addicts will tell you, in order to stay sober we must keep our spiritual connection. Addicts also know that we have to act our way into right thinking, just as the *mitzvot* teach us. For most of us, our thinking is a little off at times. Many of us allow our thoughts and emotions to direct our actions rather than allowing our souls and God to lead us. This is not the way to experience divine grace. When we receive divine grace, we are obligated to be properly responsive. I am sober and decent with the help of God, and I have to do the next right thing to continue to be worthy of this divine grace.

In your recovery, how are you acting like a priest, doing the next right thing with a humble, positive attitude?

When do you allow your actions to be guided by your higher self and God?

What does divine grace mean for you?

Thus the priest shall make expiation
for him before Adonai.

—Leviticus 14:18

Divine grace is not a permanent state. We are all entitled to divine grace; in fact, it is a birthright for all of us. However, we must live in a way that honors this gift, otherwise we leave this state of grace. Many people think that divine grace is the same as luck. This is untrue; divine grace is something we receive because of our conscious choice to do the next right thing and to continue to be responsive to the call of God and God's creations. Too often, we go into a default mode of unconscious living. This is not appreciating and responding to the gift of grace. When we say, "There but for the grace of God go I," we have to be aware of our good fortune and use this grace appropriately. This is not to say that we will not receive the gift again; it just means that we cannot take our gifts for granted.

When are you most aware of the divine
grace that God and others show you?

How do you remain conscientious in your actions?

How are you being responsible to the
divine grace you are given?

Then he shall be pure.

—Leviticus 14:20

Another reason for performing this anointing ritual is to let the *metzora* know that with healing comes responsibility. Just like spiritual leaders are required to be messengers of light, when we are healed we must bring the message of healing, doing *t'shuvah,* and taking appropriate action back to our communities. We are now responsible to carry the message, as the twelfth step of Alcoholics Anonymous states. We who have been healed must care for and teach others that healing is possible. We have to reach out and help others heal. We are responsible for creating a plan of action to ensure we will not make the same error again. We are also responsible for becoming more attuned to the silent desperation of people who feel lost. We must remember and reach out to all to spread the message of the power of *t'shuvah* and divine grace. In Judaism today, there are no more priests. Therefore, the *metzora*, like the *baal t'shuvah* (master of return or returning), is required to do the work of the High Priest. We must reach out and bring all those who are lost back to community, to healing, to God, and to life.

How are you being responsible to the gift of your healing?

What actions do you take to help others heal?

When and where do you carry the message of *t'shuvah*, healing, and hope?

Metzora—day five

An eruptive plague upon a house
in the land you possess ...

—LEVITICUS 14:34

In this parashah we also learn that a home can become impure. I am struck and stuck trying to discern what this means, and here is how I have come to understand impurity: being impure means that people and places can become otherworldly. Here, otherworldly is defined as anything that does not fit into God's plan or blueprint for how we should act and care for the world. This is not meant to indict anyone for errors in judgment or action. In God's world there is ample room to make mistakes, because we were given the ability to do *t'shuvah*. The impure world is one where people knowingly and consistently make judgments and take actions that they know are wrong. This is a world in which we, with malice and intentionality, go against what is good for humankind and engage in activities that are totally self-centered.

How do you most often act in impure ways?

What fears are you reacting to when you act in this manner?

How are you contributing to and caring
for God's world and creations?

Metzora—day six

It seems to me there is a disease in the house.

—Leviticus 14:35

The house that becomes impure is a house that is not a home. It is a place where God, decency, and community have been replaced by slavery, hatred, and narcissism. It is a house in which the people living in it are *metzoraim*. They have a spiritual malady and do not want to be healed. As Maimonides, the greatest Jewish thinker of the Middle Ages, says, they are suffering from a soul sickness. Most people who are suffering do not know it, thinking everyone else is wrong rather than that they are ill. Maimonides goes on to say that these people need a physician of the soul. This is what rabbis and clergy are trained to be, yet most people go elsewhere for healing, if they go at all.

Which of your living spaces might be demonstrating a spiritual malady?

How do you engage in healing or continuing the spiritual malady of your home, community, or world?

Whom do you trust as a spiritual physician, or are you in denial of your own spiritual maladies or think you can solve them by yourself?

Metzora—day seven

You shall put the Israelites on guard against their impurity.

—Leviticus 15:31

No one is exempt from spiritual maladies; we all suffer them from time to time, yet most of us do not do anything to heal. We think, "This is just my lot in life," or "Nothing will ever change." This is a major problem the world faces today; we cannot think our way out of these maladies, we cannot just take a pill and they will disappear. A spiritual discipline is required to find our way to spiritual health.

Do you ever take a spiritual health exam? What are the symptoms you need to check?

What are the negative thoughts to which you unconsciously succumb?

What and who helps you keep spiritually fit?

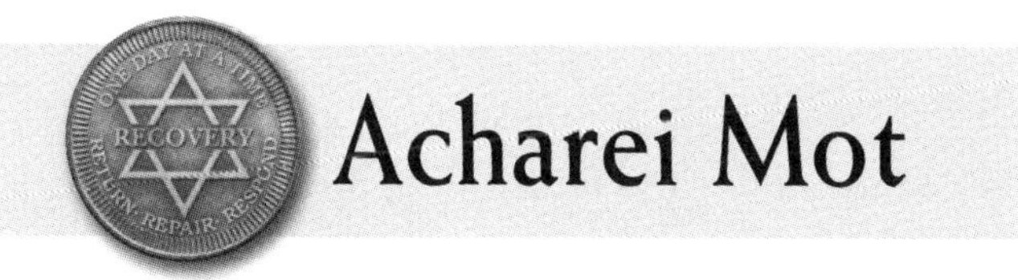

Acharei Mot

Acharei Mot—day one

Adonai … after the death of …

—LEVITICUS 16:1

This week's portion is *Acharei Mot* (after the death) and refers to the death of Aaron's two sons, Nadav and Avihu. The Torah says that they died because they drew too close to the presence of God. This is an interesting explanation of the reason for their death. To me, it proves that they were not bad boys, as some commentators have said. They were not trying to outdo their father, Aaron, nor their uncle, Moses. They knew of their separation from God and longed for a complete union. They thought that they could remove all barriers to God and be one with God while still being human. Many of us today believe this is the definition of being spiritual. Torah is teaching us, I believe, that part of the experience of being human is about learning where we stop (our finiteness) and where God and other humans begin. In this way, Torah is teaching us that some separations are important and necessary.

How are you trying to remove all separations and be one with God?

What is your way of being one with God while still being able to remain human?

When have you tried to be at one with another person and ended up losing yourself?

Acharei Mot—day two

When they drew too close to the presence of Adonai.

—Leviticus 16:1

Needing to remain distinct is not a punishment from God; rather, it is God teaching us that in this human form we have a place. Our place is to make this world better because we exist here. We are God's partners in perfecting creation. We have to stay in our human form in order to do our unique work and complete our corner of the world. When we try to eliminate the distance between ourselves and God, we are attempting to be God and to be human at the same time. We cannot be both. We have to remember that God has God's place in the world, and the world cannot exist without God in God's place. We also have a place in the world, and the world does not exist well without us in our place. These verses teach us not to be upset that we are not God; rather, we should rejoice in having our own place and in having our portion. Do we? We do when we live well and live the script of our own soul. We do when we care for others and treat others as divine images rather than as objects for our pleasure and use. We do when we study, pray, and live the teachings of Torah and our tradition. We all need to take a *cheshbon hanefesh* (accounting of the soul) to make sure that we are following the path to become our best selves.

How are you rejoicing in your portion and place in the world?

In what ways can you see that you are both a divine image and not divinity, at the same time?

What will it take for you to ensure that you follow your unique path and live your divine place in the world?

Acharei Mot—day three

That he come not into the holy place at any time …

—LEVITICUS 16:2

Let's consider another idea about this parashah. In the beginning of *Acharei Mot*, we learn that the reason for the death of Aaron's oldest sons, Nadav and Avihu, was that they tried to draw too close to God. This seems strange—isn't our whole existence supposed to be about drawing closer to God? I think the Torah is teaching us that we cannot try to get too close to God through artificial means and going through the motions of ritual. We cannot physically get too close to God; rather, it is through our actions that we feel closer to God. It is important to remember that when we approach God in prayer, in action, and in thought, we have to stay rooted, keeping our feet on the ground and not trying to leave our bodies and our world.

How am I approaching God with the actions that I take?

How am I trying to approach God through superficial rituals, magic, and smoke and mirrors?

How do I know the difference between true connection and false efforts?

Acharei Mot—day four

Aaron shall enter the Shrine with a bull of the herd for a purification offering.

—LEVITICUS 16:3

This parashah teaches us about Yom Kippur (the Day of Atonement). The first offering that the High Priest makes is for himself and his household. What a concept—in our tradition, no one is perfect. The High Priest is taught that just because he has an elevated position in the community, he is not above the law; he is taught that he is not above reproach. He is taught that he is still human and takes human actions that miss the mark. While the High Priest has a role that is different from the roles of others in the community, he, too, is human, according to our Torah. We have to remember that just as the High Priest is prone to error, so are we. There are no gurus in the Jewish tradition. When we try and make ourselves gurus or be perfect, we are missing the most important lesson of our tradition: as humans we will make mistakes and miss the mark. We are not hardwired to be perfect. We have to accept our imperfections and flaws. We have to accept that we can do *t'shuvah* and be forgiven. God wipes the stain of error and shame from us. We have to accept being forgiven and be responsible to, and for, this forgiveness.

How can you act like the High Priest, making atonement for yourself?

When do you find yourself still needing to be right, carrying resentments toward the people you have harmed?

Have you accepted the forgiveness that God and others have offered you?

Acharei Mot—day five

And the other lot for Azazel.

—Leviticus 16:8

We are also taught that after we make atonement, we must send out a goat to Azazel. We do not know what Azazel is. We do not have any goats in synagogue on Yom Kippur. So, what is the story about this ritual? This is another powerful teaching for us: not only do we have to confess our sins, not only do *t'shuvah*, but we must also have a plan for restitution of the dignity of the other person, not simply a flimsy plan not to repeat the same action. We have to separate ourselves from negativity. We send out the negativity with the goat for Azazel. We have to distinguish ourselves from the negative energy that helps us make the same mistakes. We have to create enough distance from the negativity that it no longer has power over us. We also have to make sure that we do not chase after the negativity once we have removed ourselves from it. We run after negativity in both overt and covert ways. One way we do this is by forgetting that negativity has power over us. Another way is by repeating the same actions, in slightly different ways, thinking that we can control the outcome. A third way is not accepting the truths we have learned about ourselves and other people.

How can you see the dignity of all human beings,
even those you don't particularly like?

In what ways are you still chasing after negativity?

What are some ways you know help you create distance
from your own negativity or negative situations?

Acharei Mot—day six

Let him go to Azazel.

—Leviticus 16:10

Here's another lesson about the goat for Azazel. We do not know what or who Azazel is. We can infer that it is a place, rather than a person, because the goat is taken to a region in the wilderness and released. This goat is the original scapegoat. We attach our errors to the head of the goat and send it away from us. What could this be about?

Torah always teaches us about taking personal responsibility, so how is it possible that we are also allowed to push our errors off, placing them on something else? Rather than viewing this as an example of how we are shirking responsibility for our errors, placing their onus on something or someone else, we can see this as a way to actually take action and responsibility for our mistakes, separating ourselves from the errors of which we are consciously aware.

When and where do you find yourself still blaming someone else for your own errors?

What are your fears of taking responsibility for your actions?

Whom or what are you using as a scapegoat, and what is your reward for doing so?

Acharei Mot—day seven

Confess over it all the iniquities … putting them on the head of the goat, and it shall be sent off to the wilderness.

—Leviticus 16:21

This week's parashah is the antidote to excessive guilt, hostile narcissism, and malignant shame. When we take responsibility for our errors, fix them directly with the people we have harmed, mend the damage within ourselves and with God, we can be and we are forgiven. The problem is that most of us don't accept the forgiveness from others and from God. We are given this week's ritual of sending the errors out of our reach as a way to take responsibility for our mistakes, not to avoid acting responsibly. We are being told that the harm that we have corrected, fixed, and apologized for no longer has to define us. This is essential to comprehend. Too many of us don't let go of our past errors, continuing to hold on to them tightly. Doing this allows malignant shame to grow and flourish within us. By sending the errors out of our camp, we can separate ourselves from these mistakes and acknowledge that they are still in the world. The difference is, we are no longer bound by our mistakes or to them, we don't have to repeat them, and we can let go of the power to rule us we have given them.

How are you demonstrating your ability to accept the forgiveness of God and others?

When and how are you continuing to define yourself by your past errors?

What stops you from letting go of your guilt, shame, and narcissism?

Kedoshim

Kedoshim—day one

You will be holy.

—Leviticus 19:2

This week's parashah is *Kedoshim* (holiness). I love each and every Torah portion, and *Kedoshim* is one I feel especially fond of because it has the most uplifting, hopeful, and loving two-word phrase in it—*kedoshim tiheyu* (you will be holy). Think about this for a moment: no matter where you are, nor what your past and present are, you will be holy. We are all commanded and promised that we are and will become more holy. The Hebrew word for "holy" means "to elevate," "to separate," and "to connect." So, the promise is that we will all separate ourselves from our negativity and use this energy for good. We will elevate and connect our everyday activities to serving God, others, and our souls. What could be more uplifting?

When are you most aware of your innate holiness?

How are you allowing your holiness to uplift yourself and others?

How can you connect more with others as a holy act, rather than fear connection by falsely believing it leads to unwelcome vulnerability?

Kedoshim—day two

Do not turn to idols.

—LEVITICUS 19:4

Many people ask: what does it take to be holy? Holiness in our tradition is quite simple. One of the ways we can be and become more holy is not to worship idols. This is one of the hardest actions to live, because there are so many idols today. When we worship only God, we are fulfilling the action of being holy. This does not mean that we don't look up to people who are doing great things in the world and in our lives. It means that role models are just that, models for how to live well. They are not gurus; they are not the be-all and end-all. When I am able to see the flaws as well as the greatness of others and appreciate both, I do not worship them. When I respect that having a nice house, car, mate, and job may be important for my well-being while still not worshipping any of my things, I am being holy.

What are some of the false idols you have caught yourself becoming enchanted by?

Have you ever mistaken someone in your life as a guru and who was he or she?

How are you practicing the actions of being holy? Stay away from how you are not or do not, and focus on how you are.

Kedoshim—day three

When you sacrifice an offering of well-being …

—Leviticus 19:5

When I know that I have had much help to reach the place I am and when I want what I have, rather than needing to have what I want, I am being holy. When I am not greedy and share my good fortune with others, I am being holy. When I am recognizing and relating to all of my disparate parts, I am being holy. When I am living *my* life, I am being holy.

How have you acted grateful to and for God and the beauty that is your life?

How have you shared this gratitude with others?

How can you use gratitude for your gifts, coupled with humility, to share more of yourself and your unique strengths with your loved ones, community, and the world?

Kedoshim—day four

Do not place a stumbling block before the blind.

—LEVITICUS 19:14

Do not place a stumbling block before the blind: When I see someone's disabilities and do not take advantage of them, I am holy. When I tell the whole story, I am holy. When I ask people to do only that which they are capable of, I am holy. When I see all of my parts and being-ness and the whole person in front of me, I am holy. When I do not set unrealistic expectations of and for myself, I am holy. When I do not get disappointed when people do things to the best of their ability, appreciating their offering even if it isn't the way I would have performed the same action, I am holy. When I appropriate trust, money, energy, kindness, justice, and love in proper measure for myself and for others, I am holy. When I clear away the things that will block me (and others) from both material and spiritual pathways, I am holy.

How are you able to both notice people's weaknesses or disabilities and still give them appropriate opportunities?

What are some of your own shortcomings about which you are able to be accepting and honest with yourself?

What things can you do today to clear away some of the clutter that separates you from being connected with God?

Kedoshim—day five

Do not stand idly by the blood of your neighbor.

—LEVITICUS 19:16

Do not be a talebearer, and do not stand idly by the blood of your neighbor: When I engage in uplifting speech, I am holy. When I walk away from malicious gossip, I am holy. When I do not use someone else's foibles to make me seem or feel better, I am holy. When I take action to help another, I am holy. When I do not needlessly and recklessly embarrass others, I am holy. When I aid someone who is hurt, I am holy. When I visit the sick to bring them comfort, I am holy. When I help my enemy, I am holy. When I allow others to help me, I am holy. When I speak up for the powerless, I am holy.

Where and when do you find yourself connecting with others by participating in gossip because it is easy to use judgment of others to feel better about yourself?

How can you foster connection by focusing on shared interests or a desire to create more positivity?

What action(s) can you take today to help someone you are not close to, a stranger, or even someone you dislike, without coming from a place of pity?

You shall surely rebuke your neighbor, you shall not bear guilt because of him or her.

—LEVITICUS 19:17

You shall surely rebuke your neighbor, you shall not bear guilt because of him or her, and you should not hate your neighbor in your heart: When I lovingly tell someone that he or she is doing the wrong thing, I am holy. When I listen to others rebuke me, I am holy. When others come to me to amend any harm they have caused and I accept their *t'shuvah*, truly forgiving them, I am holy. When I am able to speak the truth to others, not just placate them because of my own self-interest and fear, I am holy. When I accept the foibles of others as their actions and not their essence, I am holy. When I see the *tzelem Elohim*, the divine image, in another, I am holy. When I do my own *t'shuvah* and do not worry about the reaction of the other person, I am holy. When I separate myself from my own errors and do not carry inappropriate guilt, I am holy. When I have spoken to others in every way that I can and they still can't hear me and I feel *rachmones* (compassionate pity), I am holy.

Rather than being defensive, what are some ways you can listen to others' concerns or criticisms of you from a place of gratitude?

How are you able to distinguish action from essence in yourself and in others?

What are some reminders that help you be able to let go and be at peace, knowing you have done your best to repair the damage from your mistakes?

Kedoshim—day seven

Love your neighbor as you love yourself.

—LEVITICUS 19:18

Love your neighbor as you love yourself: When I treat myself and other people with dignity, I am holy. When I can connect to another person spiritually, physically, and emotionally, I am holy. When I love and care for myself so I can do the same with and for others, I am holy. When I realize and live the distinctions between being separate from you and erasing the margins, as Father Greg Boyle speaks about, I am holy. When I embrace that we are all kinfolk and neighbors, I am holy. I can do this when I realize the other ways in which I am holy.

How can you act with more dignity today?

What are some ways you are taking the same care of yourself as you would for a dearly beloved friend?

How have you treated all others today as kinfolk, as cherished members of the same family?

Emor

Emor—day one

Speak to the priests …

—Leviticus 21:1

This week's parashah is *Emor* (to speak). God commands Moses to speak to the priests and teach them about defilement. What strikes me so much is the name of the parashah, *Emor*. Why does God have to command Moses to speak? Perhaps it is because Moses wanted to show proper deference to the priesthood and to his older brother, Aaron. Yet, God is telling Moses and us that we are commanded to speak in order to instruct others. We are commanded to speak when we see someone doing something that is not good or right. We are commanded to speak when we would like to hide instead.

About what are you inappropriately staying silent because of self-centered fear?

To whom are you afraid to speak?

How has your silence harmed you and others?

Emor—day two

None shall defile themselves for any dead person.

—Leviticus 21:1

Why spend so much time on death and mourning this week? It is important to realize that there is never an excuse to retreat from God and decency. Too often people use the pain brought about by natural events to deny God and defy authority. Just as stoicism is not appropriate in the face of loss, neither is running rampant because of your feelings of sadness and anger. I say this with some authority, as I let my feelings cause me to run out of control after my father's death. All this did was cause more heartache and pain, hurting a lot of people and dishonoring my father. This week's parashah reminds me that there are never any excuses for the type of behavior that I exhibited after my father's death. It reminds me that I have to be careful not to defile myself or those whom I love. In recovery, we learn to deal with life on life's terms, not our own. I am a holy soul, as are we all, and we are also God's partners. I have to take care not to dishonor myself, losing my place and path.

How are you honoring the memory of your deceased loved ones?

How are you lifting yourself and others up in the name of those you love?

What are some examples of how you are living life on life's terms, not your own?

Emor—day three

They shall not shave smooth any part of their heads.

—LEVITICUS 21:5

The priests are told not to act like pagan priests. They are not to shave their heads or cut themselves when they are in mourning. We are taught that death is not an excuse to stop following God, which is an important concept. We are taught that death is to be consecrated in a certain manner. Today, we have the seven-day mourning period called shiva. During this time mourners are exempt from all manners of everyday life, except for prayer. During shiva we are not supposed to care how we look or worry about our work. We are only to allow ourselves to be comforted by our community. Torah recognizes our need to mourn, and it also recognizes our need both to stay connected and to be bereft. This both/and is the reason that there are prohibitions on what we are permitted to do to ourselves. As every mourner knows, we are in tremendous psychic and spiritual pain after the death of a loved one. Our tradition recognizes this and takes measures to prevent us from taking extreme actions because of our pain and confusion.

How do you mourn?

How are you prolonging your suffering rather than allowing yourself to feel and move through the pain?

How are you using the death of a loved one as an excuse to stop living or, conversely, as a reason to be more alive?

Emor—day four

They shall not ... make gashes in their flesh.

—Leviticus 21:5

Judaism teaches us that we don't have to hurt ourselves to validate our pain; rather, our pain is, and we can let it out through tears, silence, and even singing. Our tradition teaches us that death is part of life, and it is not a punishment. It is, however, a time when people could stop following God because of anger and sorrow. Cutting ourselves is not going to help us or the deceased person; perhaps this explains the prohibition against shaving or getting our hair cut. Judaism teaches that while we can never be totally whole after the death of a loved one, we can be consoled and comforted by our family and community. This healing process happens through prayer and visiting the person in mourning.

Why people die is not a question that we can answer. What was the purpose of their life and how we can help to fulfill their mission is one that, I believe, we do have to answer.

How are you answering this question
for those you have lost?

What and whom do you look to in order
to feel consoled and comforted?

How are you accepting comfort and giving solace to others?

Emor—day five

Cut the side-growth of their beards.

—LEVITICUS 21:5

The *Kaddish* prayer, said in mourning, makes no mention of death. It is a prayer that extols God's virtues. *Kaddish* comes from the root word *kadosh* (holy). Saying this prayer helps keep us connected to the sacred memory of our loved one and to God. When death occurs, our tradition has us praise God so that we remember that God is not a punisher. God gives us life, and at some point we return home to God. In *Man Is Not Alone* (295–296), Rabbi Abraham Joshua Heschel, *z"l*, teaches that when our lives are an answer, death is a homecoming. While those of us left behind are in pain, the deceased has been released from pain and is back home with God. The *Kaddish* prayer reminds us of this truth.

How are you using *Kaddish* as a means of connection rather than as a way to stay in grief?

Being part of a minyan allows you to be with others who know your experience. How do you let your community bring you comfort?

How are you an answer to God's question, "What is life getting out of you?"

Emor—day six

No man ... who has a defect shall do an offering.
—Leviticus 21:17

The parashah goes on to tell us that people with disabilities cannot do the work of the sacrifices. If someone who is of the priestly class is unable to physically perform the duties necessary, he is exempt from the work. While this seems unfair and goes against our current sensibilities, seemingly demeaning the disabled, I think that the Torah is giving us an example of an earlier law. In the Holiness Code in *Parashat Kedoshim*, we are told not to put a stumbling block before the blind (Leviticus 19:14). Here, in this parashah, Torah is giving us an example: if we ask disabled persons to perform deeds that they are physically unable to do, aren't we setting them up for failure and embarrassment?

This example does not show discrimination; it is a way of respecting the abilities of each person. We are being taught that we should not ask others to do something that we know they are unable to do, which is the same as putting a stumbling block before the blind. It is our responsibility to help people succeed in life, not set them up for failure. Recovery is about finding one's rightful place in the world and not living out someone else's hopes or design.

How are you setting yourself up for failure by asking yourself to do things that are beyond your means or capabilities?

How are you helping others by letting them know that they can stretch themselves and accomplish more than just the bare minimum?

How can you ensure you are living your life and not someone else's vision for you?

Emor—day seven

These are My fixed times.

—LEVITICUS 23:2

This parashah also teaches us about time. We are again told about the set times in the year for holidays. These holiday times are spoken about more than once, reminding us that we have things to celebrate in every generation. Holidays mark times of remembrance. They teach us the importance of being linked to the past, to a tradition. Too often we think that we are so far advanced that we do not need to remember or learn from our past. In fact, many of us see the past as something to run away from. Instead, Torah seems to be telling us that we have to learn the lessons of the past. We have to remember to rejoice in the joys of the past and bring them into our present awareness. When we celebrate the harvest festivals, we remember to be grateful that the earth produces the crops we need for food and clothing. We also come together to celebrate in our homes or synagogue, reminding us to keep family and friends close and to stay in touch with them and our community. Time goes forward; by celebrating the holidays we remain connected to our past, allowing us to enhance our present and plan for our future.

How often do you gather with friends and family to celebrate the joys of life?

How often do you set aside time to be grateful and share your bounty with others?

How can the past inform your present and enhance your future?

Behar

Behar—day one

Adonai spoke to Moses on Mount Sinai.

—Leviticus 25:1

This week's parashah is *Behar* (on the mountain). The Torah is talking about God speaking to Moses from Mount Sinai. Torah makes it clear that we need to receive and take direction from God and from other people who have more experience. We do not have to go up on a mountain to hear God's direction, but we do have to take ourselves out of our normal hearing to be open to God's guidance. We have to go beyond the usual noise or chatter in our head; we have to tune it out in order to hear direction from God and others. Our natural reaction when we are able to hear this kind of guidance is to think, "yes, but ...," further chasing after our own thoughts. When the chatter in our head is turned down, we can usually hear direction clearly and are able to either understand it or ask the proper questions so that we are able to follow. Moses was able to hear God and usually take the direction he received, although even he had times when the noise of his thoughts was louder than God's voice.

How do you stop the noise or chatter in order to receive God?

When and how do you hear the voice of God within you?

How often do you take direction from your soul?

Behar—day two

The land shall observe a Sabbath of
Adonai.... It shall be a jubilee.
—LEVITICUS 25:2, 10

Behar also deals with the seventh year, known as the Sabbatical year, and the fiftieth year, also called the Jubilee year. These years are counted from the time we entered the Land of Israel. What is so remarkable about this parashah is that we are taught that even the land has to have a rest and celebrate a Sabbath. What an interesting concept for us consumption junkies. So many of us just want to consume and consume; we never think about conserving or that anyone or anything else needs to rest. Torah is teaching us that the land must not be used for one whole year out of every seven. In fact, we are told that the land has to celebrate a Sabbath for God. Even the land has to answer to God. This teaches us that as God's partners, we have to care for and about all of God's creatures and creations. While we have the intelligence to rule and subdue the earth, as we are told in Genesis, this does not give us the right to abuse the earth. We have to care for it and treat it with respect and love, just as God does. Because God knows us, God gave us this commandment to ensure that we would all be conservationists, another way in which we are being partners with God.

How are you caring about yourself and others enough to take a break?

Do you use your abilities to rule and have dominion over or to care for and grow other humans, creatures, and the land?

How do you appreciate what you have, rather than continually search to consume more?

Behar—day three

You shall proclaim release throughout the land.

—Leviticus 25:10

This parashah is about release as well. We have to release the land from its work for a year. We have to release others from the debts that they have incurred. We have to release our resentments toward others and toward ourselves. In the fiftieth year, we have to release all slaves and return any land we have bought back to its original owner or his or her family.

What are you releasing this year?

How are you returning to your original, more authentic self?

When do you help others return to their true selves?

Do not wrong one another; have awe of your God.

—Leviticus 25:17

We are told that we have to release people from their debts to us. Unfortunately, even in the Land of Israel, in the good old days, we were unable to do this. It came to be that people would not loan money in the fifth and sixth years before the Jubilee because they knew that they would not get totally repaid. Think about this: God tells us something we do not want to comply with, because we are afraid that we will lose something, so we look for a loophole. Sound familiar? How many times do we not do the next right thing because we are afraid that we will lose something or not gain as much as we would like? This is completely counter to this command.

Which is more important to you, winning or doing the right thing? Why?

How can you allow doing the right thing to become synonymous with winning?

In what ways are you holding people hostage for old, unpaid debts that should be released?

Behar—day five

The land must not be sold beyond reclaim, for the land is Mine; you are strangers resident with Me.

—LEVITICUS 25:23

Herein lies the heart of this parashah: release. When we are unable or unwilling to release our negativity and our hold on things, we are in violation of a basic principle of community. As Jews, we know that we have to live in and with community because so many of our practices and *mitzvot* require community for fulfillment. I ask the residents of Beit T'Shuvah to write down three resentments that they have—one or two of them could and should be toward themselves—and how they are going to release these resentments. I suggest that you do the same. If you think you have no resentments toward yourself or others, you are probably lying to yourself. This does not make you a bad person; it makes you like the rest of us—imperfect beings who are trying to be God's partners.

How are you releasing the need to be perfect?

What resentments toward yourself are you willing to let go?

What do you know you need to release that requires you to seek help from your community or God?

Behar—day six

Let him live by your side.

—LEVITICUS 25:35

Rabbi Hillel came up with a compromise more than two thousand years ago, called the *Prozbul*. This is a legal fiction that allows the *bet din* (literally, "house of judgment"), the court, to assume the loan and collect it so that the lender can get paid in full and people who have means will still lend in the fifth and sixth years. It is sad that we cared more about our money than we did about helping others. It is sad that we have not grown out of this ungodlike condition.

What fictions do you devise so that you do not have to help others?

How are you voting for the sake of your pocketbook rather than voting for your soul?

How are your actions this week promoting God's will or your own, self-centered will?

Behar—day seven

One of his kinfolk shall redeem him.

—Leviticus 25:48

Another way to relieve people of their debts, I believe, is to release others from owing us something because we helped them. Many parents think that their children owe them because they raised them. Many people think that if I helped you, you have to help me. We live in a tit-for-tat society where people keep score. I have a request for and of you: write yourself a letter congratulating and thanking yourself for giving freely to help another individual. Be grateful that you can give without expecting anything in return. Be surprised when the person gives freely to you or to another, and be joyous of the truth that you and others do give freely without needing to keep score. When we do this, we avoid and release resentments. When we do this, we get out of the slavery of comparison and competition. When we do this, we are growing in our path of imitating God a little bit better.

Make a list of people you think owe you something. Why do you think this and how can you release them from their debt?

What will it take for you make this a daily or weekly practice?

When do you give freely, and when have you attached strings that no one knows about?

Bechukotai

Bechukotai—day one

With my laws you walk.

—Leviticus 26:3

This week's parashah is *Bechukotai* (by my statutes). This parashah is about blessings and curses. Blessings happen when we live decently, and curses when we do not, according to the text. From this chapter, people get the wrong idea that God is a punishing God. I do not believe God is punishing us. I believe that the curses, or *tochechah* (admonitions), in this part of the Torah are meant as warnings. This parashah gives us the vision of what our actions, as a people, will bring about, both positive and negative. Torah is teaching us that our actions cause reactions; we must be aware of what we are doing and the repercussions of our actions. We have to live with our actions and their ramifications. This vision that Torah is giving us arms us with the ability and power to ask ourselves, "Is this action going to lead to further decency or further destruction?" We get to choose.

When do you know you have confused curses with warnings?

How are you being responsible for the blessings you have been given?

How often do you ask yourself if your actions are constructive or destructive?

Bechukotai—day two

But if you do not obey ...

—Leviticus 26:14

The truth, that bad things happen to good people, has been thoroughly explored by Rabbi Harold Kushner in his book by a similar title, *When Bad Things Happen to Good People*, which I highly recommend. The parashah is much more about the entire people Israel, in my opinion, than each individual. We are all supposed to see ourselves as if we were at Mount Sinai, which means we all received the Torah both individually and collectively. Some laws can only be carried out individually, and many can only be carried out communally. I believe that this *tochechah* is for the community and that each of us must be accountable for our own actions and for the actions of our community. When senseless hatred, *sinat chinam*, was happening in the early part of the first century BCE, it was up to the community to make it stop. Because we did not, we were conquered by the Romans. Paraphrasing from philosopher Edmund Burke, "Evil flourishes when good people do nothing." We as a community of Jews, as a community of Americans, and as a community of the world must intercede to stop people from perpetrating evil on others and on the world.

How are you contributing to goodness and holiness each day?

When do you exercise your responsibility to know and participate in what is going on in your community?

Which of your contributions to negativity and evil do you find yourself repeating frequently?

Bechukotai—day three

And if … I will go on to discipline
… I will break your pride.

—LEVITICUS 26:18–19

God tells us that we will stray from the commandments. God knows that not only will we stray, which is bad and expected because we are human and imperfect, but we will also keep going far away from God, decency, and our intended path. This event at Mount Sinai is an important one for everyone, and all of us in recovery can understand and remember our own descent into the hell of losing our way, losing our decency, and losing our connection to God and others.

How do you notice when you are straying
from walking your path with God?

How do you handle your imperfections?

What does it usually take for you to stop
your descent into proverbial hell?

Bechukotai—day four

Your strength will be spent for no purpose.

—LEVITICUS 26:20

We are told that when we lose our way, there are consequences. We do not get a free ride. For many people, this parashah proves that God is a vengeful and punishing entity. Viewing God this way is a cop-out and a clean-up excusing our own bad behavior. When we conceive of God in the above manner, we are trying to avoid taking responsibility for our own actions. This parashah is telling us that there are consequences for our actions.

How are you blaming others, including God, for the consequences of your inappropriate actions?

What is your fear of taking responsibility for these consequences?

Can you recall, list, and find gratitude for harsh consequences that have helped you get back on track?

And with this, you still don't listen
and don't walk with me.
—Leviticus 26:27

As we all know, when we first start to err, the consequences are not usually so bad. For many people, this leads them to believe that what they are doing is okay because a lightning bolt from the sky has not struck them. We lie to ourselves so that we can continue to do what we want even if we know that it is not the next right action to take. Then, as the consequences get worse, those of us who are unable to take responsibility for our own actions blame everyone and everything around us. God tells us in this parashah that we actually have a choice; we do not have to continue to do the wrong action.

How do you show your arrogance toward God and others by continuing to act badly even though these actions bring negative consequences to you and those around you?

What are the lies you tell yourself? Make a daily list.

What does it take for you to exercise your free will and do the next right thing?

Bechukotai—day six

And you will be scattered into other nations.

—Leviticus 26:33

Too often we are so stuck in our ways that we can't even see the consequences that we are experiencing or the consequences those around us are experiencing because of our actions. When God gives us a little nudge, many of us are so focused on what we are doing that we do not feel this gentle reminder from God. Many times we are also unable to hear the cries of those around us who see our errors, see our consequences, and experience consequences of their own because of our actions.

How are you blocking yourself from hearing the cry of your soul and the souls of others?

What nudges from God and others are you currently ignoring?

How do you give gentle nudges, reminding others to hear the call of God?

They shall atone for their errors. I will remember My covenant.

—Leviticus 26:41–42

Each time we ignore the consequences and refuse to return to God, our path, and our community, the consequences get worse and worse. Many of us have lived through this experience as either the perpetrator and/or the person who has experienced the repercussions of another person's bad behavior. God keeps calling us back, and we refuse to heed the call. In this parashah, God tells us that eventually we will hear the call and a part of us will return. We are taught that as soon as we begin our return, God accepts us back. This is what the Torah teaches us this week, and it is what the prophets Jeremiah and Hosea also teach.

How are you seeing all of the subtle ways that you are going astray?

Have you started your return to God, your path, and your community?

Can you acknowledge the wonderful experience of being welcomed back and use this experience to start your return more quickly the next time you stray?

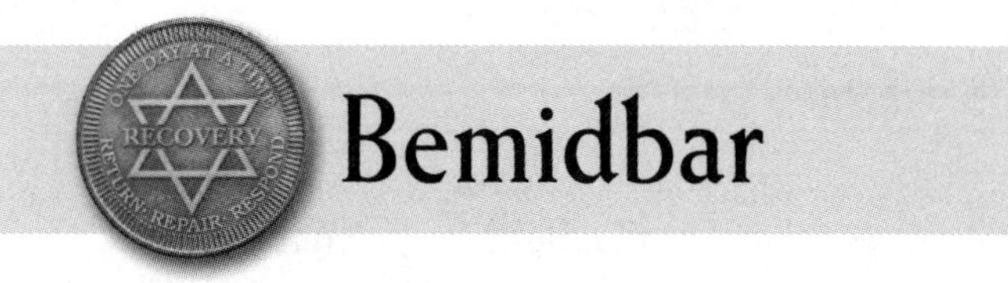

Bemidbar

Bemidbar—day one

Adonai spoke to Moses in the wilderness of Sinai.

—NUMBERS 1:1

This week's parashah is *Bemidbar* (in the desert/wilderness), the first portion of the fourth book of the Torah. A desert is a place that is hot and arid. Not much is able to survive in the desert, and many people would die trying to travel across a desert without a large supply of water and a way to find shade. A wilderness is wild and uncultivated. Many people would die if they were not careful about where they were walking or the wild beasts that live in the wilderness. There are dangers in both places. On their journey to the Promised Land, the Israelites went through the desert or wilderness.

In your journey through life, how do you recognize these kinds of dangerous places when you are in them rather than only after you get through them?

How do you get stuck in the desert or wilderness of life?

How are you able to keep moving forward?

Bemidbar—day two

In the second year following the Exodus from Egypt …

—Numbers 1:1

What the Torah is teaching us is that while we can create and use and enjoy comfort and ease in our travels, living life is not always about ease and comfort. While some people like to believe that they have to live in ease and comfort, the Torah is telling us that this is a fantasy. We do live in both the desert/wilderness and the Promised Land. Sometimes life is green, lush, a seemingly endless well of water and nourishment, that is, the Promised Land. Sometimes life is arid and inhospitable, and we feel parched and almost dead from the heat and elements. The Torah is teaching us that no matter what we think, no matter what our socioeconomic status is, all of us live both in the desert/ wilderness and in the Promised Land. We all need to find our way out of the wilderness at times, and Torah is the path that helps us find our way out. Often we are damaged by our time in the desert, and Torah helps us repair our inner wounds. This is one of the reasons that Torah is the original recovery book. From it, we learn how to recover from the brokenness inherent in being human.

How has believing you should always be in a state of ease and comfort caused problems in your life?

How do you define the Promised Land for yourself?

How are you still comparing yourself to and feeling envious of others because they have it better than you?

Bemidbar—day three

Take a census of all the congregation.

—NUMBERS 1:2

Another important lesson from this is that we can and do live through and in both the wilderness and the desert of life. Both give us enough nourishment to survive. This nourishment comes from being an actively participating member of a community. As my friend Leonard Shapiro taught me, we have to be aware that life goes up and down; what is important is to be surrounded by people to lean on when we're down and celebrate with when we're up. Our challenge is to save enough (money, energy, strength, friendship, and love) when times are good to live well when times are not so good. This is the lesson that Joseph taught us and the Egyptians in Genesis.

What do you think will help you be more able
to remember that things will always change,
no longer suffering or clinging to how they are,
thinking it is how things will always be?

How do you nourish yourself and others
during both good times and bad?

What actions are you taking today to conserve
for the inevitable rainy days ahead?

Bemidbar—day four

All those in Israel who are able to serve in the army.

—Numbers 1:3

We also have to take care to nourish our spiritual lives. To live a life of spirit, to live from our souls, we have to live true to God's principles in good times and not so good times. The times that try men's souls never have to defeat us when we remember that spiritual living encompasses a whole paradigm, not just fleeting moments. To paraphrase a story that my rabbi and friend Ed Feinstein shares, there is a king who sent his ministers on a search for the ring that held all the answers to life. All of his ministers gave up the search except for one. As this last minister was on his way back to the castle, he spotted Shlomo's Pawn Shop. He figured, "Why not try?" He went in and asked Shlomo if he had this ring. Shlomo said, "Yes, I have been waiting for the king to send for it so that he can tell everyone the answers to life." The minister took the ring and Shlomo back to the king. When the king saw the ring, he knew instantly that this was the one he wanted. He looked at the writing on it and asked Shlomo to translate the Hebrew: *Gam zeh avar*, "This too shall pass." The king smiled and laughed to himself. He had forgotten this simple lesson: no matter what was happening in this moment, it too would pass.

How are you able to live honorably in good times and bad?

How are you laughing at and with yourself?

How are you using your past to strengthen today and enhance tomorrow?

Bemidbar—day five

Do not take on any account and
enroll the tribe of Levi.

—NUMBERS 1:49

This parashah also tells us that the Levites do not have their own land. Rather, they are to live among all of the tribes so that each group has people to minister to and for them. The Levites are consecrated to God as the firstborn of all the Israelites. They represent the redemption of the firstborn. Their place, their job, is to help all of us redeem ourselves when we go astray. They remind us that we can all return, we can all be redeemed. No one is so lost that she cannot find her way back to God, to her community, to her family, and to her place in this world.

How are you asking for help today to redeem yourself?

Which rabbis, teachers, and spiritual guides do you turn to when seeking wisdom and guidance?

What actions do you need to take to return to your proper place in this world?

Camped on the east, the flag of Judah …
—NUMBERS 2:3

In this parashah we are told where each tribe is to be stationed when the people Israel are encamped, and the order in which they are supposed to march. It is fascinating that so much detail is given describing where each tribe is placed and that there even is a certain place for each tribe. Torah reminds us that we each have a specific place in the world. It comes to teach us that there is no place inherently better than another. We learn from this that our place is important. When we are in our rightful place in the world, in our community, and in our family, everything is safe, and life is lush and green. Since this is the lesson we are being taught, it also stands true that when we are not in our place, we and others are not safe, and life is arid and inhospitable. We have the power to make life lush and green or barren and dry. Right now, the world seems to be going through this arid phase. Why? Because too many countries and leaders want to overconsume, hoard, and live in someone else's place. We also do this when we try to control everything around us. We do this by needing to be right all the time. We do this by being stingy with our money, our resources, our time, and our love.

How and in which areas of life are you living in your proper place?

Where and how are you living with your tribe?

How are you contributing to either taking the water and the joy out of life or nourishing your soul, the souls of others, and the soul of the world?

Bemidbar—day seven

I consecrate every firstborn in Israel.

—NUMBERS 3:13

Finally, the parashah teaches us about the ritual of *pidyon haben* (redemption of the firstborn). If the first child that a woman bears is a male, the parashah tells us that at thirty days, we have a ceremony to redeem this child. This redemption is our way of acknowledging that the firstborn always belongs to God. In the Middle Ages, a Christian firstborn often became a priest in the church. In our tradition, only the Levites and *kohanim* became priests; the firstborn sons of the other tribes of Israel were redeemed when their families gave five silver shekels to one of the *kohanim*. What is this child's family really saying? By paying this amount, they are demonstrating that they are going to stand with and for this child, in essence affirming, "We are going to help him find his proper place in God's world and raise him according to his soul's calling, not according to what we want him to become."

How are you standing with and for your children and other loved ones?

How are you helping them find their proper place and livelihood?

How are you living in your proper place in an authentic life?

Naso

Naso—day one

Take a census of the Gershonites also.

—NUMBERS 4:22

This week's parashah is *Naso* (literally, "lift up"), which can be understood to mean "lifting up to be counted." We are still counting the Levites and finding out about each person's job. The beginning of this portion is teaching us how important it is to be counted and that we all have a unique purpose. We need to be reminded of this often because we seem to forget this teaching. The beginning of this parashah and last week's parashah teach us that we can make a difference, and just as each journey begins with one step, each change and every improvement in the world begins with one person. Look at our history—individuals have caused change to happen; consider Thomas Edison, Albert Einstein, Theodore Herzl, and many others. We are all obligated to see ourselves as important people who count, and we need to stand up and be counted. By doing this we fulfill the first command given to us by God: become God's partner in making our corner of the world a little bit better.

How do you know that you matter or count in this world?

What do you stand for?

What changes have you brought about to make life better for yourself and others?

Naso—day two

Record them from the age …

—NUMBERS 4:23

All of the Levites are counted. None of them hide from Moses and Aaron during this census. None of the other Israelites hide from being counted either. Even though they have no idea what the future will hold for them, they stand up and are counted. This is so important that Torah devotes the first four chapters of Numbers to this concept. When we stand up and are counted, we know that we belong some place. We also know that we are not afraid to go forward in our lives and our living. Additionally, being counted means that we want to be seen and noticed. We are no longer willing to hide in the shadows, worrying about being right or wrong. We are more concerned with being present than with how we look to others.

What are you still hiding from?

How are you answering God's call of *ayecha* (where are you) with *hineni* (here I am)?

How are you moving forward in your life by being seen, by counting, by having your presence count for something?

Naso—day three

Each one was given responsibility for his service.

—NUMBERS 4:49

The Levites are given the obligation of caring for the Tabernacle, and they are not given any land of their own. This seems a little unfair. They have to depend on the *tzedakah* (meaning "righteousness," it signifies charitable giving) of the rest of the tribes for survival, and they also have to minister to the *kohanim* and the rest of the Israelites. In fact, some historians tell us that some Levites were placed in each tribe's area to help people on the spot, rather than making the other Israelites trek to Jerusalem every time they had a question or problem. So, the Levites have to work and serve others, and they have to depend on God and the rest of the Israelites for their sustenance. They are the only tribe that is given their direct purpose and place by God. So, they have the best of both worlds; they get to know their place, and they are able to be sustained simply by fulfilling their purpose.

Are you aware of your place in the world?
What do you believe it to be?

How are you accepting your place
graciously, fulfilling its requirements?

How are you using the spiritual guides available to
you to help you continue to grow and thrive?

Naso—day four

Anyone with an eruption … put them outside the camp.

—NUMBERS 5:2–3

Another teaching this week is to put infectious people out of the camp. What does this mean? Some people get offended, interpreting this to be about physically handicapped people. I understand the Torah differently. Who is to be put outside the camp? Those who indulge in *lashon hara* and inappropriate sexual activities should be separated. These are not physically challenged people; rather, they are people who have forgotten that they are counted on and need to stand up and be counted. Furthermore, these people are not thrown out or away; they are ministered to spiritually so that they may relearn their own importance and take their proper place in their community.

How are you helping people in need?

How are you avoiding and/or indulging them?

How are you helping them receive the spiritual, physical, and emotional help that they require?

Naso—day five

Both male and female shall you take out.

—Numbers 5:3

Inappropriate sexual behaviors also destroy the world. When people treat each other as objects to meet their desires and fill their needs, they are destroying the world. When they don't care about their partners except as vehicles for their pleasure, they are destroying the world. So, just as with those who engage in *lashon hara*, we have to give them guidance and comfort. We have to help them relearn and return to their place in the world and guide them to see the divine image of each and every person. We have to help them see that each person is worth an entire world and we are all here to be a community, not for one to simply fulfill another. We also have to comfort them so that they know they can do *t'shuvah* and return home.

With whom and how do you still treat others as objects?

With whom and how do you allow others to treat you as an object?

Are you actively engaged in doing *t'shuvah* every day? How?

Naso—day six

Speak to … anyone who vows the vow of the *Nazir*.

—NUMBERS 6:2

Also, we learn in this parashah about the Nazirite. This is a person who takes a vow of abstinence from all intoxicants for a specific period of time. How long this period is depends on each person's life circumstances and desires. For some of us, being a *Nazir* lasts our lifetime, please God. The *Nazir* might be a person who has made mistakes because of poor judgment. We are being taught that in order to make really gross mistakes, to ignore basic truths that God and Torah are teaching us, we must be confused and our sight cloudy. The only reason this happens, according to my understanding of our tradition, is because we are intoxicated.

For some of us, this intoxication is caused by drugs, alcohol, gambling, sex, food, or any number of other things. We are the lucky ones. For others, more subtle substances like power, money, property, prestige, negative thoughts, or faulty logic cause their intoxication. These are the tools of the Angel of Death. These are the intoxicants that society endorses, allowing us to think we are doing the right thing by pursuing these at any and all costs.

What intoxicants are you still indulging in that cloud your vision?

How can you know the difference between truth and the lies you tell yourself?

Which spiritual practices do you believe you need to adopt in order to stay clear-sighted?

Naso—day seven

The chieftains ... drew near and brought
their offering before God.

—Numbers 7:2–3

The end of the parashah tells us about the gifts that each of the tribes brought at the time of the consecration of the Tabernacle. Each tribe brought the same gifts but in different manners, allowing them all to feel equal and unique. According to our tradition, no two people do the same thing in the same way. One of our human challenges is to know that we are equal in value, worth, and dignity to everyone else and to accept that we are also different and unique. While we all can bring gifts to the world, none of them should be exactly the same. I bring a different and unique service to people than does my friend and teacher Rabbi Ed Feinstein. This doesn't make me better or worse, just different and unique. I have been nominated for awards that I have not gotten; this doesn't make me less than, and it doesn't change my worth. The fact that those organizations chose others doesn't make them wrong or bad; they had a lot of people to evaluate. I can't make my self-image dependent on popularity. I have to keep my self-image dependent on living in a way that is holy and good.

In which areas of your life are you
comparing yourself to others?

What do you get from competing with others to be more,
or less, like them than to be precisely like yourself?

How is your self-image dependent on what others
think or on what you contribute to life?

Behaalotecha

Behaalotecha—day one

When you rise yourself up to the lamp …

—Numbers 8:2

This week's parashah is *Behaalotecha* (when you rise up). This is an intriguing parashah for me and I hope for you. We first learn that Aaron has to rise up to light the wicks of the menorah. In thinking about this, I was struck by the idea that to light something holy, I have to rise up. Each morning, we arise. Are we seeing ourselves as holy, rising ourselves up each day to light our lives and the pilot light that is our soul? If not, we are stuck in the rut of "same stuff, different day." What a terrible existence this is. In *God in Search of Man*, Rabbi Abraham Joshua Heschel, *z"l*, teaches that "indifference to the sublime wonder of living is the root of sin." Not only is it the root of sin or negativity, but it is also the root of misery.

What are some ways you are living a life of tolerable misery?

How are you living in such a way that while you have happy times, basically you feel that life is hard and then you die?

What principles, practices, or people help you to rise and ignite your own inner light?

Take the Levites … and purify them.

—NUMBERS 8:6

"Well, Rabbi, how do we change?" you may ask. Rabbinic Judaism teaches that we each have the menorah inside of us, in our spine and rib cage. Therefore, we are able to light our own menorah each day by the way in which we get up and out of bed. We are taught to say the prayer *Modeh Ani L'fanecha* (I thank You) each morning when we open our eyes. This is the prayer that proclaims our powerlessness and our obligation. This prayer says we are grateful to God for returning our souls to us with compassion; great is God's faithfulness. By saying this, we are both acknowledging that we live by the grace of God and we are stating our commitment to live in a healthy manner. The fact that this indicates a both/and shows our powerlessness. Many of us know people who have died in their sleep, and because we have not, we are acknowledging that it is not by our own doing alone that we are alive. This admission helps us realize that we have to continually light our own internal menorah by having a healthy lifestyle. It means that we cannot carelessly engage in risky behaviors that can kill us physically, emotionally, and/or spiritually just because we want to or because we think it's cool.

What are your commitments upon waking?

How are you either adopting an attitude of wonder or acting like it is just another day?

How do you honor the gift of life each day?

Behaalotecha—day three

This is what you shall do to them.

—Numbers 8:7

The part of the *Modeh Ani L'fanecha* prayer that directs us to obligation comes because just as compassion is shown to us, so too do we have to show compassion to others and ourselves. This prayer helps us light our menorah and elevate each action we take to a higher plane; as Rabbi Abraham Joshua Heschel, *z"l*, says in *Man Is Not Alone*, "We ennoble the common." The way in which we do this is significant as well. We demonstrate compassion by not condoning our own or other people's bad behavior; rather, it is by acknowledging misconduct, believing it can be changed, and helping ourselves and others adjust our actions. Compassion is knowing that we are not perfect and not hating ourselves or others because of our imperfections. Compassion is accurately discerning what others are capable of doing and offering them help if it is needed. Compassion is seeking to understand, not to hate, a person with whom we have been in conflict. Compassion means not being judgmental. There are no stereotypes in God's world; there are no absolutes, except God. Compassion is understanding that many times, there but for the grace of God go I.

How are you demonstrating compassion for yourself and for others?

When and with whom do you most often default to being judgmental instead of discerning?

What are some ways in which you are ennobling the common?

Behaalotecha—day four

Let the Israelites lay their hands …

—Numbers 8:10

In this parashah, we are told that the Levites are installed in their positions as ministers to the people and are the *kohanim*, the priests. The whole community lays their hands on the heads of the Levites and installs them in their posts. It was so easy if you were born into a Levite family—you knew your purpose from birth and you spent the first twenty-five years of your life learning how to fulfill this purpose and the next twenty-five years doing it. You spent the rest of your life mentoring and teaching the younger generation how to fulfill their purposes. Pretty easy for them; not as easy for us. Yet, how many of us spend time and pay attention to discovering and fulfilling our purpose? Too many of us run away from our purpose and our authentic script. I spent more than twenty years running away from my place in the world. I did not want to accept that I had a specific place and that fulfilling my purpose might not always be fun and exciting. A purpose is always rewarding, but not always fun, or exciting, or easy. The prophets provide an example for us; they didn't want their jobs, but they were called and they answered the call.

Do you believe you know your purpose(s) on earth? If so, what is it?

How might you be running from something you know your soul or God wants for you?

Today, how are you listening to the call from God?

Behaalotecha—day five

The people took to complaining.

—NUMBERS 11:1

Later on in the parashah, the people start to complain again. God gets angry, and Moses pleads with God. Then we are told that the riffraff get gluttonous feelings and the Israelites weep (Numbers 11:4). What is the relationship between riffraff—that is, negativity—becoming gluttonous and the Israelites weeping? I understand this as a meaningful teaching, even though it may seem strange. When our inner negativity gets gluttonous, hungry, and greedy, the other parts of us weep in false fear and dread. Why? Because the riffraff inside of us has coalesced and become so strong that it gets the rest of us to buy the lies of being not enough, a victim, hopeless.

What lies does your inner riffraff tell you?

How can you rise above the riffraff inside of you?

What do you need to do today to remember the light of Torah, decency, God, and community?

Behaalotecha—day six

The riffraff in their midst …

—NUMBERS 11:4

What about the outer riffraff? What is it that makes us go along with the riffraff, doing evil and sometimes believing it is good? The external riffraff makes us weep for two reasons: one is that we feel powerless against this riffraff and its negative power; second, we buy into the lies and cry over our perceived lack.

Who are the people in your life who feed these fears and lies, and how?

What actions must you take to stay away from the power of negativity?

How can you use the light of the Ark to remember these words of the psalmist, "God is my shepherd; I lack nothing" (Psalm 23:1)?

Behaalotecha—day seven

Moses heard the people weeping.

—NUMBERS 11:10

Another obligation in this prayer is faithfulness. Just as God stays faithful to us, so, too, do we have to stay faithful to God. We do this by staying faithful to our principles and values. We do this by staying faithful to our souls. We do this by not prostituting ourselves for financial or emotional gains. We do this by accepting both the claim that God has on us and the related claim that all of us have on each other. This claim is to make our corner of the world a little bit better; it stops us from leaving something or someone simply because it does not match our fantasy. It means that I stay faithful to my wife because she is my partner and I have made the commitment to be hers. It does not matter how I feel in any one moment; what is important is that I know that she is my soul mate, my *ezer k'negdo* (fitting helper; Genesis 2:18). Faithfulness means not giving up even when I am disappointed, angry, or sad. As we read in the Torah, the Israelite people disappointed God many times, and God never let them go. God thought about it and never did. The people also stayed faithful in that they never turned back, no matter how often they thought or talked about doing so.

How do you define faithfulness?

To what or whom are you keeping faithful?

List the ways you see yourself remaining faithful and the ways in which you give up.

Shelach L'cha

Shelach L'cha—day one

Send for yourself men to scout …

—Numbers 13:2

In this week's parashah, *Shelach L'cha* (send for yourself), God tells Moses to send for "yourself" (Moses) people to spy on and explore the land of Canaan. God is basically saying, "Look, I have told you what is to happen. I have promised that I will be with you and deliver you. If you have to go and check it out yourself, then go." Herein lies the problem for the Israelites and for us: the Israelites have been guided by God, protected by God, and nourished by God; they have heard the promises of God, and they have accepted God's Torah with the words "We will do and then we will understand" (Exodus 24:7). Yet, here again, they doubt God, Moses, Aaron, Caleb, and Joshua. They believe the false reports of ten of the spies. They cannot or will not hear the words of Caleb and Joshua. Instead, they start feeling sorry for themselves. This incident brings up so many questions and experiences that we all have.

What causes you not to trust the people you have relied on in the past, those who have shown you that they have your best interests at heart?

How often do you get stuck, wanting more details than are necessary, before moving forward?

Upon whom in your life can you really count?

Shelach L'cha—day two

All those were chiefs of the people Israel.

—NUMBERS 13:3

When we are told something, given advice and direction from God (through Torah, tradition, history, prayer, and/or meditation) or by another person (parent, mentor, advisor), and a part within us still drives us to know better, we are so often led astray. We have all heard the age-old adage that intelligence is the ability to learn from our mistakes, and wisdom is the ability to learn from the mistakes of others. Learning to have faith in God, and in a select group of people we have found to be trustworthy, can make such a great difference in our quality of life, allowing us to share our burdens and our successes with those we love.

In which ways and areas of your life are you trying to prove God and your mentors wrong?

What is your investment in knowing better and in going against God?

At which times do you value wisdom over personal intelligence by letting yourself trust the experiences of others?

Shelach L'cha—day three

It is indeed a land flowing with milk and honey.

—NUMBERS 13:27

The spies come back with great fruit and great fear. They tell the whole people that the land is great, flowing with milk and honey, and that it is too difficult for them to overtake the people who live there now. The spies do not go to Moses and Aaron to give them the report and get debriefed; rather, they report their ideas and fears to the entire people, spreading fear and evil among the nation. Why? I think that because the spies were princes of the tribes, they thought that they knew it all and could do things their own way. They were sure that they were right and trying to save the people. When we think too highly of ourselves, we are not teachable. When we are not teachable, we are dangerous. We can and do create havoc and ruin when we put ourselves in God's chair and in the place belonging to our leaders and mentors.

How are you remaining unteachable?

In which areas of your life do you know it is best to be selective about the people with whom you share sensitive information?

How do you create fear, havoc, and ruin by your need to be right and live as if you know everything?

Shelach L'cha—day four

We looked like grasshoppers to ourselves …

—Numbers 13:33

Next the Israelites are surveying the land, unable to accept that God has told them the truth. God told them that the people who were in the land were going to be disposed of because of their actions. God told them that God was going to help them. God told them not to worry. The spies and the people cannot hold on to this promise and cannot hold on to their experience of leaving Egypt and having been cared for ever since. Rather, they have kept their self-perception of being slaves and small. This is evidenced in their statement, "We looked like grasshoppers to ourselves, and so we must have looked to them" (Numbers 13:33). How unbelievable is this statement! The Israelites were told by God that God has chosen them for this mission and that they were created in the image of God; they were told that they are partners of God—so how can they be grasshoppers? The spies are being arrogant in their assessment because they are saying that God is not going to fulfill God's promise and also that they are not worthy and holy souls.

How are you still seeing yourself wrong-sized?

Do you see yourself as too big or too small?

From whom might you be able to get an accurate assessment of your strengths and weaknesses to help you fulfill your unique purpose?

Shelach L'cha—day five

The whole community broke into loud cries.

—Numbers 14:1

The whole Israelite community has held on to their slave identity, as evidenced by their statements upon hearing these words from the spies: "The whole community broke into loud cries.... 'Let us go back to Egypt'" (Numbers 14:1–4). How could they have thought for a second that Egypt was better than freedom? How could they have been willing to turn their lives over to the pharaoh and not to God?

How are you holding on to a self-perception that no longer reflects who you are today? Why?

When do you choose familiarity over freedom?

How and in what areas are you turning your life over to God?

Shelach L'cha—day six

And Joshua and Caleb rent their clothes.

—NUMBERS 14:6

Caleb and Joshua are the only two out of twelve spies that believe God will make good on God's promise. The other ten, and the rest of the people, have forgotten the proof of God's ability to make good on promises. Caleb and Joshua keep truth uppermost in their minds and souls. They saw the same things as the other ten, yet, because they looked through the lens of truth, they are not afraid.

How are you still buying the lies and fears of others as truth?

How are you seeing life through the lens of truth today?

What fears allow you to deny some of the miracles, successes, learning, and teachings of your past, both individually and collectively, as family, community, and kinfolk?

Shelach L'cha—day seven

But Adonai is with us. Have no fear of them!

—NUMBERS 14:9

This story reinforces the difference between truth and honesty. The spies and the community are being honest. They are voicing their perceptions. Many of us call this our truth. Our perceptions are extremely narrow in scope; they include our denials, the lies we tell ourselves, and our own biases. Also, our perception is only a small part of the whole picture. Truth is the whole picture. "Truth" in Hebrew is *emet*, which starts with an *aleph*, the first letter of the Ten Commandments. *Anochi* is how God refers to God in the first person. In Hebrew, we humans refer to ourselves as *ani* in the first person singular. When you take the *aleph* away from the word *emet*, you are left with *met*, which means "death" in Hebrew. Truth is God. To live in the search for truth, we have to learn to see more of the picture than we can observe by ourselves. We have to be open to changing our perceptions when we are in dialogue and communion with God and with other people. Truth is realized by being in communion with community and being open to learning more and incorporating more into our view of life.

In which areas of your life can you shift from being honest to telling the whole truth?

How are you staying comfortable in your denials and narrow perceptions?

How are you seeking to widen your base of knowledge and view of situations and of life?

Korach

Korach—day one

All the community are holy, all of them.

—NUMBERS 16:3

This week's parashah is *Korach*. This is the name of one of the descendants of Levi. Korach was assigned to be one of the Levites who cared for the Temple and ministered to the people. This parashah is also referred to as Korach's rebellion. The first lesson is about how we project onto others the things we do not like about ourselves. Korach and his cohorts, Dathan and Abiram, tell Moses and Aaron that they, Moses and Aaron, have separated themselves from the community and taken on too much for themselves. They think that everyone else is less than them because of their stature as leaders. We know from the text that this is not true, but it is exactly how Korach and his friends think of themselves. Korach is jealous of Aaron's role and wants it for himself. Dathan and Abiram are jealous of Moses's status. To try to procure these roles for themselves, they stir up the community. Jealousy causes senseless and unfounded hatred and slander.

Do you act out when you feel "less than" compared to others? If so, how?

How do you project disagreeable qualities about yourself onto others?

Of whom are you most jealous?

Korach—day two

Is it not enough for you that God has set you apart?

—Numbers 16:9

This jealousy, and I believe most jealousy, comes because Korach and his cohorts are not able to accept their place and purpose in life. Accepting one's place and purpose in life does not mean settling. Acceptance means that I want what I actually have. In wanting what I have, I am able to find ways to grow my soul and improve myself and my actions to better fulfill my purpose each day.

Too many of us are stuck in the fantasy of "if only, if only I had ..." This fantasy does at least two things: one is that we do not fulfill our actual purpose—staying dissatisfied with life, ourselves, and everything around us—nothing is ever good enough, including us; the second is that it leads us to destroy the souls of others around us. We get stuck in the cycle of constantly making someone else bad so that we can look good. We forget a basic principle of Torah: we are all created in the image of God. When we engage in destroying another soul and forfeiting our rightful place, we are going against this principle.

How are you accepting your place and living your purpose at home, at work, with loved ones?

How are you helping others find and live their authentic lives?

What are some of the ways in which you are trying to destroy others because of your own discontent and lack of acceptance?

Korach—day three

For which cause both you and all your company are gathered together against Adonai.

—NUMBERS 16:11

Another lesson is how we use truth to lie to ourselves and to others. As most of us know, every great lie is rooted in some truth. Korach exemplifies this by saying that Moses and Aaron are separating themselves from the community. He states, "The whole community is holy, all of them. God is in their midst" (Numbers 16:3). This is true—the whole community is holy, and God is in the midst of the entire community. The lie is that Korach is also part of the community; he is separating himself by using the phrase "all of them" and the word "their." Korach is trying to set himself up as a defender and man of the people, but all the while he sees himself above them. He uses truth to paint an untrue picture. Dathan and Abiram do the same thing when they say to Moses, "Is it a small thing that you took us out of a land flowing with milk and honey to die in the wilderness?" (Numbers 16:13). It is true that Egypt was a fertile land; the lie is that the Israelites were not enjoying any of the milk and honey of Egypt because they were slaves. They use the truth about Egypt to make it seem as if Moses and Aaron harmed everyone by taking them out of Egypt.

How are you using bits of truth to lie to yourself?

How do you use select aspects of the truth to lie to or about others?

In which areas of your life do you most often bend the truth and create a lie?

Korach—day four

Moses sent for Dathan and Abiram …
they said, "We will not come!"
—Numbers 16:12

One lesson learned from Dathan and Abiram happens when Moses calls to them to counsel them and tries to get them to stop their rebellion, and they refuse to even listen. Too many of us become deaf to the advice of others because we want to do what we want, not the next right thing. Also, many of us don't even seek advice from others; we want to do everything ourselves. How foolish. We are so afraid of looking weak and needing help that we want to project an image of assuredness. In doing this, we forget another basic principle of life as stated in Genesis 2:18, "It is not good for humans to be alone." We all need help and advice; seeking them demonstrates strength, not weakness.

Whom have you chosen as your guide(s)?

When do you take their counsel?

How and when do you isolate yourself because
you have to do it your own way?

Korach—day five

When one man sins, will You be wrathful
with the whole community?

—NUMBERS 16:22

Moses and Aaron show themselves as part of the Israelite people. When God wants to annihilate the people for rebellion, they fight for the people. They do not separate themselves; they include themselves. Here, again, we are taught that our own egos must be sublimated so that we will do the right thing. Moses and Aaron could have easily agreed with God and said, "Enough is enough." They could have gone along with the plan to start over with just themselves and their families, but they do not. Arguing with God, they fight for the soul and the lives of the entire community. They are able to do this because the first thing they do upon hearing of both the rebellion and God's wrath is to fall on their faces so that they can take a moment to respond rather than react.

When are you able to sublimate your
ego for the greater good?

How can you include yourself even when you have
hurt feelings or don't agree with the majority?

What are some of the ways you are able to take a
breath and respond to life rather than react?

Korach—day six

Move away, I beg, from the tents of these …

—Numbers 16:26

The people still don't learn their lesson. They start to back Korach and the other rebels. It sounds good when someone who promises to deliver and says what the people want to hear wishes to lead, even though his or her promises are lies. This is quite prevalent today. Too many of us go along with people who say what we want to hear, rather than listening for the truth. Why is it that whenever people are promising us the sun, moon, and stars, we believe them and are willing to follow them? Because it is harder to deal with the work of reality; it is harder to make life better, one grain of sand at a time, than it is to believe in magic.

What lies do you still believe in because they are what you want to hear?

What spiritual practices do you need each day so that you do not choose to believe magical lies?

How are you dealing with reality and making your corner of the world a little better each day?

Korach—day seven

You must not profane your gifts.

—NUMBERS 18:32

This parashah reminds me of the importance of being in truth. I see here how easy it is to lie to others and to myself. It only takes a slight turn of the dial of reality. This is why I am always afraid to say that I have the true way to go toward God and authenticity. Beit T'Shuvah (literally, "the house of return," an addiction treatment center in Los Angeles, California) demonstrates an honest path and, I believe, is dedicated to practicing truth in all of its affairs. I also know that we are human, therefore we make mistakes. I am dedicated to acknowledging our mistakes as well as our successes so that I am not lying to myself or anyone else. I have a path to God and authenticity, and it is truth, and it works. It is just not the only true path. There are many paths to God, decency, and authenticity; we have to find the one that fits us.

Today, how are you seeking a path to God, decency, and authenticity?

What changes do you make when you become aware of the lies you are telling yourself?

How often are you checking in with yourself spiritually, emotionally, and intellectually?

Chukat

Chukat—day one

This is the statute …

—NUMBERS 19:2

This week's parashah is *Chukat* (statutes or decrees). A *chok* is a law that is given by God that makes no logical sense. In fact, the sages say that we could not understand the reasoning behind a *chok*, and this makes observing it that much more important and holy. Why is this? Once something is explained and rational or logical to us, we find it easier to observe. It takes a strong sense of surrender, acceptance, and faith to follow a precept that does not make sense to us. Therefore, following a *chok* is the Jewish path of surrender.

To what are you willing to surrender?

How do you let your soul override your intellect?

How do you define acceptance and faith?

Chukat—day two

Instruct the Israelite people to bring you a red heifer.

—NUMBERS 19:2

The *chok* that is explained is how to help someone who is in mourning get clean and be able to spiritually rejoin society. This is the ritual of the red heifer. The red heifer is burned, and the ashes are used in a mixture to help the person who is in mourning or who has had contact with a dead body to become spiritually clean. The mourner needs a ritual because after a death, everything seems tainted and dirty. An interesting event happens, however. The person who burns the red heifer and the one who ministers to the mourner both become unclean. I have no idea how the ashes of a certain kind of cow can make someone clean. I believe that it would not matter what the ritual was; simply having any ritual allows me to feel that the impurities and the dirty feelings I have can be removed. Today, on the seventh day of observing shiva, we lift mourners up and walk around outside of their house with them so that they know they have to get back to living and that there is a community that cares for them. I do not know how or why this works; I just know that it does. The same is true of the red heifer ritual. The power of a *chok* is not in having to know how or why it works; we just know that it does, and that is enough.

How do you help someone lift himself or herself up?

How do you get clean after helping another such person?

What do you do to rejoin your community after you have been on the outside?

Chukat—day three

One who touches a corpse … he shall purify himself.

—NUMBERS 19:11–12

Another lesson from this parashah is that the words "pure" and "impure" do not have the same connotation that most of us assume. Someone who touches a dead body is actually performing a great *mitzvah*, as there is no reciprocity from the deceased. It is one of the most selfless *mitzvot* we can offer, yet we then become impure. "Impure," in this context, must mean "out of the normal world." The same is true for people put outside the camp for all other maladies of the intellect, emotions, and spirit. Most of us look down upon people who are sick in the intellect, emotions, or spirit. These illnesses happen to all of us, and we are obligated to help rather than demonize the person suffering.

Our culture has demonized alcoholics, addicts of all kinds, and others with mental deficiencies, emotional problems, and spiritual maladies. Mental deficiencies and emotional illness are less stigmatized now because of advocacy; yet alcoholics, addicts, and people suffering from other spiritual maladies are still reviled. Addiction is not about a lack of willpower.

To whom and what are you demonizing
rather than ministering?

How can you better understand those whom you malign?

How can you do your part to advocate for the
spiritual and emotional health of all?

Chukat—day four

The pure person shall sprinkle it upon the impure.

—NUMBERS 19:19

"Pure" also takes on a new meaning as we take this chapter seriously. The one who is pure becomes impure. This must mean that when we minister to, when we visit the mourner, when we visit the sick, when we counsel the lost person, it is imperative that we take some of their suffering away from them and take it on ourselves. As a rabbi, if I am not affected and a little bit more impure after each counseling session with someone who is in spiritual and moral need, then I am not being present, and I have not really helped the other person. If the doctor is not weighed down with the illnesses that he or she has seen, then the doctor has not really been involved in healing. If the therapist is not saddened at the end of the day, then he or she has not been available and involved in the client's spiritual and emotional maladies. I also believe this to be true of us as friends. When our friends are in trouble and we are with them, if we are present and involved, then we will be helping them find a solution to their current issues.

How are you being present enough in your interactions with others to be affected by their moral, emotional, intellectual, and spiritual challenges?

What are some of the daily practices that help you stay grounded in the here and now?

How are you valuing yourself enough to reach out and ask for the help you need from others in the areas of your life in which you are struggling?

Chukat—day five

The community was without water,
and they joined against Moses.

—Numbers 20:2

In this case, the fears of the people are that they are going to perish for lack of water. Even though their entire experience has been that God cares for them, when they experience the death of Miriam, their fears overtake this knowledge. Letting their fears run rampant causes the Israelites to blame Moses and bemoan leaving Egypt. Interestingly, this time, God does not get angry. God understands that death causes a split in people. We are split between the world of the living and the next world. This split, left unhealed, will cause us to forget everything we know and revert back to our primal fears. God knows this and instructs Moses to talk to the rock so that the people know they are not alone. Talking to the rock will cause the people to remember that God cares about them and that the death of an individual does not mean that God has left the individual or the communal survivors. Moses, in hitting the rock and speaking to the people as if it were he and Aaron who brought forth the water and other miracles, reinforces the people's fear rather than assuaging it. It is in this way that Moses does not sanctify God's name and beingness.

When faced with the pressure of caring for others, do you forget where your strength and support come from?

When do you become so arrogant, you catch yourself thinking that you are omnipotent?

When have you taken sole credit for doing something great for which you know you received much assistance?

Chukat—day six

And Moses raised his hand and struck the rock twice.

—NUMBERS 20:11

In looking at Moses striking the rock, I think that it is important to put this moment into context. This chapter starts out with Miriam dying. In it we are told that she died and was buried in the wilderness of Zin. A midrash tells us that when Miriam was alive, a well of water followed the Israelites, and when she died, the well dried up. There is no mention here, however, of any mourning for Miriam. This is the problem. Miriam was one of the Big Three; it was Miriam, Aaron, and Moses who were the leaders of the Israelites. It was Miriam who watched over Moses on his trip down the Nile as an infant. It was Miriam who led the dance after the crossing of the Red Sea. It was Miriam who was the advisor to the women and even, I believe, Moses himself. Moses lost his sister, his confidante, and his best friend. The people lost one-third of their leadership, and the one who watered their souls. Yet, there is no mention of any mourning, no time given for the expression of grief and pain. What is recorded, however, is the fear of the people.

When do you take the time needed to express and deal with your grief and pain when you lose someone or something dear?

How are you still letting your fear and emotion overtake you, reacting to those instead of the actual feeling of loss?

How do you act out, seeking escape in any form, when dealing with a major loss?

Chukat—day seven

Therefore you shall not lead this
congregation into the land.

—NUMBERS 20:12

At this point, God realizes that Moses and Aaron are not able to handle all of the responsibilities that have been given to them. God realizes that the loss of Miriam is too much for them to bear. God realizes that the people have become too dependent on Moses and Aaron. God realizes that in order for the people to be free, they are going to have to depend on and do the work themselves.

Whom do you need to release from the burden of doing everything for you?

When you find yourself overwhelmed, to what or whom do you reach out?

How are you going to realize and develop the faith that you really are capable of caring for yourself and for others?

Balak

Balak—day one

Balak son of Zippor saw all that Israel had done to …
—NUMBERS 22:2

This week's parashah is *Balak*. This is the name of the king of Moab. I believe this parashah is named after him because he is a great teacher for us. The story is that Moses and the Israelites have defeated the Amorites and the king of Og, and they are on their way toward Moab. There is no indication that they will make war with the Moabites and the Midianites, yet Balak is worried that they will. He has made up his mind that he will have to go to war with the Israelites and that he will lose.

What causes you to make up scenarios in your mind before you have all the facts?

How do you defeat yourself prior to beginning a task?

When do you allow your fears to overrule your spirit and/or intellect?

Balak—day two

Spend the night here, and I shall reply as Adonai says.

—NUMBERS 22:8

Knowing that he is alone, even with his Midianite neighbors, and thinking he cannot defeat the Israelites, Balak sends for a prophet named Balaam. Balaam is known as a prophet of God who can bestow both blessings and curses. As the text says, whomever Balaam blesses is blessed and whomever Balaam curses is cursed (Numbers 22:6). Balak sends his representatives to Balaam to hire him to curse the Israelites. When they come to Balaam, he tells them that he has to ask God for permission to go with them. That evening, God comes to Balaam and asks who these people are and what they want. Balaam tells God, and God tells Balaam that the Israelites are God's people and they are not to be cursed. Balaam tells the representatives of Balak that he cannot go with them. Balak is enraged.

What causes you to use or try to use magic to accomplish something?

When have you sought out a magician of sorts to do for you what you can actually do for yourself?

How do you react when people refuse your request to do what you want them to?

Balak—day three

Balak sent more distinguished messengers.... I will reward you.

—NUMBERS 22:15, 17

Balak is a king, and he thinks that he has control and authority over everyone. He is so full of himself that he sends more representatives and offers Balaam a lot of money. He is sure that Balaam will not be able to refuse the monetary reward. Balak is right; Balaam tells the new representatives to wait overnight and see if God instructs him to go with them. God comes to Balaam and asks who the people are again, and this time God tells Balaam it is okay to go with them, but he has to speak only the words that God puts in his mouth. Balaam tells the representatives that he can go and leaves very quickly. While this seems innocent enough, this story reveals something important about Balaam and about us: Balaam already knows the answer from God, yet he goes again to see if God has changed God's mind.

When have you kept upping the ante to entice someone into doing your bidding?

What causes you to sell out to the highest bidder when you know the task is wrong?

How often do you go to different people trying to get the response you want, rather than the one you need?

Balak—day four

Let me find out what else Adonai may say to me.

—NUMBERS 22:19

There is a paradox found in yesterday's lesson. We have to learn from God and others, and in order to do so, we must try to understand their way of reasoning and seeing a situation and its solution. For many of us, the only way to do this is to question. Questioning our guides, our elders, and even God is not bad. What is important and ultimately determines whether or not we learn is how and for what we are questioning. Too often, we are trying to be right rather than seeking truth. Too often, we get mad at the person who is trying to help us see more of the picture, which forces us to give up what we want in order to do the next right thing. Balaam wants the money, or the prestige, or the challenge. He is not staying true to his gift and using it for the purpose for which God gave it to him. While he is like Abraham in having the power to bless and curse, he does not have the wisdom to use his gift for the sake of others; he uses it for his own sake. He goes against what he knows to be true in order to get what he wants.

When do you ask questions, seeking to learn more?

When do you ask questions, seeking to be right?

What are you willing to give up in order to be in truth?

Balak—day five

"But whatever I command you. . . ."
Balaam saddled his ass.

—NUMBERS 22:20–21

We have to look at ourselves and be able to acknowledge that even though we want something, we are able to forgo it for the greater good and to serve truth rather than our own interests. Balaam gets blinded by money. He forgets whom he is serving and starts to serve himself and his desires. Balaam is so befuddled that he rushes off without considering what God is saying. Instead of telling the representatives that he has to speak the words that God puts in his mouth, he lets them believe that he is going to curse Israel. God sends an angel with a sword to stop him as he is leaving his home. Balaam is so blinded by the money; he, a prophet who talks with God, cannot see the angel that even his donkey can. The donkey saves him three times from certain death, and Balaam can only beat him for this gift. The donkey starts to talk to him and, Balaam, not realizing that donkeys do not usually talk, answers his donkey. Talk about being focused on what one wants and not seeing any other signs! When God lifts the veil covering Balaam's eyes, Balaam realizes what has happened. He immediately offers not to go and is told again to go and speak only what God tells him to say.

What is blinding you to the truth?

When have you sacrificed your integrity
to get what you want?

Whom in your life do you beat when they
try to protect you from danger?

Balak said to Balaam, "Don't curse
them and don't bless them."

—Numbers 23:25

A lot of people say staying focused is imperative. "Keep your eyes on the prize" is a sales slogan. Yet, this is not about winning and losing, it is about truth and lying. Balaam and Balak represent most people who keep trying to hold on to their lies and status. This reminds me of Rabbi Joseph B. Soloveitchik, *z"l*, who states in *The Lonely Man of Faith* that redemption happens when we allow ourselves to be confronted and defeated by a Higher and Truer Being (God). I call this act surrender. Balak is unwilling to be confronted by truth. He is unwilling and unable to allow himself to be defeated by truth. What does it mean to allow oneself to be confronted and defeated by a Higher and Truer Being? It means we humans have to participate in our surrender. Surrender, in this definition, is not giving up because we are beat down. Rather, surrender is letting go of our need to be right and our need to play God. Surrender is joining the winning side. Balak is too in love with himself and his position to admit that there is a Higher and Truer Being.

How do you allow truth to confront and defeat you?

How are you participating in your surrender?

When do you fight truth for the sake of prestige?

Balak—day seven

How good are your tents!

—Numbers 24:5

One of the truths that I have been defeated by is that I have and am enough. When I get like Balak or Balaam, thinking that I don't have enough and need more, I remember how blessed I am and experience gratitude for my life, my work, my purpose, and my passion. Then, my next experience is giving a blessing to the other person/people for the work, purpose, passion, and life they live. In fact, I ask God to bless them in their work, rather than to curse them. When I come to appreciate them for who they are, they are no longer the other or my enemy; they become a fellow traveler on the path of life. For me, this growth began with no longer being in competition with my brother Neal and has extended to most areas of my life most of the time. I am not perfect. Golda Meir said about peace in Israel between Arab and Jew, "We will only have peace … when they love their children more than they hate us." This is the challenge for Balak, for all of us really.

When and how will your love trump your hatred?

When and how will your compassion trump your rage?

When will your desire to live free and care for the poor, the stranger, the widow, and the orphan trump your desire for power, prestige, and wealth?

Pinchas

Pinchas—day one

Say, therefore, "I give him My covenant of peace."

—NUMBERS 25:12

This week's parashah is *Pinchas*. At the end of last week's parashah, Pinchas kills an Israelite who had brought a Midianite woman into or near the entrance of the Tent of Meeting and was having sex with her. Pinchas is still given the High Priesthood as an inheritance. He was the eldest son of Eleazar, so he would have inherited it anyway, and this does not seem to be a reward. God gives Pinchas a *b'rit shalom* (a covenant of peace) which gives Pinchas what he needs to be a whole person, to be someone who is now armed and able to deal with all of life's circumstances in proper measure. Becoming a member of the priesthood causes Pinchas to help people who have erred come back and return to God, decency, and community. God is telling us that to be a priest, to be someone who helps others return, we must ourselves have had the experience of straying from the path.

What errors have you made that have enabled you to help others return to a better path?

How are you still trying to defend your life rather than learn from each of your experiences?

How does your need to be perfect stand in the way of your need to be real?

Pinchas—day two

Because he was zealous …

—NUMBERS 25:13

In the world today, Hamas, Hezbollah, ISIS, and other fundamentalist groups believe that killing anyone and everyone who does not agree with them and does not live according to their interpretations of God's will is justified and right. In our own country, there are people who believe that if you do not follow the law exactly the way in which they interpret it, you belong in jail, in prison, or dead. Zealotry allows us to kill and destroy others physically and spiritually. Zealotry is the ultimate act of arrogance. Zealots feel powerful under the false belief that they know the will of God. Because God is infinite and we are finite, with that reasoning zealots are really saying that they are God.

In which areas of your life are you being arrogant enough to believe you know the only way?

Whom are you killing through your zealotry?

How can you be more godlike, seeing the whole picture?

Pinchas—day three

The name of the Israelite who was killed …

—NUMBERS 25:14

We learn the names of the two people Pinchas killed in this parashah, also. One is Zimri, a prince of the tribe of Simeon, and the other, Cosbi, a Midianite princess. In Genesis, Levi and Simeon were the ones who tricked the men of Shechem after the rape of Dinah, massacring the entire town. Jacob, at the time of his death, was still angry about this event and tells both Levi and Simeon that they are to be scattered among the tribes. The action in killing these two, taken by Pinchas, is the split in this alliance. For us, these types of alliances take the shape of gossip groups and resentments that are fueled by others. No longer will the tribes of Levi and Simeon plot together to take vengeance and killing into their own hands.

In what alliances of negativity are you still engaged?

How can you detach yourself from
the grips of gossip groups?

Are there people in your life from whom
you know you should be separated?

Pinchas—day four

For they show hostility by the trickery
they practiced against you …
—NUMBERS 25:18

I know that most immorality causes more destruction and spiritual death than even idolatry. When we deceive someone, we seduce ourselves into believing that we are stronger than the other person and even stronger than God. When we take advantage of others, through lies and unethical behavior, we are strengthening our false beliefs in our power. When we tidy up unethical business practices by saying, "Everyone does this" or "This is how it is in business," we are giving a powerful boost to the lies we tell ourselves. When we blame others for our immorality, like our parents or God by saying, "This is the way I am," we are bastardizing the divine image in which we are created and letting our evil inclination run wild.

In which areas of your life are you still trying to trick others? What excuses are you using to explain this bad behavior? How are you dishonoring your divine image?

Because of the affair of Peor …

—NUMBERS 25:18

Rabbi Samson Raphael Hirsch, a famous commentator of the nineteenth century, in his book *The Pentateuch*, says that the fact that in the Torah we are told three thousand people died because of the Golden Calf and twenty-four thousand people died because of sexual immorality shows that sexual immorality is more dangerous and destructive than idolatry. This is a powerful statement. In consideration, I have found that I agree with Rabbi Hirsch for the most part but would amend his statement a little: I believe that all types of immorality are more destructive than idolatry. Here we see the lure and seductiveness of acting out sexually. We see in our own time how sexual acting out destroys marriages, families, and individual lives. Yet, we continue to engage in this type of behavior. Sexual immorality is not about having an affair or consensual sex between two single, willingly engaged adults. Sexual immorality is using sex as a weapon or tool to get what we want from others. It is using sex to lure and seduce someone into behavior that is harmful and possibly destructive to others.

How are you using your sexuality to seduce others?

How are you succumbing to the seduction of another?

What have you destroyed by seducing and/or being seduced?

Pinchas—day six

Moses brought their case before Adonai.

—Numbers 27:5

One of the messages that I receive from this part of the parashah is that we all have to see our own flaws and, through our return and our covenant with God, repent and do *t'shuvah* for our errors. Only then can we help others to return to themselves and God. Many people think that we need saints and people who are perfect to be able to help us come back from our errors. This teaching of the Torah, in my opinion, disagrees with this idea. We are all flawed. We need to search inside and ask ourselves some difficult questions.

How often do you do an inventory of your life?

What causes you to hide from your flaws?

What is the covenant you need to make in order to become more whole?

Pinchas—day seven

Go up on the mountain.

—NUMBERS 27:12

Another lesson in this week's parashah is about acceptance. Moses is told by God to go up on the mountain and look at the land of Canaan, Israel's inheritance, because he is not going to go into the land. Instead of complaining and appealing, at this moment Moses accepts God's decree. Not only does he accept this instruction, but he also stays concerned about his people. He asks God to appoint someone in his place so the Israelites are not sheep without a shepherd. Even when Moses does not get what he wants, he is still living his purpose as a leader and ensuring that the Israelites have what they need to get into and stay in the land.

What pieces of guidance have you been able to receive and accept?

How do you deal with not getting what you want?

In what ways are you training someone to take your unique place in the world so that transitions are more seamless for your community?

Matot/Mas'ei

Matot/Mas'ei—day one

Moses spoke to the heads of the tribes of Israel …

—NUMBERS 30:2

Each year we come across some weeks in which we are given two Torah portions together like we have in this week's Torah portions, *Matot/Mas'ei*, a double *parashiyot. Matot/Mas'ei* translates to "tribes and marches." Let us begin by looking at the first parashah, *Matot* (tribes). In it we are told that Moses is speaking to the heads of the tribes of Israel. We learn from this that we are all part of a tribe. Again in this parashah, as in the first parashah of this book, we learn of a census being taken. As we are about to enter the land, God, the leadership, and the people themselves have to know who is standing up and being counted. They have to know whom they can count on. Each of us needs to do this, not just for war, but so that we and everyone else knows whom to count on for what. It is imperative to stand up for and be counted as a member of a community, a shul, a family. We must stand up for ourselves, for the ones who cannot stand up for themselves because of oppression, fear, or terror, and for God.

With what tribes do you identify?

What is your responsibility as a member of your tribe(s)?

For what do you and your tribe(s) stand?

If a man makes a vow ...

—NUMBERS 30:3

We also learn about vows in this parashah. We are told that any vows we make, we have to keep. What a concept. We are reminded of the lesson that just as God spoke and the world came into being, our words have the power to create and destroy. When we make a vow, we are committing ourselves to an action. We are then counted on to fulfill this vow because if we don't, we suffer from our sin. The suffering is not some external punishment; rather, the suffering is the sin itself. The suffering is that we give power and credence to the negative voice that tells us we are not good enough. When we fulfill our vows, this negative self-talk is quieted. Also, when we commit to do something, others count on us. When we don't fulfill our commitment, we cause a chain reaction of negativity.

How are you using your words as swords, and how are you using them as plowshares?

When and in what ways has negativity been created when you have not kept your commitments?

When and in what ways has good been created by honoring your vows, in word and deed?

Matot/Mas'ei—day three

Takes an oath imposing an obligation on himself …

—NUMBERS 30:3

Our vows allows us to live our life with and on purpose. Many people think so little of themselves that they say, "Who cares? What does it matter?" This type of thinking leads to not caring about oneself and others. This then leads to living life by accident. As we all know, accidents can cause damage. We have the ability, and are taught this week, that fulfilling our vows lifts up ourselves and others. There are times when we make vows that we learn later we cannot fulfill. If we immediately, upon our own awareness, let people know, this is still fulfilling our vow. We are taught that fulfilling our vows causes the world to become more complete and, therefore, a better place for us to live.

How are you living your life on purpose?

How are you living your life accidentally or unconsciously?

Which vows have you made that no longer work and must be annulled?

Matot/Mas'ei—day four

He must carry out all that has crossed his lips.

—Numbers 30:3

The great scholar Moses Maimonides said, "What is on your soul should be on your lips." I am reminded of these words whenever I read this parashah. God is telling us that deceit is not okay. God is telling us that using language to obfuscate truth is not okay. The Torah is telling us that we have to be congruent beings; otherwise, we are not really being human. We have to stop telling others and ourselves what we want to hear in the moment just so that we can achieve what we want. Rather, we have to be in truth and keep our commitments and our obligations. Without following Maimonides's dictum, we can have no integrity. Without integrity we can have no meaningful connection. Without meaningful connection, we cannot be truly human.

About what are you still being deceitful?

How are you obfuscating truth or making false promises, in order to "get yours"?

How are you living with integrity and meaningful connections?

Matot/Mas'ei—day five

The Reubenites and the Gadites ...

—NUMBERS 32:1

Two tribes come to Moses in this parashah and tell him that they are content to stay on this side of the Jordan River and not cross over into the land that was promised. They see the land as good for cattle, and not knowing what is on the other side, they ask permission to settle there. Moses is angry. He accuses them of doing what their ancestors did when they listened to the ten spies and did not want to go into the Land of Israel. These two tribes, after hearing Moses's words, say, "Okay, you are right; we will go and fight for the land, but let us build here pens for our flocks and towns for our children." The lesson that we learn here is that we can redeem the errors of our past and of our ancestors before us.

What errors do you need to redeem that you, your family, or your ancestors have made?

What particular legacy do you or your family seem to have that you are either proud of or ashamed about?

What can you do to either enhance or shift this legacy so that you are passing on a gift to future generations, either of your own lineage or the world at large?

We will build here sheepfolds.

—Numbers 32:16

Another nuance to this conversation is that the tribes say, "We will build here sheepfolds for our flocks and towns for our children" (Numbers 32:16). Moses tells them that as long as they agree to fight alongside their kinfolk, they may go and "build towns for your children and sheepfolds for your flocks" (Numbers 32:24). The difference here is that Moses is more concerned with caring for human life and then taking care of material wealth, while the tribes are most concerned with their material wealth and then taking care of human life.

What is more important in your life, material wealth or the wealth and worth of human life?

How do you demonstrate your answer on a daily basis?

Today, how can you view caring for human life as ultimately beneficial in all ways?

Matot/Mas'ei—day seven

These are the marches of the Israelites.

—NUMBERS 33:1

Mas'ei is the last parashah of the book of Numbers. This parashah also ends the narrative of the story of our ancestors' journey from Egypt to the borders of the Promised Land. One of the interesting and telling lessons of our Torah is that it ends without us entering the land. It is, in my opinion, teaching us that the road map for living, which includes all of life's joys and sorrows, trials and tribulations, doesn't depend on reaching our "ultimate" goal. What is important, our Torah is teaching us, is how we live on the way to the goal. The end can never justify the means in our tradition.

How does your joy in life depend on whether or not you reach your ultimate goals?

How do you see yourself as a success or failure, by the way in which you are living or by the attainment of your goals?

How are you living according to the "means" or the "ends"?

Devarim

Devarim—day one

These are the words …

—DEUTERONOMY 1:1

This week's parashah, *Devarim*, begins with the sentence "These are the words that Moses addressed to all of Israel." In fact, since the name of this parashah is actually *Devarim*, meaning "words," we can assume that it emphasizes the importance of words actually spoken.

How are you actually aware of the importance and weight your words carry with others?

How do you fool yourself into thinking that your words do not matter?

How are you uplifted when you pay attention to the impact of your words?

Devarim—day two

You have stayed long enough.

—Deuteronomy 1:6

God says, "You have stayed long enough," expressing impatience and eagerness for Israel to enter the land immediately. There are many ways in which we procrastinate in the process of living. Due to fear and self-will we can stagnate and get tripped up on our own path. Just like the people of Israel, we get waylaid on the way to our destination. While it is imperative that we embrace the journey and gather all important new information about ourselves, it is also crucial that we give ourselves the greatest chance for living well by listening to the people in our lives who are attempting not to be God, but to be Moses. Our sponsors, our advisors, our guides, our rabbis, and our counselors all have direction to give us, and in our journey toward living well, it is critical that we actually take guidance into account and follow it. I say this not as an admonishment, but as a prayer for all of you to avoid some of the mistakes I have made along my way. The most momentous mistake I have made happened because I was not listening to some profoundly wise words that came my way.

In what ways do you frustrate God by refusing to move forward with your life?

What is still holding you back?

What comforts of the status quo are binding you to a life of stagnation and torment?

Devarim—day three

We set out from Horeb.

—Deuteronomy 1:19

In this parashah, Moses recounts the happenings since the Israelites left the wilderness of Sinai. It seems that his memory and the earlier texts are a little different. I don't think this is by mistake. I believe two things are at work here: one is that Moses has the gift of time to reflect and gain perspective on earlier actions; the second is that Moses is still wrestling with the reasons he is not going into the Promised Land. The time to reflect has given Moses the opportunity to see that he was constantly seeking to do what was best for the people, even when they thought otherwise. This is the mark of a great leader.

How do you consistently seek what is best for the people you serve?

How do you care for others in a moral and ethical manner?

How often do you take time to reflect on the actions you take?

Devarim—day four

Then all of you came to me and said ...

—DEUTERONOMY 1:22

Moses tells us that the people asked him to send spies to scout out the land, which makes the parashah in Numbers, *Shelach L'cha* (send for yourself), more sensible. The people wanted to know which way to go, and Moses thought that this was a good idea. He blames them, however, for their fears after hearing the report from the spies, leaving out the fact that he himself said nothing during this entire exchange. Moses also blames them for God having gotten angry with him, at this point, because of their rebellion and not letting them into the land.

How are you still trying to blame others for the consequences that you experience?

Who gets the brunt of your disappointment when you do not get what you want?

What are some of the ways you take your frustrations and anger out on those around you?

Devarim—day five

When Adonai heard your loud complaint …

—Deuteronomy 1:34

This parashah, *Devarim*, is the one that precedes the observance of Tishah b'Av (the ninth day of the eighth month), which is the commemoration of the destruction of the First and Second Temples. So it is appropriate that we speak about our own destruction. When we think of ourselves and our bodies as temples, we realize that we are harming not only ourselves when we participate in this demise, but also the people who may have come to us for comfort, for sanctuary, for a place to just be.

How have you participated in the destruction of your temples?

Who has been displaced or abandoned in the wake of your destruction?

What might be some consequences from your harmful actions that you are still unaware of?

Devarim—day six

No one of this evil generation …

—Deuteronomy 1:35

We are taught that the Second Temple was destroyed because of *sinat chinam* (senseless hatred). As I look upon my life and the world around me, I ask myself: how am I still practicing this type of hatred? I realize there are times when I have to stay away from someone because he or she is an evil friend, as our morning prayer teaches us. Yet, I do not have to have resentment, anger, and hatred toward others because of their success and/or failure. I do not have to engage in *sinat chinam*. I can and must have joy and compassion for all.

How are you practicing senseless hatred of others?

Of whom are you resentful because of their success?

What will it take for you to have compassion and joy for others?

Devarim—day seven

Your children ... they shall possess it.

—Deuteronomy 1:39

Now it is incumbent upon us to figure out how we can rebuild our personal temples. As we remind ourselves of the importance of the words of Moses and of the sadness at the destruction of our Temples, let us have continued strength and hope for the coming days. While we must never forget the destruction we are capable of, we must always remember that we can be magnificent and glorious palaces in which to dwell.

What are you actively doing to participate in the rebuilding of your life and temples?

How do you use Judaism to make sure your foundation is solid?

How do you show gratitude on a daily basis for your magnificent life?

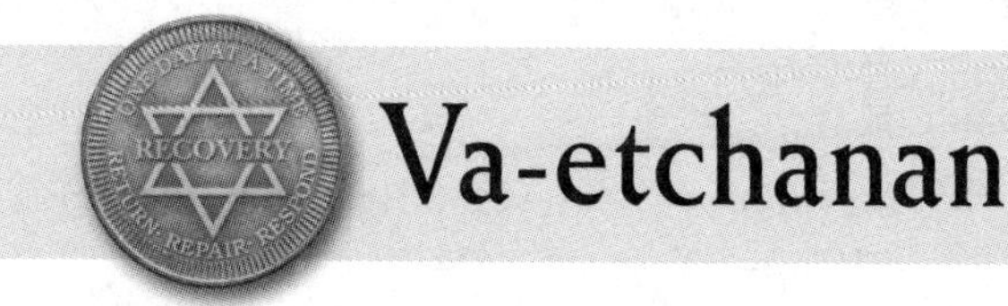

Va-etchanan

Va-etchanan—day one

And I pleaded …

—Deuteronomy 3:23

This week's parashah is *Va-etchanan* (and I pleaded). This parashah has much in it, including the *Shema/V'ahavta* and a repetition of the Ten Commandments. As I sit here writing this, I am awakened by the truth of my own pleadings. I pled for mercy from a judge and received a prison sentence. Was this mercy? Yes, the prison sentence allowed me the necessary time to reflect on my life and find a path of change. Was it mercy that my father died when both he and I were young? Yes, it was merciful because of his health, and he died peacefully.

What makes you plead for grace?

When you plead for something, how often is it for yourself versus for another person?

When you plead for something, do you see the mercy in the result, or are you fixated on getting the result you think you want?

Va-etchanan—day two

But Adonai was wrathful with me on your account.
—DEUTERONOMY 3:26

An interesting note here is that Moses is still blaming the Israelites for the decree. Much like many of us and our leaders, Moses is unable to accept responsibility for his actions and the consequences of his actions, so he has to blame someone else. The people Israel were no more to blame for Moses hitting the rock than the Jewish people are to blame for one Jewish person's bad behavior or a family is to blame for one of its member's active addiction. Yet, even Moses, the greatest of all prophets, succumbs to a base human frailty of blaming others for his own errors.

Today, whom are you still blaming for your own errors?
What actions can you take to release them from this blame?
How are you living in recovery by taking responsibility for your life and your own actions?

Va-etchanan—day three

Adonai said to me, "It is too much for you!"

—Deuteronomy 3:26

God's response to Moses is *Rav 'lach* (it is too much for you). God is telling Moses, and I believe teaching us, that pleading for a change by blaming others is taking too much upon himself. When we blame others for our errors, we are trying to make ourselves look too good. Blaming others is a way of trying to look and be perfect. When we do this, we are not just saying that we are godlike; we are saying that we are God.

How can you accept your own imperfections?

When will you take responsibility for your foibles?

In what types of situations do you find yourself taking on too much?

Va-etchanan—day four

You shall not add or subtract …

—Deuteronomy 4:2

We are told not to add or subtract from anything that we are commanded, and we are not to go to the left or to the right of the path that we are given by God. What does this mean? It is evident that this is not meant literally, because there are commandments that we cannot fulfill regarding the Temple, there are commandments that have been changed (e.g., Hillel's *Prozbul*), and the Rabbis added laws concerning how to fulfill the different commandments. I understand these two directions to mean that everything we need to make a just, compassionate, truthful, and loving life and world is contained within the Torah. The old saying "If it ain't broke, don't fix it" applies here. We don't need to find new ways to live; rather, in order to live well, we need to follow the path that has been laid out for us by God and to learn from our ancestors and elders about the ways they did and did not follow the right path. Too many people think that if something is old, it is not needed today. These two directions from God teach us that there is truly nothing new under the sun.

What ways of living from Torah are you still rejecting because they don't seem hip and cool enough?

When do you reject God's ways, believing you know better?

How are you actively seeking to recover the lessons of your elders to build a better life?

Va-etchanan—day five

The land you are about to go in and inherit.
—Deuteronomy 4:5

This parashah also teaches us that the land we are to enter is an inheritance to and for us. We are admonished to carefully guard and adhere to the laws that were commanded by God. This ensures that life will go well for us and we will be able to live in our proper place. Here, I believe, the Torah is teaching us to stop living life by accident. Too many people today have decided either to know what God's will is and try to enforce their ways on everyone else—that is, terrorists and fundamentalists—and/or to live according to whatever whim/impulse that comes over them without considering its consequences. Both of these groups then are able to blame others for whatever goes wrong without ever looking inside themselves. We are being taught to live life with and on purpose. We are being told that each of us has a unique place/lane on the path of life, and we have to keep watch of ourselves in order not to stray from our place/lane and do the inner and outer work necessary to live well.

How are you guarding against the inner demons that want you to relapse into despair?

What triggers you to remember your proper place?

What is the inner work you need to do in order to remain teachable?

Va-etchanan—day six

Hear, Israel, Adonai is our God, Adonai is One.
—DEUTERONOMY 6:4

This parashah also has in it the *Shema/V'ahavta* prayer. In *Man's Quest for God*, Rabbi Abraham Joshua Heschel, *z"l*, writes that the *Shema* epitomizes what prayer is: "Jewish prayer is an act of listening." What a great concept; "prayer" in Hebrew means "to look inside or discern for oneself." It is only by listening to our souls that we can do this. The *Shema* guides us to hear all of our soul's messages. It guides us and teaches us to listen for the call of Adonai our God, not the call of all the false idols and gods we have set before us. The *Shema* makes it imperative to understand that God is One and that we are part of the oneness of the world. Therefore, when we recite the *Shema*, we are acknowledging that we are part of God, God is part of us, and this truth encompasses all humans.

How do you use daily prayer as a daily inventory?

How do you know when you are hearing the call of Adonai as opposed to the call of false idols and gods?

What are the ways in which you are treating others as your brothers and sisters, kinfolk united in a return to oneness?

Va-etchanan—day seven

You shall love Adonai your God …

—Deuteronomy 6:5

The first line of the *V'ahavta* says, "You shall love Adonai your God with all your heart, with all your soul, and with all of your everything" (Deuteronomy 6:5). If we love with our heart and our soul, what else is left? I realize that I have to love God even when I am feeling doubtful, apathetic, and negative and ruled by my *yetzer hara*. Because everything we are and everything we have comes from God, all of our parts can be transformed to serve the greater good. In Arthur Green's translation entitled *The Language of Truth*, the *S'fat Emet*, a famous Hasidic rebbe, says that "it is in our very nature to love God with full heart and soul but that inclination is buried deep within us." I believe we are given the commandments to provide direction so that when we meet obstacles and distractions, we will know how to pursue our deep longing to dwell with God, and our souls can find the path home. When we love God with everything, all of our being, even our *yetzer hara*, we can do the next right thing no matter how we feel. Doing this allows us to love the oneness and godlike image in others and ourselves and to take our proper place in the oneness of the world.

Whom do you love with your whole being?

How can you embrace your *yetzer hara*?

What actions do you take daily to remove the obstacles and distractions that prevent you from giving and receiving love freely?

Eikev

Eikev—day one

It will be when you heel and obey …

—Deuteronomy 7:12

This week's parashah is *Eikev* (heel or obey). It is also the root of the name Yaakov, Jacob. Moses tells us to obey all of the teachings found in the Torah. As we get deeper into the book of Deuteronomy, we get more and more teachings from God and from Moses. The teachings are not always the same. This is an important lesson; not all of what I say, what any rabbi says, what any clergyperson says, what any leader says, what any parent says, comes from God. We all do the best we can to understand, interpret, and hear God's words and teachings, and none of us is perfect at it. This simple truth is one that we, as listeners, have to be reminded of and we, as speakers, have to be committed to.

How do you differentiate between your way and God's way?

How do you practice being open to others' views in order to hear their godlike voice?

How do you know when you are speaking with your soul, your godlike voice, and when you are speaking from a self-serving voice?

Eikev—day two

Heel to the social ordinances …

—Deuteronomy 7:12

This parashah starts out by telling us that we must "heel to the social ordinances" that we are given today. We must guard them and perform them—in Hebrew, *shomer v'oseh*. This is critical to living well. Social ordinances are the laws for how we live together, how we create a just and decent society. Each day there are different social ordinances that we have to follow, and each day there are some consistent ordinances. People say to me, "Rabbi, don't I just have to be a good person; isn't that enough?" I respond, "Yes and no." It depends on how you define a good person. Our tradition says that we have to practice being holy/decent in all of our affairs. Some people define being a good person as someone who does not purposely do harm to another. While this is a good start, there is much more. I believe that many of us do harm to others unknowingly and unwittingly because we don't even think about the other soul involved. We then act from our own single-minded perspective, seeking self-gratification, and we unknowingly harm others all the while still thinking that we are good people.

In which situations have you tried to justify some behavior by saying, "This is what everyone does" or "This is the way the world works"?

When do you make your own interests more important than the concerns of others?

How do you define what it means to be a "good person"?

Eikev—day three

You need have no fear of them.

—DEUTERONOMY 7:18

The parashah goes on to teach us not to be afraid of our enemies, because God is fighting for and with us. We are not being told that everyone who wants to move his or her own agenda forward is fighting in God's name. We have to be careful not to think or act as if we are the only ones who understand and are mandated by God to wage war. We are not the only ones who are right; given the climate of the world today, this is critical to acknowledge. We are told that we should not be in fear of our enemies, because God is with us. When we can truthfully know that our actions are for the sake of God and for the sake of truth, then we must not let our fears stop us from doing the next right thing. This is one of the hardest lessons to follow, I think. Everyone has some kind of fear. This teaching comes because Torah knows this and is teaching us and encouraging us not to let these fears stop us from taking the next right action.

How often do you act as if you are the
only one who knows what is right?

What fears stop you from doing the next right thing?

What do you need from God and others
to overcome these fears?

Eikev—day four

God will dislodge those people
before you little by little.

—Deuteronomy 7:22

The path to ensuring that we are doing God's will even with our fears is also taught to us in this parashah. This path is about remembering to face our enemies and our fears little by little. Torah is telling us not to bite off more than we can chew at any given time. We cannot face all of our fears and/or enemies at one time. It will be too much for us and we will be, as this parashah teaches, overcome by wild beasts. These wild beasts include our doubts, emotions, and feelings of being overwhelmed.

How are you living one moment at a time?

How are you trying to do too much or too little?

Can you think of a situation that seems too big to handle all at once but can be broken into digestible actions that make it much more manageable? Write out those action steps.

God will deliver those people up to you.
—Deuteronomy 7:23

The difficulty with this teaching is to know when we are living for the sake of God and when we are bastardizing the words of God. In order to be right, for fear of being or looking wrong, many people wrap themselves in the words of the Torah, the Christian Bible, or the Qur'an. This is a knee-jerk reaction to our fears. Torah is telling us that we have to take a breath and analyze whether or not we are doing God's will and then go forward. Rabbi Abraham Joshua Heschel, *z"l*, in his book *The Insecurity of Freedom*, tells us that we have become a society that equates desires with needs. This was written in 1958. He reminds us that we have forgotten that the Hebrew Bible is an answer to "What is life getting out of you?" This question is awesome and makes me tremble. It also keeps me right-sized when I remember to ask it of myself.

How are you continually taking inventory of your actions to ensure that you are following God's teachings and not your own desires?

What are the spiritual or religious teachings that you twist to support or justify your actions that you need to think about reinterpreting?

What is life getting out of you today, tomorrow, and every day?

You shall guard and do all the *mitzvot*
I command you today.

—Deuteronomy 8:1

Appropriate social ordinances are different each day because we encounter different situations each day. When we see each day as the same as every other, we are indifferent to the sublime wonder of living, as Rabbi Abraham Joshua Heschel, *z"l*, teaches in *God in Search of Man*. We have to treat each person with the dignity and respect that God deserves, because each of us is created in the image of God. We also have to see which of the social ordinances apply to a particular situation. Sometimes we have to be firm and hold people accountable, and sometimes we have to be compassionate, forgiving ourselves and others. Sometimes we have to tell people how they are missing the mark, and other times we have to hear from others about how we are missing the mark. Sometimes we have to give *tzedakah*, and sometimes we have to share our gratitude for the gifts we have been given. Sometimes we have to demand truth, and sometimes we have to accept that another person cannot see the whole picture.

What are you noticing about the sublime wonder of living today?

Which social ordinances do you make part of your everyday living?

How do you try to determine what is required of you in each situation you encounter?

Revere Adonai your God, walk in God's ways, love God, and serve God.

—DEUTERONOMY 10:12

Another teaching in this parashah is about learning what God wants from us. Moses tells us that God wants us to walk in God's path, to love God, to take on all of these actions, laws, opportunities, and obligations with our whole being and take care of the orphan, the widow, and the stranger. In order to do this, we are told to circumcise the foreskin of our hearts and to stop being so stubborn. What does "the foreskin of our hearts" mean? It is the thin membrane that many of us have separating our hearts from clear connection with others and with God. Like a cataract obscures our physical sight, this membrane clouds our spiritual, emotional, and intellectual vision. It enables us to be self-absorbed without noticing it. Torah is telling us that we have this tendency to protect our hearts, and we need to be proactive in removing it from our being. To walk in God's path means to take care of my entire community, to pay special attention to people in need, to give power to the powerless and voice to the voiceless. It means to surrender to God's will and God's teachings rather than just follow our own ways and means.

What do you do each day to keep removing the cloudiness from your thinking and feeling so that you are truly living according to your soul?

When and how do you surrender to God's will?

How do you give dignity to all humans and ensure that you are helping everyone have a voice and be heard?

Re'eih

Re'eih—day one

See, I have set before you this day blessing and curse.
—DEUTERONOMY 11:26

This week's parashah is *Re'eih* (see). What are we supposed to see? According to one of the people I study with, we are being told to see the false gods that we are still worshipping. We have to search for them, because sometimes we are able to fool ourselves into thinking that we are worshipping God when we are really worshipping ourselves, others, or other false gods. This is one of the hardest actions to take. We see what we see and yet throughout the Hebrew Bible we are told to "lift up our eyes and see." We learn how many of our ancestors see the "wrong" things. How many times have we forgotten to really see in our lives? So, one of the teachings of this week's parashah is to see what is really happening in our daily life.

How are you seeing what is?

How do you confuse what is true and what is false?

In which areas of your life are you consistently seeing "wrong" or inaccurately?

Re'eih—day two

Blessing if you obey the commandments …

—Deuteronomy 11:27

Another thing to see is the blessings in our lives. In fact, this is the first thing mentioned in the parashah to see. What are blessings? Are they words that we speak? Are they things other people do for us? Are they actions that we take? I believe that they are all of the above. We have to see the blessings that are in our lives each day. The first is that we woke up this morning. Too many of us take getting up each day for granted. There are also many of us who are upset that we woke up. How ungrateful can we be? When we do notice these simple moments of grace, we need to say a *b'rachah* (blessing) so that we acknowledge them and implant them in our memory banks. Each day that we wake up and recognize the blessing of waking, we are following this commandment of seeing. Each day that we continue to search for and see the blessings around us, we are following this commandment. Each day that we remember to see the blessings that are right in front of our nose, we are following this commandment.

What are the blessings in your life?

What blessings are you grateful for today?

What are you seeing as trouble in your life rather than a blessing?

Re'eih—day three

Follow other gods whom you do not know.

—Deuteronomy 11:28

Another lesson found in this parashah tells us that the false gods we run after we don't really know. The word for "know" in the Hebrew is *yodei'a*. This verb is usually used in regard to knowing objects. When it is used in conjunction with humans, it means that there is a sexual union. In Genesis 4:17 it says that the man "knew" his wife and she conceived. So, what could Torah mean by using this word in conjunction with false gods? I think it means that we can never really "know" the false gods. Inherent in the term "false gods" is the concept that they are never really anywhere. They are like mist; you cannot get ahold of false gods. We cannot have union and create something holy with false gods. We can only have union with God. We can only create something holy when we are following God's path, not the path of false gods.

What false gods are you following?

When do you engage in false intimacy, not really knowing people?

How are you recovering a deep union with God, others, and yourself?

You must destroy all the sites at which ...
—DEUTERONOMY 12:2

The first action that we are told to take in this parashah is to destroy the altars, sites, and idols of the land that we are going to possess. We are told in verse 1 of chapter 12 that the land is an inheritance. The English translation is that we are to "possess" it. Another lesson from this is that we must possess our inheritance in order to really honor this gift. What does it mean to possess something? Torah is teaching, in my opinion, that to possess something is to use it for the purpose intended and to the fullest that we can. To possess something also means to want it and to honor, cherish, and respect it. I believe it also means to become one with it.

What possessions do you honor and cherish?

How do you use your inherited traits to the best of your ability each day?

Which of your gifts are you squandering?

Re'eih—day five

You shall not act as you please.

—DEUTERONOMY 12:8

We are also told to stop living in any way we want, doing what we want when we want. This type of living is going to lead us astray again. Why? Because when we do this, we fall into the trap of lies and believing that we are the arbiters of right and wrong, blessing and curse. Look at the world—so many people want to force everyone to do what they think is the right thing, not what God tells us is the right thing. We are commanded to sacrifice (today we use prayer) in certain ways, at certain times, and in certain places. This seems counterintuitive to me. If I am moved to prayer or sacrifice, why do I need a formula or place? I understand this commandment to be telling us that we have to have a set routine and a set path. It is too easy to do what we want when we want and not really put our meaning and commitment behind our desires. Yes, we might mean it and be committed for the moment, but without a structure we will not know the steps or see the path to continue to follow through in our lives. To have this routine and commitment starts, according to this parashah, with being on the path of God. The blessings come in and on the path of serving the Holy One in the ways that God has shown us.

How many things do you start and never finish because you do not have the commitment that comes from serving God?

How are you following the path that God has given you?

When you fulfill your commitments, how do you experience the blessings and see the joy of living?

If there is a prophet or dream-diviner …

—Deuteronomy 13:2

Another teaching from this week's parashah is to know when someone is a false prophet. Torah is teaching us that there are many people who will lie to us, and the lie will sound good. In fact, sometimes it will sound so good that we will want to believe it. Torah tells us to listen with our soul so that we can discern the truth from lies. This is an important principle. Too often we either want to believe someone else and/or we lie to ourselves so that we can believe it. Why is this so important to Torah? Because whenever we follow the lies of someone else or of ourselves, we are following other gods. This is the great sin. Remembering the beginning of the parashah, we can only have blessings if we follow God, not false gods. When we follow lies, which are false gods, we curse ourselves.

What is the reward for believing someone else's lies?

What is the reward for believing your own lies?

How can you tell the difference between a false prophet and a true prophet?

Re'eih—day seven

You shall not eat anything abhorrent.

—Deuteronomy 14:3

The parashah goes on to talk about *kashrut* again. We are told which foods are permitted and which ones are not. Eating is such an important part of life; we do it often, and we do it to nourish and grow our bodies. Torah recognizes this and wants us to treat it as an elevated action, not just something we do without thinking. *Kashrut* reminds us that we have to pay attention and put thought into all of our actions. In this way we continue to be yoked to God's will and continue to improve the world. *Kashrut* means "fitting and proper." The reminder of tithing follows the part regarding *kashrut*. We are told that we have to tithe and care for the Levite and the poor. From this I understand the reminder of *kashrut* to be about much more than food. We have to live a life that is fitting and proper. We are obligated to spend our money in fitting and proper ways. We have to give the first of our fruits (or money) to the ones who are in need as an action of gratitude to God for being able to sustain ourselves.

How conscious are you of what you are eating, with whom you are eating, and your level of conversation?

Is your money "kosher"—are you earning it in a fitting and proper manner?

How are you sharing your money with those in need, and how are you hoarding it?

Shofetim

Shofetim—day one

Judges and officers give for yourself at all your gates ...

—Deuteronomy 16:18

This week's parashah is *Shofetim* (judges). The parashah begins by saying that each of us, individually, should give to ourselves judges and officers at all of our gates and combine justice with righteousness. Each year I am struck by the power of this first verse. Being a mentor, guide, and/or judge is a gift rather than a burden. It is a gift to be used wisely and with righteousness, not as a club and a ""holier than thou" attitude. This role is to be accepted with awe and reverence, not force or entitlement.

For whom are you a mentor, judge, or guide?

Do you approach this role with awe and reverence?

How are you remembering to serve the agenda of the person who has asked you to fill this role?

Shofetim—day two

At all your gates …

—DEUTERONOMY 16:18

The parashah starts with the command to appoint judges and guards at all of our gates. However, the command is in the second person singular, not plural. Often in Torah the command is to "the Children of Israel" or "all the community," and here, in reestablishing the need for a society of justice and law, the command is in the singular. Why? I think because Torah is telling us a truth that many of us forget. We cannot have a just society unless each of us is responsible and obligated to justice. The opening also tells us that we have to judge with righteous justice. Why the qualifier? I think it is to tell us that no one can live under the strict letter of the law. We are not saints, and we are not perfect. We have to have compassion in our judgments, and we have to see each case as brand new. In *Moral Grandeur and Spiritual Audacity*, Rabbi Abraham Joshua Heschel, *z"l*, writes, "No two moments are alike"; therefore, no two cases are exactly alike either. We have to use prior situations to guide us, and we have to see each occurrence and individual as brand new. This is why the Torah goes on to tell us not to accept bribes or favor the rich or poor. Each case and each experience is to be seen as new.

As an individual, how do you take responsibility for what is happening in your world?

How are you living in an obligated manner of doing righteous justice in all your affairs?

How are you seeing each moment as new?

Shofetim—day three

They shall govern people with righteous justice.

—DEUTERONOMY 16:18

This entire parashah is about creating a just society. In order to do this, we have to have a rule of law. However, this rule of law is not just for the society; it is also for each individual. The Torah is brilliant, I think, in the way it goes back and forth between the plural and the singular. This is a portion that is so rich, it is impossible to do it "justice" in only one writing. So, I will highlight a few parts that are well known and a few others that I have come to appreciate this year.

How are you creating a just society within yourself?

How are you creating a just society in your family, community, and the world?

Which judges, literal or figurative, help you stay on course?

Shofetim—day four

You shall not judge unfairly; you
shall not show partiality.

—Deuteronomy 16:19

We are also told in the opening verses of this parashah to judge fairly, to not judge a situation one way or the other because we are familiar with the person(s) involved, and to not accept a bribe. All of these actions, we are told, blind the eyes of the wise and overturn the words of the righteous. To judge fairly means that I have to see the whole picture. To remove any bias I have because I know the players involved is really difficult. This tells me that I have to see each situation anew and for what it is. I have to remember that God's agenda is what is important, not my likes and dislikes. Finally, I have to be careful not to accept a bribe. Bribes come in many forms; one of the most insidious, I believe, is in the form of friendship/flattery. It is hard to live justly. It is hard not to give in to our baser emotions and rationalizations. That is, I believe, the reason that this portion is the first parashah in the month of Elul (the ninth month, roughly corresponding to September, although based on a lunar cycle). Let us all take these next forty days and review our year with both discernment and compassion so that we can repair the harms we have wrought and find realistic ways to grow even one grain of sand better in the coming year.

In what ways are you still judging yourself unfairly?

When are you blinding yourself from your own wisdom as well as the wisdom of others?

How do you overrule doing what you know to be the next right thing?

Shofetim—day five

Bribes blind the eyes of the wise.

—Deuteronomy 16:19

The second concept that strikes me is that appointing someone else to help me is not a statement of incompetence; rather, it is a gift that I give to myself. When I give myself judges and guards, I am saying that I am human, and it is possible for me to let my intellect or emotions overrule what my soul tells me and, in so doing, live falsely. In this way, I am recognizing my ability to lie to myself and to others. I am also admitting that there are times when I practice willful blindness in order to satisfy my feelings and desires. By remembering that I can gift myself people to help me see, I am acknowledging that I am not God and I need help in life.

In what areas of life do you acknowledge your need for help?

Where in your life and the lives of others are you still trying to play God?

How are you giving yourself the gift of guides?

Shofetim—day six

Thus you will sweep out evil from your midst.

—Deuteronomy 17:7

Another aspect of justice taught to us in this parashah is what to do with people who spread evil in the community. We are told that we have to root out these people because they will infect the entire community. What is the basis of this evil? Worshipping other gods. Why is this such a pronounced theme throughout the Torah? What is its meaning for us? I believe, from my experience and the experiences of our ancestors, that worshipping other gods is the basis of evil because it allows us to lie to ourselves regarding our responsibilities and our obligations. Worshipping other gods perverts my sense and knowledge of what is just and right. Even a king is not allowed too many horses, wives, gold, silver, or belongings, so as to prevent him from straying from the path. Even the king has to read and follow the laws of Torah, so that he does not follow false gods.

How are you perverting justice and truth?

When does the pursuit of things get in your way of pursuing righteousness?

Who is infecting you with negativity, and whom are you infecting with your negativity?

Is there anyone who has …

—Deuteronomy 20:5

Another lesson of righteous justice found in this parashah is about who is to go to war and how we wage war. We are told that before we go to war, there are certain questions that we have to ask the warriors: is there anyone who has built a new house and not dedicated it; is there anyone who has planted a vineyard and not harvested it; is there anyone who has become engaged and not consummated the marriage; is there anyone who is so afraid that he will spread fear among his fellows? If so, let these people go back and finish what they have started before they go to war. It is not just or right to allow people who have started things that create life and sustain life to go to war and possibly die before they have enjoyed the fruits of their labors. Today, we send our youngest to war with little regard for the life they have not yet lived. This is not living justly or righteously, according to the parashah.

What fruits of your labors do you take the time to enjoy?

Does faith apply only when it is in your own self-interest?

Where are you with respect to justice and righteousness when it goes against your self-interest?

Ki Teitzei

Ki Teitzei—day one

When you go out to war …

—Deuteronomy 21:10

This week's parashah is *Ki Teitzei* (when you go out). This parashah has many different laws for us, ranging from how to act in war to how to build a house. We are taught that we have to build a parapet around our roof so that we don't incur guilt for spilling blood. Huh? Why is the Torah worrying about how our homes are built? This comes to teach us that every aspect of living has the potential to preserve and enhance life or to destroy life. The parapet is a fence that is eighteen inches tall and eighteen inches in from the end of a flat roof. It serves as a warning that we are getting close to the edge of the roof and could fall over. It also is far enough in that we can stop ourselves. This is important because many people use flat roofs to entertain and sunbathe. When we do not put up a parapet, we are not doing all that we can to protect life. It is so easy to get too close to the edge and fall off.

What fences are you putting up to protect yourself from relapsing to your baser instincts?

What laws or roads are you following that help you recover your life?

What fences are you enforcing so that others recovering their own lives are enhanced?

Ki Teitzei—day two

And you see a beautiful woman …

—DEUTERONOMY 21:11

This parashah starts out by telling us how to act when we go to war. If the man sees a beautiful woman, he is not allowed just to take advantage of her. Rather, he has to bring her home, have her cut her hair, listen to her mourn for her family for thirty days, and then decide whether he wants to make her his wife. What a concept. The usual way of soldiers was/is to take advantage of the women captives and not care or be responsible after they, the soldiers, were satisfied. Wrong, says Torah. It is so interesting to start the parashah with this reminder that even in war, where we have to kill, there are still rules of decency and respect for persons that have to be upheld. While most of us are not soldiers right now, we can still apply this to our lives. In business, just because I can take advantage of another, I have to remember and live by an ethical code. In my home life, while I can stop listening to my family because I am tired, busy, or bored, I have to remember that my covenant with my wife, children, siblings, and parents is to be present in their lives and in our family life.

When are you acting from a "because I can, I will" attitude?

How are you remembering your covenant with God and others to take the next right action?

How are you being present in your life and the lives of others?

Ki Teitzei—day three

If a man has two wives, one loved …

—DEUTERONOMY 21:15

We then go on to learning that when we have a second family, even though we may not love our first spouse, we cannot forget our obligation to our first family. Just because we divorce our spouse, that does not allow us to divorce our children by that spouse. How important are children? Extraordinarily important—so important, in fact, that, as parents, we are prohibited from abusing them emotionally or physically. We are not to put a burdensome yoke on them. There are many other laws regarding how we are to care for our children. In this week's parashah, we are told that when we cannot speak to them in a way that they can hear, when we have to teach them so that they learn, we cannot just beat them. We also learn about the rebellious child in this parashah. When our children are drunks or gluttons and we cannot help them change, we have to take them to the elders in the gates of the city. We cannot push them away. This is what Alcoholics Anonymous and treatment centers are for. This is why Beit T'Shuvah was created. Every life matters, and each person is to be ministered to, not thrown away. We are taught to ask for the help of the community to raise our children.

When do you forget your obligations to others
because you have moved on in your life?

Whom have you forgotten about
who might need your help?

How are you being like an elder and helping
the lost children in your world?

Ki Teitzei—day four

If a man is guilty ... and is put to
death, don't let his corpse ...
—DEUTERONOMY 21:22–23

When we live these principles in all of our affairs, we have to ask ourselves questions. How am I cutting out those who were in business with me earlier and are no longer part of my circle? How am I forgetting them, not honoring their dignity, not giving them their share of my success because I no longer like them? We learn from these principles that dignity and fairness are not based on popularity. Principles trump feelings, according to this parashah and the entire Torah. This parashah goes on to teach us about dignity even more strongly and poignantly. We are taught that when someone is convicted of a capital offense and is put to death, the person's body has to be buried immediately. We learn from this that anything that could possibly take away from the inherent dignity of someone alive or dead is forbidden.

How are you honoring those whom you do not like?

How have you continued to honor and give
dignity to those you love who have died?

When do you know your principles trump the
way you feel about someone or something?

Ki Teitzei—day five

If you see your fellow's ox ... you must take it back.
—DEUTERONOMY 22:1

Also, we learn about our responsibilities to our fellow citizens in this parashah. Chapter 22 of Deuteronomy begins with the laws of lost objects. In America, as kids we say, "Finders keepers, losers weepers." In Jewish living, we say that if you find a lost object, you have to try and find its owner, and if you can't, you have to take care of the object for when the owner becomes known and then return it. Even though we could keep it and not tell anyone, we are not allowed to. We learn that hiding anything is not a healthy way to live. Torah teaches us to be transparent. To paraphrase what Rabbi Abraham Joshua Heschel, *z"l*, wrote in *Man Is Not Alone*, to be human means that the interests of others have to be our concern. Why? Because we have to remember that we live in community. It is not okay to capitalize on someone else's misfortune. While this may seem counterintuitive in business, it is one of the basic ethical principles of Judaism. This is a principle that we have to practice in all of our affairs.

What are you still hiding from others?

How do you capitalize on the misfortune of others and live an unkosher life?

How are you making the interests of others your concern?

Ki Teitzei—day six

You shall not abhor an Edomite, for he is your kin.

—DEUTERONOMY 23:8

A second law from this parashah is not to hate the Egyptian and the Edomite. This also seems counterintuitive. These are our enemies; why not hate them? Torah states that the Edomite is our kin, therefore we have to ensure *shalom bayit* (family harmony). Even though Edom became an enemy (not sure why or how), we have to remember that Esau is our brother and did well by us. How amazing that Torah reminds us to be grateful for and to the people who later on became our enemies.

How do you remember the good that your relatives have done for you?

When do you rise above the base emotion of hatred and find the gratitude for the earlier assistance of others?

What are some ways you are working to ensure there is harmony within your family?

Ki Teitzei—day seven

You shall not abhor an Egyptian, for
you were a stranger in their land.

—Deuteronomy 23:8

The Egyptian is even harder to understand and forgive. They enslaved us for four hundred years. But we shall not hate the Egyptians because we were a *ger* (stranger) in their land. Even though we became slaves in Egypt, we have to remember the good they did for and to us. Torah tells us to see the whole picture. They gave us a place to live when we needed it. They also allowed us to be fruitful and multiply. People who are our enemies now, in many cases, started out as friends/helpers. We have to remember this. We have to, according to Torah, find compassion in our hearts and souls and extend this compassion to our enemies.

Whom do you have to give compassion to
and remember how they helped you?

What is your plan to restore these friendships
and relieve hatred with these people?

How do you continue to see this situation in
the context of the whole story of your life?

Ki Tavo

Ki Tavo—day one

When you come into the land …

—Deuteronomy 26:1

This week's Torah portion is *Ki Tavo* (when you come in). This parashah tells us the laws that we have to observe when we enter the land of Canaan. Moses delivers the second *tochechah* (rebuke), telling us what will happen when, not if, we go away from God and follow other false gods. He has spent the last forty years defending the people Israel. He has looked for and found reasons for their bad actions and talked about what they do well. This is a new generation of people; these people who are entering the land are not the same people who lived under slavery in Egypt. Most of these people were not at Sinai to witness the giving and receiving of Torah. They do not remember the hardships of slavery. He is telling them, do not think that you have a free ride because of the merit of your ancestors.

When someone rebukes you, how can you see it as loving and consider what is being said?

What causes you to believe that the rules do not apply to you?

When you rebuke others, do you also acknowledge the good they have done?

Ki Tavo—day two

That God is giving you as an inheritance
and you possess and live in it.

—DEUTERONOMY 26:1

At the beginning, the parashah teaches us that we each will have a place in the land of Canaan and we are obligated to bring the first fruits as a tithe. At that time, we are told to affirm that we know that we are in our land and our place, just as God promised to our ancestors. What this tells me is that I am entitled to live in the world. I am entitled to earn a living, and this is an eternal inheritance from God to and for all of us. The parashah goes on to tell us that we must recite a formula that reminds us of what it took for us to get to our place. We first wandered and then were enslaved. We had to cry out to God for help. God heard our plea and redeemed us and brought us to this land flowing with milk and honey.

How do you affirm that you belong in this world?

How are you remembering your wanderings
and enslavements as paths on the road
to finding your very own place?

What are your daily actions of gratitude and respect
for the bounty that you have been given?

Ki Tavo—day three

You shall then recite the following …

—DEUTERONOMY 26:5

We are taught to remember where we came from and how good things are for us now. It is a very important teaching for all of us. We, people in recovery, know that we have to remember what it was like, what happened to change us, and what we have now. I have spoken to many people who have relapsed, and interestingly, the core action is always the same. They forget where they came from, a miserable life of being addicted, and what happened to change them, a life of recovery, community, and principles. Some of them lie to themselves that they can drink like a gentleman or don't need meetings anymore, and so on. This parashah is teaching us that each time we tithe, each time we reap the harvest of our actions, we have to be grateful and say a prayer remembering where we are and how to share our bounty with the poor, the widow, the stranger, and the orphan. We have to take care of the Levites and the people who serve us spiritually. "Never forget," a phrase that many people use, is an outgrowth of this chapter. However, we are never to forget where we came from and how God saved us from our addictions, and we must continue to be grateful.

What situations make you forget where you came from?

How are you slipping into relapse by not continuing to grow in your spirituality?

When do you feel most grateful for what you have?

Ki Tavo—day four

You shall declare before Adonai your God …

—Deuteronomy 26:13

The month of Elul calls for us to do an accounting of our souls. We have to see the spiritual and moral capital that we have spent and deposited. We can add to the bottom line of our spiritual/moral bank accounts through doing *t'shuvah*. This is the month and now is the time. We can't seek forgiveness from God without seeking forgiveness from those we have harmed. We can't stand *panim al panim* (face to face) with God without knowing our merits as well.

When you do your inventory, *cheshbon hanefesh*, are you including the good as well as the not so good?

What have you learned from your spiritual inventory this year?

How are you going to repair, change, and/or enhance yourself this year?

Ki Tavo—day five

God commands you this day … observe them faithfully with your heart and soul.

—Deuteronomy 26:16

Herein lies a great problem for many people: too many of us believe that because we have it good, we are entitled to do what we want. Too many of us born in the United States do not understand the gift of freedom. Too many of us who have not had to suffer poverty don't know or understand the blessings that we have. Too many of us think, and act, as if we have no responsibility to nourish, feed, and grow our blessings. Too many of us believe that we have an endless supply of gifts and entitlements. Moses is teaching all of us that our ancestors learned lessons for us to imbue and put into action. Moses is exhorting us to appreciate the moral capital that our ancestors have deposited for us. We learn that we have a duty to our ancestors, and respecting them means learning from them. Too many of us think and act as if we should have everything coming to us, just because of our lineage. This parashah is telling us this kind of thinking is wrong.

How are you spending the moral capital of your ancestors?

In what ways are you using the material capital you inherited to help others?

How are you living—as a productive member of your community or in a life of indulgence?

Ki Tavo—day six

Heed the word of Adonai your God and observe …

—DEUTERONOMY 27:10

Moses and Torah are worried about entitlement becoming a state of mind and being. Moses is afraid that the expectations of the Israelites will become so great that they will believe that simply because God chose their ancestors, they will not have to do anything to continue to merit unending bounty. The mind-set of entitlement is not relegated only to the rich, however. There are poor people who feel entitled to receive help without any responsibility on their part to use the help wisely. There are people who were abused who become abusers. Criminals believe that if they can take it, then it is theirs. Trauma victims sometimes use past experiences as weapons. Alcoholics refuse the help available to them. Not all people in these categories do this, of course, but some do. It is important to realize that this state of mind of entitlement is not relegated to one group. Many years ago, I heard a psychiatrist by the name of Dr. Stephen Marmer say, "We have spent the moral capital of our ancestors and have not put anything back in the bank account." How true his words are now, and how true they were even some thirty-three hundred years ago.

What deposits are you making in your personal spiritual or moral bank account?

What are you feeling entitled to that is not yours for the taking or even asking?

When do you give away some of your capital to those in need so you can keep your balance?

Ki Tavo—day seven

But if you do not obey …

—DEUTERONOMY 28:15

What this parashah does is give us the information/prophecy of our choices. Moses lays out the different paths we can take: following Adonai or following false gods. He then tells us the consequences of each path. What makes many people see God as punishing is that they want to follow false gods and not experience any negative consequences; they want only good consequences. How childish is this? In reality, what this parashah does is give us the information with which we can make truly informed choices. The childish thinking of not experiencing negative consequences is one of the great traps of our time. Albert Einstein said, "Insanity is doing the same thing over and over again and expecting different results." The beauty, grace, and gift of this parashah is that we get a glimpse into the future that we can choose for ourselves.

How are you making informed decisions?

When do you listen to the counsel of others so that you don't make the mistakes of earlier generations?

Knowing the previous consequences of your choices, do you still relapse into the trap of insanity?

Nitzavim

Nitzavim—day one

You stand here today …

—Deuteronomy 29:9

This weeks parashah is *Nitzavim* (standing). Before we start walking, we have to know where we are standing. When we do not take note of where we are standing, what is going on around us, and what the appropriate response to our current situation is, we can easily walk/go to a place that is not ours. In order to reach a destination, we have to know where we are starting from; to reach our proper place, we have to see where we are standing right now. Without knowing where we are standing and what we are standing for, each experience will produce a reaction rather than a response. A reaction is just that—acting in the same manner. A response is taking a breath and making an informed decision to do things differently and use our past learning/experience to have a new response this time.

With respect to where you want to go with your life, are you standing now in a place that will help lead you or keep you in your proper place?

If you know you are not in your proper place right now, do you have the road map to get there?

How do you make your next action a response rather than a reaction?

Nitzavim—day two

All the men of Israel, your wives, your children …

—DEUTERONOMY 29:9–10

We start out by learning that everyone is standing in front of Moses—the heads of tribes, elders, men, women, children, servants, strangers—everyone from all stations of life. No one is exempt from being in the covenant, according to Torah. Each of us had and still has the opportunity to cut a covenant with God and enter into it this day. This day is so important because it gives us the message that each day we can enter into the covenant, and each day we must make a choice to enter into the covenant. This is Judaism's teaching of one day at a time.

What covenants have you entered into in your life with God and with your community?

What is your family covenant, and how are you living it?

How are you choosing to be in covenant each day?

Nitzavim—day three

To enter into the covenant of Adonai your God, which Adonai your God is cutting …

—DEUTERONOMY 29:11

Moses talks to the entire people of Israel, from the tribal leaders to the water carrier, the women, children, and strangers. He reminds the people that they are entering this day into the covenant with God. This day the entire community is cutting this covenant with God. He goes on to say that they, the people, are making this covenant for themselves, their ancestors, and their descendants. I tremble with awe, wonder, and dread when I read this. I am being told that my actions affect my ancestors and my descendants as well as the people around me right now. By taking this seriously, I can no longer say, "This is my life and I can do anything I want to because it does not affect anyone else." Not only do my actions affect those around me, but they also affect both those who lived so that I could and my descendants who are yet to come.

Do you realize that your actions have long-lasting effects?

What are your descendants going to inherit from you based on your actions?

What have you inherited from your ancestors that you need to pass on as is or transform for later generations?

Nitzavim—day four

To establish you this day as God's
people and be your God.

—Deuteronomy 29:12

Even though this parashah is only two chapters, it is chock-full of teachings and lessons. Moses is getting near the end of his life, and we are getting near the end of the Torah. Moses is giving us a prophecy; he is reminding us of who we are because he is afraid we will forget for Whom and what we stand. Prophecy in our tradition is an insight into the future in truth. Prophecy does not sugarcoat what is going to be and does not give only doom and gloom. While the prophets do tell us of the doom and gloom that is going to befall us, they also give us the solution to avoid it. They give us hope that with our *t'shuvah*, we will return. This formula for prophecy is initiated by Moses and is prevalent in this portion.

What guidance from Torah are you not following that you know would enrich your soul?

What guidance from others are you ignoring?

Where are you standing right now, and do you need to change that stance?

Nitzavim—day five

If there is among you … whose heart is now turning away from Adonai our God …

—Deuteronomy 29:17

This verse is the exact description of what happens in relapse/prelapse. Almost all who relapse tell the story of how their heart and soul turned away from their program, doing the work, and God. When they return to recovery they realize how many people were affected by their "going out." In speaking to people who have relapsed and come back, I have heard some variation on this same story countless times: "I began to believe that I was 'normal' and I just wanted to be able to drink or use like everyone else." Their hearts had begun to turn away from the program and the truth about themselves and their situation. Their hearts turned away from the redemptive experience of sobriety and their hearts turned away from the spiritual act of surrender. All relapses happen because our hearts turn away from God and from our program of recovery and the wisdom of the Torah.

What are some of the signs that show you are beginning to turn away from your program of recovery?

How can you take better ownership of your truth and responsibility for your recovery today?

Whom have you hurt by not wanting to accept some truth about yourself, and what can you do about the damage you caused?

Nitzavim—day six

I shall be safe though I follow my own heart.

—DEUTERONOMY 29:18

This verse is so important to our growth in recovery. Too often we follow our willful heart and believe we are going to be able to deceive everyone around us that we are sober while we continue to use and/or cheat. Some people look good from the outside, like they are living decently, when all the while they are leading a double life. This particular verse seems like God knows that alcoholics and addicts need to be reminded that they can try to fool some people but that is not a good long-term strategy for living. I have watched many people try to live like this and then become surprised when their duplicitous nature defeats them. I have seen the pain that people living this type of double life have caused to their families and friends. I have also experienced the chaos that living a double life has on community. Living a double life is not relegated to alcoholics and addicts, however. We see this behavior in people from all walks of life: doctors, lawyers, politicians, clergy, employers, employees, and so on. With this verse, Moses and God remind us that being part of the covenant is making a commitment to living transparently. Too many of us are still trying to hide from ourselves. Doing this does not allow us to fulfill or find our true place in the world.

In which areas of your life are you still living from the place of a willful heart?

How are you living a false life, a life of hiding, and from what or whom are you hiding?

What truth are you hiding from yourself?

Nitzavim—day seven

Concealed acts are for Adonai our God, and overt acts are for us and our children ever to apply the provisions of this teaching.

—DEUTERONOMY 29:28

We are told in the last verse of chapter 29 that God knows the secrets of this willful heart. We are told that our community has to see us for who we truly are and help us to rejoin our covenant in truth and commitment. The parts of us that we are hiding, God still knows. The parts of us that are hidden from us have to be, and with God's help will be, revealed to us. The parts we know and the parts that we do not yet know about ourselves all enter into the covenant. This puts upon us the obligation and responsibility to continually reveal ourselves to others and to ourselves. We cannot hide from God, and therefore we should not hide from others and ourselves. We can and must join together to help the one who is living from willfulness, and if we are this person, we must join with others to break our own willful heart. Rabbi Joseph B. Soloveitchik, *z"l*, in *The Lonely Man of Faith*, explains redemption as being possible only when a person lets him- or herself be confronted and defeated by God. This is what it takes to save our own selves and others from ruin.

What prevents you from surrendering to a higher truth?

What are your fears about being confronted and defeated by God?

How is not surrendering harming you and those around you?

Va-yelech

Va-yelech—day one

Moses went and spoke these words to all Israel.

—DEUTERONOMY 31:1

This week's parashah is *Va-yelech* (he went). This beginning has at least two meanings: one is that Moses went and spoke to the Israelites; the second is that Moses is about to die "and he went" to God to receive the last instructions.

How would you describe the place from which you are going?

How are you using the opportunity to bring meaning, comfort, and aid to another person whenever and wherever you go?

How have you heard God's call when you went out from your own selfishness?

Va-yelech—day two

You shall not cross the Jordan.

—DEUTERONOMY 31:2

Moses starts out by telling the people that God is not letting him lead them into the land, and he will not even enter the land. He tells them to have no fear and be resolute, because God is with them. He even tells them that God will not forsake them. According to the thesaurus, other words for "forsake" are "abandon," "disown," "renounce," "relinquish," and "give up." It is an interesting word to use in connection with God. I have a new understanding of Moses's plea to the Israelites. Later on in this parashah, Moses tells the Israelites that they will go after false gods, and they will be scattered. Our future exile is told to us. So, if God is going to let us be exiled, doesn't this mean that God is forsaking us? No, it means we have forsaken God. God keeps and remembers God's covenant with us.

How often have you blamed someone else for the consequences of your actions?

What do you gain from blaming God for your troubles and/or saying it is God's will that such and such is happening?

When will you take ownership for all of your actions, including those that cause exile, pain, and destruction?

Va-yelech—day three

Be strong and courageous, be not in fear or dread.

—DEUTERONOMY 31:6

In this Torah portion Moses tells us all to be strong and have courage, to not be in dread or fear of our enemies, because God is with us. This is the crux of living, I believe. Too many of us think that we have to do everything ourselves. We don't need any help, because if we do, then we are weak and vulnerable. Torah is teaching us that we are always vulnerable. We can't live life in a vacuum. We can't live well alone. We need God and community. We need people who love us enough to see our souls. We need to love others enough to see their souls. To do this takes great strength. To do this takes great courage. We have to have the strength to ask for help. We need the courage to accept the help and reach out to others when they need help.

What help do you know you can be to others,
and are you in fact helping them?

What help do you need?

Whose help will you both ask for and accept?

Va-yelech—day four

You shall read this Torah aloud
in the presence of Israel.

—Deuteronomy 31:11

When we enter the holy day of Yom Kippur, we are in the *aseret y'mei t'shuvah*, the ten days of repentance/return/new responses. Is it not time for us to take responsibility for our errors and stop blaming others or our past? Is it not time to abandon our need to find fault with everyone else for our choices? Most of us have experienced some trauma in our lives; how many of us are still blaming our "stinking thinking" and bad behaviors on these old traumas? This is not to say that these old traumas were not horrendous or terrible; rather, I am asking if it is time to leave these traumas in the past and stop basing our actions today on them. I know that some of you will be upset thinking about this. I am not minimizing the traumas; rather, I am saying that we can leave them in the past so that we can be healed and not have to keep repeating the same behaviors now because of them. Let us take this time to forgive others and ask for forgiveness for our wrongdoings. Let us clean the slate that is our soul and allow our light to shine rather than hide it because of old traumas. When the old traumas are present in our lives now, they hide our light and our soul and therefore prevent us from living well.

From which traumatic experiences in your past do you still need to heal?

How can your community help you heal?

What *t'shuvot* do you need to make, and whose *t'shuvah* do you need to accept?

Va-yelech—day five

This people will go astray.
—Deuteronomy 31:16

Our exile is caused by us, ourselves, and Torah says that we will forsake God. It is our actions that cause our downfall. God then says that God will leave our midst because we have left God's. However, as we know from earlier Torah portions, God will wait for our return. In fact, the Shabbat between Rosh Hashanah and Yom Kippur is called Shabbat Shuvah, "the Sabbath of Return." So, we can forsake in a few different ways. We, humans, usually disown and desert when we forsake God; God does not leave us. Since God is always waiting for our return and, as the prophet Hosea says, heals our backsliding and loves us freely, God never truly leaves us or forsakes us. We turn our backs on God, and then we get upset that God left us. How ridiculous is this? What is it about our nature, our need to be right, our inability to face ourselves, others, and God that causes us to blame others for our errors?

From whom are you in exile?

What will it take for you to recover your path out of exile and onward to freedom?

How can you ensure that you will not forsake God, others, and yourself any longer?

Va-yelech—day six

When Moses put down in writing
the words of this Torah …

—DEUTERONOMY 31:24

Another instruction that Moses went to give us was to write our own Torah. This, according to my teacher Rabbi Edward Feinstein, is the 613th commandment. What does this mean? It means that we have to write for ourselves the way to serve God and community. We have to see in our own handwriting how to be the best partner with God that we can be. We have to read, write, and learn from our own hand all of the different ways for us to become whole, to not follow other gods, to walk in God's ways, and to live our authentic words of Torah. Rabbi Feinstein also teaches that each of us has a word of God within. Each of us has something to bring to the world that no one else can. By writing our own Torah, we are better able to learn, live, and share this word of God with everyone else.

What is the Torah written by your actions?

What is the Torah written by your words,
the ones you say you live?

What, if any, discrepancy exists between your
words and your deeds in this respect?

Va-yelech—day seven

I know how defiant and stiff-necked you are.

—DEUTERONOMY 31:27

If we do not stay strong and have courage as a community, we are told that we will surely stray from the covenant and worship false gods. This is the bane of our existence today. We think we are strong and have courage, yet we are weak and susceptible. When we are not going out together as a community, as people working together, we do get weak. We have taken this teaching and twisted it to mean we have to show individual strength. We are so busy bowing down at different altars—money, power, prestige, looking good, needing to be right—that we get totally lost. Getting lost usually means some degree of ruin. This ruin can come in many forms—financial, emotional, and spiritual.

At what altars do you find yourself in worship, false or otherwise?

In what state of ruin is your life or its components?

What forms does this ruin take in each of those areas of your life that you identified?

Haazinu

Haazinu—day one

Give ear, O heavens.

—DEUTERONOMY 32:1

This week's parashah is *Haazinu* (give ears). This represents our ears hearing. It is Moses's last poem. Just before Moses is going to die, he is afraid that the message of God, as he has transmitted it, has not been fully received. He is so afraid that his message will not be heard. What is so important about what he is saying, and what can we learn from it?

What are your ears open to hearing?

What truths might your ears be blocked from hearing?

When do you know your message is being heard and understood?

Haazinu—day two

Let the earth hear the words I utter.

—Deuteronomy 32:1

This portion begins with Moses calling on heaven and earth to be witnesses to his words. This example points to an ancient directive letting us know the importance of having observers when vital words are being spoken. An alternative explanation could be that Moses is asking both our earthly part (our body) and our heavenly part (our soul) to hear his words. I believe that Moses is calling to all of our parts to come together and hear. He then asks that his words fall on the ears of the Israelites like water, rain, showers, dew, and droplets. Immersing myself in this metaphor, I have come to believe Moses and God want us to absorb these teachings and words, like raindrops are absorbed into the ground and the dew gets absorbed by the grass.

What major lessons from your inventories can you absorb in your life this year?

How have you brought your spirit and your physical body together this year?

What are some ways that you can be a witness to recovering and spreading the message of God and Torah?

Haazinu—day three

May my discourse come down as rain
and my speech distill as dew.
—DEUTERONOMY 32:2

Moses's opening plea is for his words to "come down as rain" and to "distill as dew" (Deuteronomy 32:2). This conjures up some wild imagery. In this plea, I believe Moses is saying that I have to be pelted with the words and principles of God. They have to hit me over and over again and then be taken in like dew in the morning. This provides such a vibrant visual. These words tell me that I cannot say, "I read Torah once, so I know it all and don't have to read it again." These words remind me that I cannot think that I have reached the mountaintop and so have nowhere left to climb. These lies that I tell myself are smashed by these words of Torah. We have to continue to study and learn so that we can remember and remain faithful to its teachings.

In which areas of your life do you need
to be pelted by truth each day?

When do you get so full of yourself that you cannot or
will not take in the teachings of God and others?

How do you stay open to experiencing anew the
words/love/teachings of Torah each year?

Haazinu—day four

For the name of God I proclaim …

—Deuteronomy 32:3

Another lesson that Moses is giving to us is that we have to proclaim in God's name. We have to know and say that God's ways are simple, just, never false, faithful, and righteous (Deuteronomy 32:3–4). Wow, what a tall order. How do we do this? How can we do this when we feel that life is unfair? This is where simplicity comes in. Life is not fair; we must accept that. At least, it is not fair in the ways that most of us understand the concept of fairness. We proclaim God's ways by how we choose to live. It is not fair that people die of the disease of addiction. Some addicts even have survivor's guilt. We need to realize that life is a gift, and each day we must do our best to honor this gift.

In what ways do you honor the gift of life?

Answer thoroughly: what are the areas of being alive that you still feel are unfair?

How will you live with more joy, wonder, and radical amazement today and for all the days to come?

Haazinu—day five

Children unworthy of God …

—Deuteronomy 32:5

This parashah contains Moses's final words to the Israelite people. Reading it after Yom Kippur is a brilliant move by the sages. On Yom Kippur we renew our covenant with God, and then on the next Shabbat, we read about Moses's fear and knowledge that we will stray again. I guess it is part of our struggle as people to stay faithful to God. Yet, it is not just God with whom we struggle to stay faithful. Fidelity to God means acting in accordance with the principles of God. God's principles are rooted in the practice of compassion, love, justice, and service.

How are you living with faithfulness, compassion, and love?

When does justice get confused with revenge in your life?

What services are you performing for yourself and others?

Haazinu—day six

That crooked and perverse generation …

—DEUTERONOMY 32:5

Another teaching from this parashah is that Moses is telling us that we will err. In fact, Moses tells us that we will be crooked and perverse and will play God. He goes on to tell us that when we get our lives together, we will get fat, gross, and coarse. Just when we get to the place we want to be, we screw ourselves up by leaving God and thinking we did all of this without any help. Yet, as the verse says, it is/can be only one generation that is crooked and perverse. We can always do *t'shuvah* and return the world to its proper state and return to our authentic selves.

What are the signs you must be aware of, otherwise you will get fat, crooked, gross, and perverse?

What are the steps you need to take to turn back when you are on the path of these behaviors?

How are you staying humble and being of service, especially when everything is going well?

Haazinu—day seven

So Jeshurun grew fat and kicked.

—Deuteronomy 32:15

It is amazing how the Torah knows and describes humanity so well. Moses reminds us that God helped us become a nation, gave us a land and a road map about to how to live. After all this, what do we do? We "grew fat and kicked." We "sacrificed to no-gods." We "forgot God who brought us forth" (Deuteronomy 32:15–18). This parashah is telling us, reminding us, that when things are good, we will start to worship false gods and even falseness itself. When we are feeling good and satisfied, we will start to think that we created this ourselves. We will feel like we have to stay faithful to our position and feelings in order to remain content. This, of course, always leads us to idolatry and more false living. Some thirty-three thousand years ago we were taught this lesson, given this prophecy.

How are you taking this prophecy to heart?

What prevents you from learning these lessons about seeking the easier, softer way?

How are you staying faithful to your position and feelings rather than to God and your principles?

My Covenant

Having lived Torah through these teachings and questions, now is the time to reflect and write your covenant with God, your family, your community, and yourself. The questions listed below are suggestions for helping you recognize your covenant for the past year and, using this book for next year, set the intention for both living well and growing into your best self in the year to come.

How will I honor my covenant with God?

What can I do to recover more of my
authentic self each and every day?

What single action can I take today to bring
me closer to becoming my best self?

Afterword

For twenty-five years I have heard the same comments from recovering people, their families and friends, and other spiritual seekers who study with Rabbi Mark and/or have come to Shabbat or holiday services at Beit T'Shuvah: "If my temple had been like this, I never would have left Judaism," or "Everything I learn in Alcoholics Anonymous and the Twelve Steps was in the Torah first," or even "Torah *is* the Big Book of Jewish Recovery." No one knows this better than Mark Borovitz, who found his own path of recovery in Torah during his incarceration in a California state prison.

He and Rabbi Mel Silverman, *z"l*, studied together in the chapel at California Institution for Men in Chino, where Mark was serving time for being a con man and a thief. The story of Jacob gave him hope. As he says, "Jacob was my kind of guy: a heel, a liar, and a con. But he wrestled with God and became Israel." Mark Borovitz wrestled and became a rabbi with a prophetic soul. He describes himself as an advocate for the souls of others. Helping countless addicts, convicts, and other struggling souls to discover themselves, he uses the Torah and other spiritual texts to show them the way home. They learn that all of our heroes are imperfect by divine design and the antidote is *t'shuvah*—when you are wrong, promptly admit it and make a plan to rectify your misstep and do the next right thing, no matter what you feel. Or, as Rabbi Mark bluntly puts it, "F*$% your feelings."

We are created *b'tzelem Elohim*, in the image of God, with opposing *yetzer*s—the *yetzer hatov* (good inclination) and the *yetzer hara* (evil inclination). Torah teaches us that both are from God and the evil inclination is, in fact, very good if its energy is redirected to love and being of service to others. In Rabbi Mark's words, "I'm still a hustler, but now I hustle for God, not for myself." And, indeed he does, tirelessly working to raise moncy to help Beit T'Shuvah keep its doors open for those suffering from addiction who cannot afford a pricey treatment option. Mark walks his talk; he is immersed in Torah and committed to its injunction to help those less fortunate: the stranger, the orphan, and the widow. His passion is evangelical, his energy is boundless, and his voice is big and loud.

Torah gave Mark Borovitz a life worth saving, and he wants to help you save yours.

—Harriet Rossetto

The Twelve Steps of Alcoholics Anonymous

This set of guiding principles outlines a course of action for recovering from addiction to substances and detrimental processes or behavioral patterns. They are as follows:

1. We admitted we were powerless over alcohol—that our lives had become unmanageable.
2. Came to believe that a Power greater than ourselves could restore us to sanity.
3. Made a decision to turn our will and our lives over to the care of God *as we understood Him*.
4. Made a searching and fearless moral inventory of ourselves.
5. Admitted to God, to ourselves, and to another human being the exact nature of our wrongs.
6. Were entirely ready to have God remove all these defects of character.
7. Humbly asked Him to remove our shortcomings.
8. Made a list of all persons we had harmed, and became willing to make amends to them all.
9. Made direct amends to such people wherever possible, except when to do so would injure them or others.
10. Continued to take personal inventory, and when we were wrong, promptly admitted it.

11. Sought through prayer and meditation to improve our conscious contact with God *as we understood Him*, praying only for knowledge of His will for us and the power to carry that out.

12. Having had a spiritual awakening as the result of these steps, we tried to carry this message to other alcoholics, and to practice these principles in all our affairs.

Secular Calendar of Torah Readings: 2016–2020

	2016	2017	2018	2019	2020
Parashat Va-yigash		Jan. 7			Jan. 4
Parashat Va-yechi		Jan. 14			Jan. 11
Parashat Shemot	Jan. 2	Jan. 21	Jan. 6		Jan. 18
Parashat Va-eira	Jan. 9	Jan. 28	Jan. 13	Jan. 5	Jan. 25
Parashat Bo	Jan. 16	Feb. 4	Jan. 20	Jan. 12	Feb. 1
Parashat Beshalach	Jan. 23	Feb. 11	Jan. 27	Jan. 19	Feb. 8
Parashat Yitro	Jan. 30	Feb. 18	Feb. 3	Jan. 26	Feb. 15
Parashat Mishpatim	Feb. 6	Feb. 25	Feb. 10	Feb. 2	Feb. 22
Parashat Terumah	Feb. 13	Mar. 4	Feb. 17	Feb. 9	Feb. 29
Parashat Tetzaveh	Feb. 20	Mar. 11	Feb. 24	Feb. 16	Mar. 7
Parashat Ki Tisa	Feb. 27	Mar. 18	Mar. 3	Feb. 23	Mar. 14
Parashat Va-yakhel	Mar. 5	Mar. 25*	Mar 10*	Mar. 2	Mar. 21

*Some years two *parashiyot* will apply to the same Shabbat. For these weeks, if you would like, you may read one selection from both of the portions each day.

**Holiday falls on Shabbat—no parashah assigned. You may review from any section you feel you will benefit from further reflection

	2016	2017	2018	2019	2020
Parashat Pekudei	Mar. 12	Mar. 25*	Mar. 10*	Mar. 9	Mar. 21
Parashat Va-yikra	Mar. 19	Apr. 1	Mar. 17	Mar. 16	Mar. 28
Parashat Tzav	Mar. 26	Apr. 8	Mar. 24	Mar. 23	Apr. 4
Parashat Shemini	Apr. 2	Apr. 22	Apr. 14	Mar. 30	Apr. 18
Parashat Tazria	Apr. 9	Apr. 29*	Apr. 21*	Apr. 6	Apr. 25*
Parashat Metzora	Apr. 16	Apr. 29*	Apr. 21*	Apr. 13	Apr. 25*
Pesach	Apr. 23**	Apr. 15**	Mar. 31**	Apr. 20**	Apr. 11**
Pesach	Apr. 30**		Apr. 7**	Apr. 27**	
Parashat Acharei Mot	May 7	May 6*	Apr. 28*	May 4	May 2*
Parashat Kedoshim	May 14	May 6*	Apr. 28	May 11	May 2*
Parashat Emor	May 21	May 13	May 5	May 18	May 9
Parashat Behar	May 28	May 20*	May 12*	May 25	May 16*
Parashat Bechukotai	June 4	May 20*	May 12*	June 1	May 16*
Parashat Bemidbar	June 11	May 27	May 19	June 8	May 23

*Some years two *parashiyot* will apply to the same Shabbat. For these weeks, if you would like, you may read one selection from both of the portions each day.

**Holiday falls on Shabbat—no parashah assigned. You may review from any section you feel you will benefit from further reflection

	2016	2017	2018	2019	2020
Shavuot					May 30**
Parashat Naso	June 18	June 3	May 26	June 15	June 6
Parashat Behaalotecha	June 25	June 10	June 2	June 22	June 13
Parashat Shelach L'cha	July 2	June 17	June 9	June 29	June 20
Parashat Korach	July 9	June 24	June 16	July 6	June 27
Parashat Chukat	July 16	July 1	June 23	July 13	July 4*
Parashat Balak	July 23	July 8	June 30	July 20	July 4*
Parashat Pinchas	July 30	July 15	July 7	July 27	July 11
Parashat Matot/Mas'ei	Aug. 6	July 22	July 14	Aug. 3	July 18
Parashat Devarim	Aug. 13	July 29	July 21	Aug. 10	July 25
Parashat Va-etchanan	Aug. 20	Aug. 5	July 28	Aug. 17	Aug. 1
Parashat Eikev	Aug. 27	Aug. 12	Aug. 4	Aug. 24	Aug. 8
Parashat Re'eih	Sept. 3	Aug. 19	Aug. 11	Aug. 31	Aug. 15

*Some years two *parashiyot* will apply to the same Shabbat. For these weeks, if you would like, you may read one selection from both of the portions each day.

**Holiday falls on Shabbat—no parashah assigned. You may review from any section you feel you will benefit from further reflection

	2016	2017	2018	2019	2020
Parashat Shofetim	Sept. 10	Aug. 26	Aug. 18	Sept. 7	Aug. 22
Parashat Ki Teitzei	Sept. 17	Sept. 2	Aug. 25	Sept. 14	Aug. 29
Parashat Ki Tavo	Sept. 24	Sept. 9	Sept. 1	Sept. 21	Sept. 5
Parashat Nitzavim	Oct. 1	Sept. 16*	Sept. 8	Sept. 28	Sept. 12*
Parashat Va-yelech	Oct. 8	Sept. 16*	Sept. 15	Oct. 5	Sept. 12*
Rosh Hashanah					Sept. 19
Parashat Haazinu	Oct. 15	Sept. 23	Sept. 22	Oct. 12	Sept. 26
Yom Kippur		Sept. 30**			
Sukkot	Oct. 22**	Oct. 7**	Sept. 29**	Oct. 19**	Oct. 3**
Shemini Atzeret					Oct. 10**
Parashat Bereshit	Oct. 29	Oct. 14	Oct. 6	Oct. 26	Oct. 17
Parashat Noach	Nov. 5	Oct. 21	Oct. 13	Nov. 2	Oct. 24
Parashat Lech L'cha	Nov. 12	Oct. 28	Oct. 20	Nov. 9	Oct. 31
Parashat Va-yeira	Nov. 19	Nov. 4	Oct. 27	Nov. 16	Nov. 7

*Some years two *parashiyot* will apply to the same Shabbat. For these weeks, if you would like, you may read one selection from both of the portions each day.

**Holiday falls on Shabbat—no parashah assigned. You may review from any section you feel you will benefit from further reflection

	2016	2017	2018	2019	2020
Parashat Chayei Sarah	Nov. 26	Nov. 11	Nov. 3	Nov. 23	Nov. 14
Parashat Toledot	Dec. 3	Nov. 18	Nov. 10	Nov. 30	Nov. 21
Parashat Va-yetzei	Dec. 10	Nov. 25	Nov. 17	Dec. 7	Nov. 28
Parashat Va-yishlach	Dec. 17	Dec. 2	Nov. 24	Dec. 14	Dec. 5
Parashat Va-yeishev	Dec. 24	Dec. 9	Dec. 1	Dec. 21	Dec. 12
Parashat Miketz	Dec. 31	Dec. 16	Dec. 8	Dec. 28	Dec. 19
Parashat Va-yigash		Dec. 23	Dec. 15		Dec. 26
Parashat Va-yechi		Dec. 30	Dec. 22		
Parashat Shemot			Dec. 29		

*Some years two *parashiyot* will apply to the same Shabbat. For these weeks, if you would like, you may read one selection from both of the portions each day.

**Holiday falls on Shabbat—no parashah assigned. You may review from any section you feel you will benefit from further reflection

Glossary

AA meeting: Usually held weekly, this is a gathering of people recovering from substance abuse and/or those interested in the Alcoholics Anonymous program.

***Adonai*:** Literally, "my Lords," it serves as an appellation of God, and when the tetragrammaton became too holy for utterance, *Adonai* was substituted for it, so that, as a rule, the name written *YHVH* is read *Adonai*, except in cases where *Adonai* precedes or succeeds it in the text, when it is read *Elohim*.

***aleph*:** The first letter in the Hebrew alphabet.

***ani*:** Meaning "I" or "myself," it is subtly different from *anochi*.

***anochi*:** Also meaning "I," it is usually used when emphasizing the fact that "I" is referring solely to oneself and no one else. Also, it sometimes connotes drawing near to God.

Beit T'Shuvah: Literally, "The House of Return," it is an addiction treatment center and synagogue community in Los Angeles, founded in 1987 by Harriet Rossetto.

***b'rit*:** Literally, "covenant." The most well-known example is the rite of circumcision, first described in Genesis as a covenant between God and Abraham.

***b'tzelem Elohim*:** Literally, "made in God's image." The Torah tells us that people are made as images of the Divine and therefore possess godly qualities.

Burke, Edmund (1729–1797, Ireland, England): Author, orator, political theorist, and philosopher known for his support of the cause of the American Revolutionaries and Catholic emancipation.

***cheshbon hanefesh*:** Literally, "accounting of the soul." This is akin to the process of taking a moral inventory, the recommended fourth step of the Alcoholics Anonymous program.

chok: Literally, "law." It is traditionally a rule or commandment given without clear reason.

Deuteronomy/*Devarim*: The fifth book of the Torah. The Hebrew word *devarim* translates to "spoken words."

drash: Literally, "inquiry" or "searching." This is a figurative, rather than literal, interpretation of a text, most often the Torah or Talmud.

Elohim: Most often interpreted to mean "God," it is both a grammatically singular and plural noun that can function to mean the "true God," "gods," or "powers" and is the word most often used for "God" in the Torah.

Etz Hayim Chumash: A Torah in printed form (*Chumash*) with commentary; this one is published and used by the Conservative Jewish movement.

Exodus/*Shemot*: The second book of the Torah. The Hebrew word *shemot* translates to "names."

Genesis/*Bereshit*: The first book of the Torah. The Hebrew word *bereshit* translates to "in [the] beginning."

Hanukkah: Derived from the verb meaning "to dedicate." Known best as the "Festival of Lights," this holiday is observed for eight days and nights by lighting candles in a nine-branched candelabrum, progressing to light one additional candle each night until all eight are lit on the last. This holiday commemorates the rededication of the Second Temple in Jerusalem after the Maccabean Revolt against the Seleucid Empire. It begins on the twenty-fifth day of the Hebrew month of Kislev, which may occur anywhere between late November and late December.

hanukkiyah: A nine-branched candelabrum or *menorah* made for Hanukkah, the Jewish "Festival of Lights." It holds nine candles, one for each of the eight nights of the holiday and a ninth, in the center, contains the shammes (literally, "servant").

Heschel, Abraham Joshua (1907–1972, Poland, Germany, United States): One of the great and most widely quoted Jewish religious scholars of the modern era, he was a rabbi, an educator, and a social justice advocate. A prolific author, his most famous books include *The Insecurity of Freedom*, *God in Search of Man*, and *Man Is Not Alone*.

***hineni*:** Literally, "here I am," it is often used to answer God's call of *ayecha* (where are you) and is first used by Abraham in Genesis 22:1.

Kabbalah: Literally, "reception." It is the tradition of Jewish mysticism, which maintains that there are hidden truths within the Torah. The primary resource for Kabbalah is the *Zohar*. Hasidism is based upon many of the teachings of Kabbalah.

***Kaddish*:** Literally, "holy." It is a hymn of praises to God recited at funerals and by mourners. It can only be said with a minyan, traditionally a quorum of ten men, after a psalm or prayer has been spoken in the presence of said minyan.

***kohein*:** Literally, "priest"; pl. *kohanim*. A member of the Jewish priesthood. Priestly status is conferred, as all are male Jews who are descendants of the patriarch Aaron, the first priest and Moses's elder brother. The *kohanim* performed all the sacred rituals during the era of the Temple in Jerusalem.

***lashon hara*:** Literally, "evil tongue." It is a term used to describe derogatory speech about another person or party, which is not previously known to the public, is not seriously intended to correct or improve a negative situation, and is true. It is considered a very serious sin in the Jewish tradition.

Levites: Descendants of Levi, the third son of Jacob and Leah, they are members of one of the twelve Israelite tribes.

Leviticus/*Va-yikra*: The third book of the Torah. The Hebrew word *va-yikra* translates to "and God called."

Maccabees: Leaders of a Jewish army that rebelled against the Seleucid Empire and took control of Judea in 164 BCE.

***machzor*:** Literally, "cycle." This Jewish prayer book contains the liturgical texts for Rosh Hashanah and Yom Kippur, known collectively as Judaism's "High Holy Days."

Maimonides/Rambam (1135–1204, Spain and Egypt): A physician, rabbi, and possibly the greatest Jewish thinker of all time. Among his many important works are the *Mishneh Torah*, the first written Jewish legal code, and the *Guide of the Perplexed* (*Moreh Nevuchim*), which interprets the Torah with the objective of eliminating apparent contradictions with philosophy.

Menachem Mendel of Kotzk (1787–1859, Poland): Better known as the Kotzker Rebbe, he is a Hasidic master with a philosophy of pointed honesty and wit.

menorah: A seven-branched, golden Hebrew lampstand or candelabrum used in the biblical Tabernacle and later, the Temple in Jerusalem.

Midianites: Descendants of Midian, a son of Abraham's. These were a nomadic Arabian people believed to have lived near the eastern shore of the Gulf of Aqaba on the Red Sea.

midrash: Literally, "elucidation" or "exposition"; pl. *midrashim*. A story or commentary, made by the Palestinian Rabbis from the third through tenth centuries CE, about the laws, customs, or rituals of Jewish life mentioned in the Torah.

***Mishkan*:** Literally, "place of dwelling." Also referred to as the Tabernacle, this was a portable sanctuary used by the ancient Israelites as a holy space for the Divine Presence.

Mishnah: Literally, "teaching." The foundational text for the Talmud and for the Rabbinic tradition. Most scholars date its final editing to circa 200 CE.

Mishnaic period: Approximately 10–220 CE.

***mitzvah*:** Literally, "commandment"; pl. *mitzvot*. One of the religious obligations detailed in the Torah, the majority of which fall into the positive category of religious, ethical, or moral obligations. The Torah also contains negative *mitzvot*, which are prohibitions.

***na'aseh v'nishma*:** Literally, "we will do and we will understand." This is how the Jews standing at Mount Sinai signal their acceptance of the Torah in Exodus 24:7. This has been used to impart the teaching to do first and then understand or study later and is very similar to the idea behind taking the next right action, no matter what you might think or feel.

Nachmanides/Ramban (1194–1270, Spain and Israel): A physician, halachist, kabbalist, poet, and one of the most important scholars in Jewish history. He is most well known for his commentary on the Torah.

***nishmat chayim*:** Literally, "breath of life." This phrase is used to describe how the first human, Adam, became a *nefesh chayah* (living soul).

Numbers/*Bemidbar*: The fourth book of the Torah. The Hebrew word *bemidbar* translates to "in the desert," or sometimes "in the wilderness."

parashah: Literally, "portion"; pl. *parashiyot*. A weekly portion of the Torah, which is divided into fifty-four parts—one for each week of a leap year in the Hebrew lunar calendar. In non-leap years some of the portions are combined to create double *parashiyot* that compensate for the reduced number of weeks.

Pharaoh: The common title for the kings of Egypt, in the Torah. Most scholars believe the specific pharaoh referenced in Exodus was Ahmose I, but other historical figures have been proposed.

***Pirkei Avot*:** Literally, "Chapters of the Fathers," this is a compilation of the ethical teachings and maxims of the Rabbis of the Mishnaic period.

Rosh Hashanah: Literally, "Head of the Year," the Jewish New Year. One of the "High Holy Days," it falls on the first and second days of Tishrei, the seventh Hebrew month (in September or October). Rosh Hashanah always occurs on the Rosh Hodesh (new moon) that is closest to the autumnal equinox.

Schulweis, Harold (1925–2014, United States): A contemporary Jewish philosopher, poet, author, and the longtime spiritual leader of Congregation Valley Beth Shalom in Encino, California. His books include *For Those Who Can't Believe: Overcoming the Obstacles to Faith* and *Conscience: The Duty to Obey and the Duty to Disobey.*

***S'fat Emet*:** Literally, "The Language of Truth." It is a five-volume commentary on the Torah and Jewish holidays written by the great Hasidic rabbi Yehuda Aryeh Leib Alter of Ger (1847–1904, Poland).

***Shema*:** Shortened from *Shema, Yisrael*, literally, "Hear, O Israel." This prayer serves as a centerpiece of the morning, evening, and weekly Shabbat prayers.

***simcha*:** Literally, "joy." It is often used to mean a celebration or festive occasion.

***sinat chinam*:** Literally, "hatred of grace." Usually used to mean "baseless hatred," and especially in the context of it causing the destruction of the Second Temple in Jerusalem, it is considered a serious sin.

Soloveitchik, Joseph B. (1903–1993, present-day Belarus, Germany, United States): Commonly referred to as "the Rav," he was a well-known American Orthodox rabbi, Talmudist, and major modern Jewish philosopher. Ordaining more than two thousand rabbis, he was also a prolific writer whose best-known work is *The Lonely Man of Faith*.

Steinsaltz, Adin (1937–, Jerusalem): A teacher, philosopher, social critic, and spiritual mentor who devoted his life to making the Talmud accessible to all Jews. His works include the classic text of Kabbalah, *The Thirteen Petalled Rose: A Discourse on the Essence of Jewish Experience and Belief*.

Tabernacle: Literally, "residence" or "dwelling place." See *Mishkan*.

Talmud: The central and most important body of Rabbinic literature. Combining the Mishnah and Gemara, the Talmud contains material from the Rabbinic academies that dates from sometime before the second century CE through the sixth century CE. There are two versions: the Jerusalem (*Yerushalmi*), or Palestinian, Talmud and the Babylonian (*Bavli*) Talmud. When people speak of the Talmud generically, they are referring to the *Bavli*, as it is more extensive and widely used. The Talmud serves as the primary source for all later codes of Jewish law.

***t'shuvah*:** Literally, "return"; pl. *t'shuvot*. Referring to the "return to God," *t'shuvah* is often translated as "repentance." Central to the process of atoning for sin, it is comprised of return, repentance, and a new response. It is akin to the amendments made in the ninth step of the Alcoholics Anonymous programs.

Twerski, Rabbi Abraham Joshua (1930–, United States): Hasidic rabbi, acclaimed author, and psychiatrist specializing in substance abuse.

***tzedakah*:** Literally, "justice" or "righteousness." It is usually used to signify charity and an obligation to provide for the poor, the widow, the orphan, and the stranger.

Yarrow, Peter: American singer and songwriter, Peter of "Peter, Paul and Mary."

***yetzer hatov* and *yetzer hara*:** Literally, "good inclination" and "bad inclination," respectively. Both good and evil come from God. The good inclination (*yetzer hatov*) is good. The evil inclination (*yetzer hara*) can also be good—in proper measure. You can harness "evil" energy and put it to good use. The struggle between the *yetzer hatov* and *yetzer hara* is part of what makes us human; both are necessary components of authentic living.

***YHVH*:** Abbreviation for *Yud, Hey, Vav, Hey*, the transliterated Hebrew letters known as the tetragrammaton, composing the ineffable, unpronounceable name of God.

Yom Kippur: Literally, "Day of Atonement." The most holy and solemn day of the Jewish calendar, filled with pleas for forgiveness and acts of self-denial, including fasting. It falls on the tenth day of the Hebrew month of Tishrei, which is usually in late September or early October.

Suggestions for Further Reading

Anonymous. *Alcoholics Anonymous*. 4th ed. New York: AA World Services, 2001.

———. *Twelve Steps and Twelve Traditions*. New York: AA World Services, 1981.

Borovitz, Mark. *The Holy Thief: A Con Man's Journey from Darkness to Light*. New York: HarperCollins, 2005.

Feinstein, Edward. *The Chutzpah Imperative: Empowering Today's Jews for a Life That Matters*. Woodstock, VT: Jewish Lights, 2014.

Green, Arthur. *The Language of Truth: The Torah Commentary of the* Sefat Emet, *Rabbi Yehudah Leib Alter of Ger*. Philadelphia, PA: The Jewish Publication Society, 1998.

Heschel, Abraham Joshua. *God in Search of Man: A Philosophy of Judaism*. New York: Farrar, Straus, and Giroux, 1976.

———. *The Insecurity of Freedom: Essays on Human Existence*. New York: Farrar, Straus, and Giroux, 1967.

———. *Man Is Not Alone: A Philosophy of Religion*. New York: Farrar, Straus, and Giroux, 1951.

———. *Moral Grandeur and Spiritual Audacity: Essays*. New York: Farrar, Straus, and Giroux, 1997.

Kurtz, Ernest, and Katherine Ketcham. *The Spirituality of Imperfection: Storytelling and the Search for Meaning*. New York: Bantam Books, 1992.

Kushner, Harold S. *When Bad Things Happen to Good People*. New York: Anchor Books, 2004.

Kushner, Lawrence. *God Was in This Place & I, i Did Not Know: Finding Self, Spirituality and Ultimate Meaning*. 25th anniv. ed. Woodstock, VT: Jewish Lights, 2016.

Mykoff, Moshe, ed. *The Empty Chair: Finding Hope and Joy—Timeless Wisdom from a Hasidic Master, Rebbe Nachman of Breslov*. Woodstock, VT: Jewish Lights, 1996.

Mykoff, Moshe, and S. C. Mizrahi, eds. *The Gentle Weapon: Prayers for Everyday and Not-So-Everyday Moments—Timeless Wisdom from the Teachings of the Hasidic Master, Rebbe Nachman of Breslov*. Woodstock, VT: Jewish Lights, 1999.

Olitzky, Kerry M., and Stuart A. Copans. *Twelve Jewish Steps to Recovery: A Personal Guide to Turning From Alcoholism and Other Addictions—Drugs, Food, Gambling, Sex* ... 2nd ed. Woodstock, VT: Jewish Lights, 2009.

Peli, Pinchas H. *On Repentance: The Thought and Oral Discourses of Joseph Dov Soloveitchik*. Lanham, MD: Jason Aronson, 2000.

Rossetto, Harriet. *Sacred Housekeeping: A Spiritual Memoir*. Bloomington, IN: AuthorHouse, 2012.

Shapiro, Rami. *Recovery—The Sacred Art: The Twelve Steps as Spiritual Practice*. Woodstock, VT: SkyLight Paths, 2009.

Soloveitchik, Joseph B. *The Lonely Man of Faith*. New York: Doubleday, 2006.

Steinberg, Paul. *Recovery, the 12 Steps and Jewish Spirituality: Reclaiming Hope, Courage & Wholeness*. Woodstock, VT: Jewish Lights, 2014.

Steinsaltz, Adin. *The Thirteen Petalled Rose: A Discourse on the Essence of Jewish Experience and Belief*. New York: Basic Books, 2006.

Twerski, Abraham J. *Growing Each Day*. New York: Mesorah, 1992.

———. *Lights along the Way: Timeless Lessons for Today from Rabbi Moshe Chaim Luzzatto's* Mesillas Yesharim. New York: Mesorah, 2009.

More Wisdom from the Hasidic Masters

WALKING THE PATH OF THE JEWISH MYSTIC
How to Expand Your Awareness and Transform Your Life
by *Rabbi Yoel Glick*
6 x 9, 224 pp, PB, 978-1-58023-843-4 **$18.99**

GOD IN ALL MOMENTS
Mystical & Practical Spiritual Wisdom from Hasidic Masters
Edited and translated by *Rabbi Or N. Rose* with *Rabbi Ebn D. Leader*
5½ x 8½, 192 pp, PB, 978-1-58023-186-2 **$16.95**

HASIDIC TALES
Annotated & Explained
Translated and annotated by *Rabbi Rami Shapiro*
5½ x 8½, 240 pp, PB, 978-1-893361-86-7 $18.99

YOUR WORD IS FIRE
The Hasidic Masters on Contemplative Prayer
Edited and translated with a new introduction by *Rabbi Arthur Green, PhD*, and *Barry W. Holtz*
6 x 9, 160 pp, PB, 978-1-879045-25-5 **$16.99**

THE WAY INTO JEWISH MYSTICAL TRADITION
by *Rabbi Lawrence Kushner*
6 x 9, 224 pp, PB, 978-1-58023-200-5 **$18.99**

Spirituality

THE MODERN MEN'S TORAH COMMENTARY
New Insights from Jewish Men on the 54 Weekly Torah Portions

Edited by *Rabbi Jeffrey K. Salkin*
6 x 9, 368 pp, HC, 978-1-58023-395-8 **$24.99**

MAKING PRAYER REAL
Leading Jewish Spiritual Voices on Why Prayer Is Difficult and What to Do about It

by *Rabbi Mike Comins*
6 x 9, 320 pp, PB, 978-1-58023-417-7 **$18.99**

MUSSAR YOGA
Blending an Ancient Jewish Spiritual Practice with Yoga to Transform Body and Soul

by *Edith R. Brotman, PhD, RYT-500*
Foreword by *Alan Morinis*
7 x 9, 224 pp, 40+ b/w photos, PB, 978-1-58023-784-0 **$18.99**

THE WOMEN'S TORAH COMMENTARY
New Insights from Women Rabbis on the 54 Weekly Torah Portions

Edited by *Rabbi Elyse Goldstein*
6 x 9, 496 pp, HC, 978-1-58023-076-6 **$34.95**
PB, 978-1-58023-370-5 **$19.99**

DAVENING
A Guide to Meaningful Jewish Prayer

by *Rabbi Zalman M. Schachter-Shalomi* (z"l)
with *Joel Segel*; Foreword by *Rabbi Lawrence Kushner*
6 x 9, 240 pp, PB, 978-1-58023-627-0 **$18.99**

ABOUT JEWISH LIGHTS PUBLISHING

People of all faiths and backgrounds yearn for books that attract, engage, educate and spiritually inspire.

Our principal goal is to stimulate thought and help all people learn about who the Jewish People are, where they come from, and what the future can be made to hold. While people of our diverse Jewish heritage are the primary audience, our books speak to people in the Christian world as well and will broaden their understanding of Judaism and the roots of their own faith.

We bring to you authors who are at the forefront of spiritual thought and experience. While each has something different to say, they all say it in a voice that you can hear. Our books are designed to welcome you and then to engage, stimulate and inspire. We judge our success not only by whether or not our books are beautiful and commercially successful, but by whether or not they make a difference in your life.